# THE HIDDEN RULES OF RACE

Why do black families own less than white families? Why does school segregation persist decades after *Brown v. Board of Education*? Why is it harder for black adults to vote than for white adults? Will addressing economic inequality solve racial and gender inequality as well? This book answers all of these questions and more by revealing the "hidden rules of race" that create barriers to inclusion today. While many Americans are familiar with the histories of slavery and Jim Crow, we often don't understand how the rules of those eras undergird today's economy, reproducing the same racial inequities 150 years after the end of slavery and 50 years after the end of Jim Crow segregation. This book shows how the fight for racial equity has been one of progress and retrenchment, a constant push and pull for inclusion over exclusion. By understanding how our economic and racial rules work together, we can write better rules to finally address inequality in America.

Andrea Flynn is a Fellow at the Roosevelt Institute, where she researches and writes about race, gender, and the social and economic issues that impact women and families. Her writing has appeared in *The Atlantic*, *The New Republic*, *Cosmopolitan*, *Salon*, *The Hill*, and *Time*.

Susan R. Holmberg is a Fellow at the Roosevelt Institute. She writes on inequality, climate change, and corporate governance issues. Her writing has appeared in *Democracy Journal*, *The Atlantic*, *Salon*, *The Hill*, and *Grist*.

Dorian T. Warren is a Fellow at the Roosevelt Institute, an MSNBC Contributor, and Board Chair of the Center for Community Change. His forthcoming book is entitled *The Three Faces of Unions: Inclusion & Democracy in the U.S. Labor Movement*.

Felicia J. Wong is President and CEO of the Roosevelt Institute, where she leads work on Roosevelt's comprehensive economic program and narrative to rewrite the rules. She is a political scientist with expertise in race and education politics, has held senior executive roles in the private and nonprofit sectors, and has served as a White House Fellow.

CAMBRIDGE STUDIES IN STRATIFICATION ECONOMICS:
ECONOMICS AND SOCIAL IDENTITY

*Series Editor*

William A. Darity Jr., *Duke University*

The Cambridge Studies in Stratification Economics: Economics and Social Identity series encourages book proposals that emphasize structural sources of group-based inequality rather than cultural or genetic factors. Studies in this series will utilize the underlying economic principles of self-interested behavior and substantive rationality in conjunction with sociology's emphasis on group behavior and identity formation. The series is interdisciplinary, drawing authors from various fields including economics, sociology, social psychology, history, and anthropology, with all projects focused on topics dealing with group-based inequality, identity, and economic well-being.

# The Hidden Rules of Race

*Barriers to an Inclusive Economy*

## ANDREA FLYNN

Fellow, Roosevelt Institute

## SUSAN R. HOLMBERG

Fellow, Roosevelt Institute

## DORIAN T. WARREN

Fellow, Roosevelt Institute

## FELICIA J. WONG

President and CEO, Roosevelt Institute

CAMBRIDGE
UNIVERSITY PRESS

# CAMBRIDGE
## UNIVERSITY PRESS

One Liberty Plaza, 20th Floor, New York, NY 10006, USA

Cambridge University Press is part of the University of Cambridge.

It furthers the University's mission by disseminating knowledge in the pursuit of education, learning, and research at the highest international levels of excellence.

www.cambridge.org
Information on this title: www.cambridge.org/9781108417549
DOI: 10.1017/9781108277846

First published 2017
Reprinted 2018

Printed in the United Kingdom by TJ International Ltd. Padstow, Cornwall

A catalogue record for this publication is available from the British Library.

ISBN 978-1-108-41754-9 Hardback

# Contents

| | | |
|---|---|---|
| *Notes on Contributors* | | *page* ix |
| *Acknowledgments* | | xiii |
| | Introduction: Rewriting the Rules of Racial Inequality: An Agenda for Structural Inclusion | 1 |
| 1 | American Politics and Economic Outcomes for African Americans: A Brief Historical Overview | 15 |
| 2 | Stratification Economics: A General Theory of Intergroup Inequality | 35 |
| 3 | Creating Structural Changes: The Role of Targeted Universalism | 52 |
| 4 | The Racial Rules of Wealth | 63 |
| 5 | The Racial Rules of Income | 77 |
| 6 | The Racial Rules of Education | 93 |
| 7 | The Racial Rules of Criminal Justice | 108 |
| 8 | The Racial Rules of Health | 127 |
| 9 | The Racial Rules of Democratic Participation | 145 |
| 10 | What Will It Take to Rewrite the Hidden Rules of Race? | 156 |
| | Conclusion | 171 |
| *Notes* | | 175 |
| *Index* | | 219 |

# Notes on Contributors

**Wendy Ake** directs the Haas Institute's Just Public Finance program, where her work examines how axes of difference can reinforce marginality or create opportunity for building an inclusive society. Through critiques of orthodox economic systems, her research examines changes in networks of financialization and technical issues in public finance as related to credit and debt. She is also a consultant on implementing targeted universal policies and strategy, especially for the philanthropic sector.

**William A. ("Sandy") Darity Jr.** is the Samuel DuBois Cook Professor of Public Policy, African and African American Studies, and Economics at Duke University. Darity's research focuses on inequality by race, class, and ethnicity; stratification economics; schooling and the racial achievement gap; skin shade and labor market outcomes; the economics of reparations; and the social psychological effects of exposure to unemployment. He was a fellow at the Center for Advanced Study in the Behavioral Sciences (2011–2012) at Stanford, a fellow at the National Humanities Center (1989-90), and a visiting scholar at the Federal Reserve's Board of Governors (1984).

**Alberto Dávila** is Professor of Economics and Associate Dean in the College of Business and Entrepreneurship at the University of Texas Rio Grande Valley. Dávila has recently published on U.S.–Mexico border and Hispanic topics (e.g., *Labor Market Issues along the U.S.–Mexico Border,* 2009, and *Hispanic Entrepreneurs in the 2000s,* 2013).

**Darrick Hamilton** is the Director of the doctoral program in Public and Urban Policy, and was jointly appointed as an Associate Professor of Economics and Urban Policy at the Milano School of International Affairs, Management and Urban Policy and the Department of Economics, and the New School for Social Research at the New School in New York. Professor

Hamilton is a stratification economist, whose work fuses scientific methods to examine the causes, consequences, and remedies of racial and ethnic inequality in economic and health outcomes, which includes an examination of the intersection of identity, racism, colorism, and socioeconomic outcomes.

**Trevon D. Logan** is the Hazel C. Youngberg Trustees Distinguished Professor of Economics at the Ohio State University and a Research Associate at the National Bureau of Economic Research. He specializes in economic history and applied demography, and does work that intersects with health economics, applied econometrics, applied microeconomics, and sociology. He is winner of the American Sociological Association's Section on Sociology of Sexuality's Best Article Award. His work has appeared in *American Economic Review, American Sociological Review, Journal of Economic History*, and other outlets. He is the author of *Economics, Sexuality, and Male Sex Work* (Cambridge University Press, 2017).

**Patrick L. Mason** is Professor of Economics and Director of the African American Studies Program at Florida State University. His research interests include racial inequality, educational achievement, income distribution, unemployment, social identity, immigration, well-being of families and transitions in family structure, racial profiling, and innovation and development in Caribbean economies.

**Marie T. Mora** is Professor of Economics at the University of Texas Rio Grande Valley. She has shared her research expertise on Hispanic socioeconomic outcomes with numerous institutions and agencies, including the White House, the Federal Reserve System's Board of Governors, and the Bureau of Labor Statistics, among others. Her publications include *Hispanic Entrepreneurs in the 2000s* (with Alberto Dávila, 2013), two coedited volumes, and over forty-five journal articles and book chapters.

**john a. powell** is Director of the Haas Institute for a Fair and Inclusive Society (HIFIS) and Robert D. Haas Chancellor's Chair in Equity and Inclusion at the University of California, Berkeley. Formerly, he directed the Kirwan Institute for the Study of Race and Ethnicity at The Ohio State University. He led the development of an "opportunity-based" model that connects affordable housing to racialized spaces in education, health, health care, and employment.

**Gregory N. Price** is Professor of Economics at Morehouse College. An applied econometrician and theorist, his research has been published in a wide variety of journals such as *African Development Review, Economics and Human Biology, Review of Black Political Economy,* and *Review of Economics and Statistics.*

**Sue K. Stockly** is an Associate Professor of Economics at Eastern New Mexico University with previous experience as an Associate Economist at the RAND Corporation. She holds a Ph.D. in Economics from the University of Texas at Austin. Dr. Stockly is cofounder and past president of the American Society of Hispanic Economists (ASHE). Her research interests include stratification economics, minority scholarship in higher education, and teaching innovations in economics.

# Acknowledgments

This book would not have been possible without the guidance and support of many individuals. Authors Andrea Flynn, Susan R. Holmberg, Dorian T. Warren, and Felicia J. Wong would like to thank Wendy Ake, William A. Darity Jr., Darrick Hamilton, Patrick Mason, john a. powell, Gregory Price, Alberto Dávila, Marie Mora, James Stewart, and Sue K. Stockly, who contributed to the writing.

They would also like to thank the many Roosevelt Institute staff members who dedicated their time and talents to this project: Nell Abernathy for her thought leadership and expert guidance at every stage; Marybeth Seitz-Brown for her extensive assistance with research, drafting, and editing on both the initial report on which this book is based and the final manuscript; Renée Fidz and Gabriel Matthews for their contributions to the original report; Andrew Hwang for his contributions to Chapter 5; Rakeen Mabud for her guidance and expertise bringing this manuscript to publication; and Tim Price for his invaluable editing contributions from the earliest conceptualization of this project through the publication of this book. The authors would also like to thank Roosevelt Institute Chief Economist Joseph Stiglitz for his guidance in the original planning stages of this project, and for his expertise and advice as it came to fruition. Contributions and input from Roosevelt Institute fellows Saqib Bhatti, Mike Konczal, J. W. Mason, K. Sabeel Rahman, and Todd N. Tucker helped shape the narrative and arguments we make throughout. Héctor Sáez of Chatham University and Anastasia Wilson of University of Massachusetts, Amherst provided important contributions to the initial Roosevelt Institute report.

The authors would also like to acknowledge the following people, many of whom participated in convenings that informed this work, reviewed early drafts of the publication, and/or provided input throughout the publication process (affiliations listed for identification purposes only): Randy Albelda (University of Massachusetts Boston), Kate Bahn (Center for American Progress), Dante Barry (Million Hoodies for Justice), Carmen Berkley (AFL-CIO), Annette Bernhardt (University of California, Berkeley), Raphael Bostic (University of Southern California), Jeffrey Butts (John Jay College of Criminal Justice), James Carr (Center for American Progress), Anmol Chaddha (Harvard University), Axia Cintron-Velez (Russell Sage Foundation), Lisa Cook (Michigan State University), Robert DeFina (Villanova University), Shawn Dove (Campaign for Black Male Achievement), Jennifer Eberhardt (Stanford University), Katrina Gamble (Center for Popular Democracy), Alicia Garza (National Domestic Workers Alliance and the Movement for Black Lives); Linda Goler-Blount (Black Women's Health Imperative), Pilar Herrero (Center for Reproductive Rights), Deepa Iyer (Center for Social Inclusion), Carl Lipscombe (Black Alliance for Just Immigration), Ellen Liu (Ms. Foundation for Women), Julianne Malveaux (Economic Policy Institute), Imani Marshall (Roosevelt @ Amherst), Aleyamma Mathew (Ms. Foundation), Natalia Mehlman-Petrzela (The New School), Suresh Naidu (Columbia University), Zachary Norris (Ella Baker Center), Amani Nuru-Jeter (University of California, Berkeley), Shuya Ohno (Advancement Project), Steven Pitts (University of California, Berkeley), Steven Raphael (University of California, Berkeley), Rashad Robinson (Color of Change), Rashid Shabazz (Campaign for Black Male Achievement), Purvi Shah (Center for Constitutional Rights), Thomas Shapiro (Brandeis University), Monica Raye Simpson (SisterSong), Rogers Smith (University of Pennsylvania), William Spriggs (AFL-CIO), Marbre Stahly-Butts (Law for Black Lives), Nelini Stamp (Rise Up Georgia), Jeanne Theoharis (Brooklyn College), Vince Warren (Center for Constitutional Rights), Susan Wefald (Ms. Foundation), Frederick Wherry (Yale University), Jeannette Wicks-Lim (University of Massachusetts Amherst), Irene Yen (University of California, San Francisco), and Haeyoung Yoon (National Employment Law Project).

Additional thanks to Roosevelt staff and consultants for their support and contributions: Hannah Assadi, Eric Harris Bernstein, Johanna Bonewitz, Amy Chen, Samantha Diaz, Kristina Ensminger, Joelle Gamble, Monica Gonzalez, Claire Levenson, Chris Linsmayer, Katy Milani, Marcus Mrowka, Dave Palmer, Camellia Phillips, Alan Smith, Alexandra Tempus, and Alexander Tucciarone.

The report on which this book is based was made possible with generous support from Ford Foundation, Open Society Foundations, Arca Foundation, Nathan Cummings Foundation, and the Dobkin Family Foundation.

# Introduction

## Rewriting the Rules of Racial Inequality: An Agenda for Structural Inclusion

Two dominant conversations have driven progressive politics in recent years: one centered on the moral, social, and economic injustices that have arisen from decades of unchecked economic inequality, and another centered on structural racism. A number of intersecting forces have brought these issues to the fore: frustration about Americans' worsening economic circumstances, particularly in the wake of the 2008 global financial crisis and the so-called economic recovery that followed; outrage over the deaths of people of color at the hands of police; activist movements such as Black Lives Matter, Fight for 15, Occupy Wall Street, and the Women's March on Washington; and the intellectual work of Thomas Piketty, Joseph Stiglitz, and others focused on the mutually reinforcing relationship between economic and political inequality.

At times, we have seen the people who care about these two issues work in tandem to bring questions long ignored by America's elites into the mainstream political debate. Such movements as the Fight for 15 or FedUp have united racial justice and economic justice activists against trickle-down economic policies that disproportionately disadvantage people of color. But too often, progressive leaders mistakenly assume that ostensibly "colorblind" economic policies are sufficient to address the obstacles to equal opportunity and equitable outcomes for people of color. Indeed, in the wake of the 2016 presidential election, there was a call among some progressives to abandon "identity politics" – that is, the identity politics of nondominant social groups – in favor of an exclusive focus on class and economic inequality.

In this book, we reject that notion, arguing that race and class are inextricably linked. In order to understand racial and economic inequality in America today, we must look below the surface and understand the web of rules and institutions that lead to unequal outcomes. While those unequal

1

outcomes are very clear to a large proportion of Americans, many still believe they are the result of personal ambition and individual choices, and that the solution for racial inequality is for individuals to take more "personal responsibility."

As of 2007, two-thirds of the general population, including 71 percent of whites and even 53 percent of black Americans, believed that black Americans who "have not gotten ahead in life are mainly responsible for their own situation."[1] This belief is incorrect, and a rules-based analysis illuminates how and why: our rules and institutions are rarely colorblind, and even when policy makers intend on race-neutral results, policies are refracted through historical institutions, current rules, and societal norms, resulting in disparate impacts on black Americans.

First, we must understand the scope of the problem. As we will describe throughout this book, the disparities are familiar but overwhelming: at every level of education, black Americans are paid less than their white counterparts. At every level of income, black Americans have fewer assets than their white counterparts. Compared to white Americans, black Americans have higher rates of unemployment, accrue less wealth, and have lower rates of homeownership. But just as critically, even middle-income black Americans have unequal access to the quality-of-life goods – education, health, and safety – that economic success is expected to guarantee.

These disparities also are gendered. Black women, in particular, are situated uniquely at the intersection of race, class, and gender hierarchies, historically and today. They make up a disproportionate share of minimum-wage workers. They face labor market segregation that pushes them into insecure jobs with low pay and few benefits. They bear the weight of community and familial well-being in the vacuum left by mass incarceration. And persistent racial and gender pay gaps prevent them from earning a just and equitable wage.[2]

As noted, many progressives consider economic policy alone to be a sufficient remedy for these issues. But for black Americans, higher incomes or more education do not remove the threat of injustice. Indeed, the continued shooting of unarmed black Americans underscores the limits of economic policy in addressing systemic racism.

A progressive economic agenda that seeks to raise the minimum wage, for example, will benefit black Americans, but it will not change the fact that a dollar of income in black hands buys less safety, less health, less wealth, and less education than a dollar in white hands. Nor will it address the underlying structures of racial exclusion and discrimination that cause black Americans to be overrepresented among unemployed and low-wage workers and underrepresented in the middle class, let alone "the 1 percent."

In this book, we will show that *racial rules* undergird our economy and society and are the driving force behind the patently unequal life chances and basic opportunities for people of color and women. We build on and extend the framework described in *Rewriting the Rules*, the 2015 policy report published by Joseph Stiglitz and the Roosevelt Institute. That report challenges traditional economic thinking, arguing that inequality is a choice we make with the rules we create to structure our economy. These rules, the report argues, shape the economy and thus shape a range of opportunities and outcomes. They are the "regulatory and legal frameworks that make up the economy, like those affecting property ownership, corporate formation, labor law, copyright, anti-trust, monetary, tax and expenditure policy, and other economic structures." And they quite clearly include "an entire set of rules, regulations, expenditure policies, and normative practices that excludes populations from the economy and from economic opportunity."[3]

Throughout this book, we define and outline a broad collection of these rules, many of which have deep historical roots. The historical arc of our nation's racially exclusionary and discriminatory policies is long, and remedying today's injustices will require looking backward and understanding the inextricable link between the policies of our past and present. As epidemiologist Camara Phyllis Jones writes, "the association between socioeconomic status and race in the United States has its origins in discrete historical events but persists because of contemporary structural factors that perpetuate those historical injustices."[4] As such, we trace the ways in which the wealth-building and income constraints of slavery, Jim Crow, and New Deal policies continue to reverberate in asset-poor black communities. We also examine how other rules of those periods have shaped contemporary outcomes across a range of social and economic realms.

Most of the more contemporary rules that disproportionately impact people of color are less explicitly discriminatory. Yet we argue that policies that purport to be colorblind frequently have both racialized origins and racialized consequences. It is important to acknowledge that even policies that are meant to apply equitably across our society exist in the context of racialized historical rules, ensuring that policy outcomes differ by race.

This is especially apparent in the structure of the criminal justice system, which is deeply racialized in practice despite being race-neutral on its face. Colorblind rules such as cuts to public services and the social safety net shape the socioeconomic opportunities available to communities of color, as demonstrated by the water crisis in Flint, Michigan (ongoing at time of publication). Other rules are simply norms that codify personal bias, which is often unconscious – for example, occupational segregation that results from the repeated channeling of people of color into lower-wage positions.

## WHAT OTHER EXPLANATIONS MISS

### Neoclassical Economics

Over the last thirty years, proposed solutions to disparate economic outcomes have focused primarily on either individual responsibility or developing human capital – more rigorous education standards, skilling programs, investments in prekindergarten, and so on. However, personal responsibility cannot explain the unequal life chances faced by people of color, nor can it explain the increasingly limited social mobility of poor children and children of color, which results from the widening of the inequality ladder. And, unfortunately, education has not been the silver bullet that was promised: black Americans at every level of education continue to earn less than their white counterparts.[5]

It is no surprise that solutions oriented around individual responsibility or human capital growth have failed given the faulty classical economics from which they derive. The human capital approach is based on economic models that assume compensation is driven solely by productivity – the effort an individual is willing to exert and the skill with which it is exerted. The most influential version of this theory, associated with Gary Becker's *The Economics of Discrimination*, holds that discrimination cannot exist in labor markets that have at least some employers who are not racially biased.[6]

The theory has it that in a perfectly competitive economy, as long as there are some individuals who do not have racial (or gender or ethnic) prejudices, they will hire members of the discriminated-against group because their wages will be lower than those of similarly qualified members of the not-discriminated-against group. Of course, markets are not perfect, and decades of field experiments have proven the quite common-sense observation that discrimination persists in labor markets.[7]

*Neoliberalism* is a key concept that we will refer to frequently throughout this book. At its core, neoliberalism is an economic theory that the best way to advance human well-being is to encourage individual entrepreneurial freedom and create institutions that assert strong private property rights, free markets, and free trade. Under neoliberalism, the role of the state is to oversee those functions but take a hands-off approach to all other rule making.[8] For example, neoliberalism is fundamentally opposed to government regulation and in favor of privatization (withdrawing the state from the role of providing public services). As the antecedent to this book, *Rewriting the Rules of the American Economy*, argues, "deregulation" is in fact "reregulation," and "free markets" do in fact have rules; those rules simply benefit the already-powerful corporate and financial sectors at the expense of people. We use rules to ensure that markets perform as they should, especially given forces such as structural racism that affect the way markets function. Throughout this book, we will show how neoliberalism is a belief system and economic theory that was both fueled by and reinforces structural racism and racial rules.

Other terms we will use to refer to this concept (with similar or slightly varying definitions) include *market fundamentalism*, *market freedom*, and *laissez-faire economics*.

Arthur Okun, Lyndon Johnson's chair of the Council of Economic Advisors, famously argued that there was an inherent trade-off between equality and efficiency insofar as government institutions interfered with the free market. Okun's argument has been hijacked and simplified to argue against redistribution or legal protection of human rights.

However, two facts must be noted. First, most recent research, from case studies to cross-country analysis, shows no negative relationship between redistribution and economic performance.[9] Therefore, if the chief argument against enacting the kind of policy agenda for which we advocate is a concern about long-term economic growth, we can be confident that the preponderance of evidence suggests there is no validity to that concern.

Second, even if we indulge the premise of Okun's 1970s argument, Okun himself claimed an exception to his "trade-off" was the case of efforts to reduce discrimination because it is so inefficient to underutilize human capital. As the United States moves toward a majority-minority population, continued barriers to building or utilizing human capital for people of color could increasingly impoverish our national assets.

### Observable Bias

Another set of policies to reduce the racial income gap includes a combination of improving educational outcomes and reducing discrimination in hiring. While these are more complex and effective prescriptions, they are also grounded in simplistic economic models that fail to account for the full system of racially discriminatory structures. Many economists estimate the cost of job market discrimination to African Americans as the pay differential between similarly educated white and black workers. In this tradition, economists such as James Heckman calculate that much of the disparity in earnings and outcomes experienced by black Americans is due to differences in skills rather than discrimination.[10]

However, we argue that the models and regression results underpinning these approaches mostly capture the effects of individually mediated bias. As such, they fail to account for the degree to which other tested independent variables (education, skill, experience) are themselves dependent variables produced by actions and choices that are embedded in a political economy shaped by racially exclusionary and discriminatory rules. In plain language, the education and skills of a given job candidate are outcomes of life choices made in a world constrained by racialized rules.

## Progressive Economics: A Focus on Class

A more progressive economic framework understands the role of rules and institutions in circumscribing the economic outcomes for some and privileging the outcomes for others. This approach tends to begin and end with a focus on class: it asks how best to improve the economy for the least wealthy and powerful, but rarely considers race or gender.

The latest iterations of the inequality debate in the United States derive from this framework and have zeroed in on important drivers of economic inequality: weakened financial regulations, rampant short-termism in corporate decision making and an increase in corporate power, the erosion of labor protections, and the lack of collective power of working families and ordinary people. The policy agenda flowing from this diagnosis attempts to distribute power and income more broadly, whether through tax-and-transfer redistributive approaches or through "predistribution," that is, increasing wages before redistribution or expanding access to the labor market.[11]

We certainly agree with this general approach. But we also know that even if a rising tide were to lift all boats, and even if it were to benefit communities of color proportionally more than white Americans, this approach still would be insufficient to address systemic racial inequality. For example, a significant increase in the minimum wage might positively benefit a greater percentage of African Americans compared to whites. However, it would not address the root causes behind the disproportionate representation of black Americans and other nonwhites in low-wage jobs, would not guarantee a minimum number of hours of work, and would not benefit those who are unemployed. More aggressively inclusive economic policies would benefit people of color, but they would not keep a black boy like Trayvon Martin walking down his street with a bag of Skittles from becoming a target of violence.

## RACIAL RULES: AN ALTERNATIVE FRAMEWORK

We characterize our alternative institutionalist or structural framework as a theory of racial rules. Our framework argues that rules matter and having the power to write the rules matters. We argue that the economy is shaped by choices – choices determined by legal, regulatory, and expenditure policies, among other factors. It is also shaped by institutions that codify societal norms. In this way, the values and interests of the powerful (in terms of class, race, gender, etc.) are baked into the economy and can circumscribe opportunities and outcomes for the less powerful.

When the rules are written to benefit those who already hold privilege and power, as they too often are, the incentives for preserving and reinforcing those rules increase, and more resources are devoted to shaping the rules in favor of the powerful. In this kind of "rent-seeking" economy and society, short-term gains for the privileged (the "rent-seekers") are accompanied by long-term losses for the majority of individuals and for the economy as a whole.[12] And when the rules divert resources away from black Americans and black communities, as they have for more than two centuries, they result in racial inequality. This is not only a continued violation of human rights and American values but also imposes long-term costs on families of color and, in turn, on all Americans.

Throughout this book, we describe two kinds of rules: formal and informal. Formal rules are the regulatory and legal frameworks that make up the economy and society – including those that affect property ownership, corporate formation, labor and employment laws, copyright, antitrust, monetary, tax and expenditure policy, and other economic structures.[13] These laws, policies, and regulations are enacted and enforced by political decision makers.

Informal rules are not codified but are, instead, normative practices, behaviors, and standard operating procedures that also result in unequal racial outcomes. Informal rules can be structural – for example, the well-documented practice of steering people of color into lower-paying occupations.[14] They also can become manifest as personal racial bias, as in the case of a shopkeeper who provides poor or no service, or overt hostility, to African American customers.

Especially on matters of race, formal and informal rules interact, and both have very clear effects on economic outcomes and overall well-being. Within this broader framework, this book examines three distinct categories of racial rules:

- **Exclusionary rules** include *racially explicit laws*, such as slavery, Jim Crow, and the redlining of mortgages or other services. These exclusionary rules all actively sought to keep black Americans socially and economically separate from the rest of American society. Exclusionary rules also include *racially implicit laws*, such as the omission of domestic and agricultural workers from 1930s labor provisions, or today's mandatory minimum sentencing laws, which have a disproportionate impact on people of color. Both historically and today, implicit exclusions continue to have outsized impacts on economics, health, and well-being. Also included in this category is *racial bias*, both structural and personal.
- **Inclusionary rules** are laws, regulations, and policies that advance racial inclusion and equity. These rules are often "race-conscious" remedies – such as *Brown v. Board of Education*, the 1964 Civil Rights Act, the 1965 Voting Rights Act, and affirmative action in employment – intended to address racial injustices.
- **Nonrules** are the *absence of rules*, which allows discrimination and racially unequal consequences to persist. We might think of these as regulatory gaps. For instance, in the banking sector, the lack of rules to curb a range of predatory lending behavior in the run-up to the financial crisis of 2008 was a regulatory gap that, combined with interpersonal racial bias and incentives, resulted in racialized consequences (loss of wealth and assets) harmful to communities of color. Nonrules are also domains in which rules to advance racial equity are warranted but do not exist. Finally, nonrules can be what political scientists call "nondecisions"; this is when power is exercised to keep issues off of the agenda, resulting in a lack of rule making in areas where rules are sorely needed.

Throughout this book, we examine the cyclical nature of these racial rules, illustrating how they intersect and reinforce one another, thus codifying preexisting societal norms and shaping future norms. As we discuss in detail in the following chapter, these rules are the products of distinct historical eras.

These racialized rules fuel and perpetuate different forms of racism:

- **Institutional or structural racism**, which "stresses how past mistreatment drives current inequities" and is "codified in our institutions of custom, practice, and law."[15] As Camara Phillips Jones explains, this results in racially unequal access to goods, resources, opportunities, and power.[16] It also includes informal norms, practices, and behaviors that result in racially inequitable outcomes.
- **Personally mediated or interpersonal racism**, which includes prejudice – "differential assumptions about the abilities, motives, and intentions of others according to their race" – and discrimination – "differential actions toward others according to their race."[17] As Jones explains, this type of racism can be intentional or unintentional and includes acts of "commission as well as omission."

## OUR FRAMEWORK AND ITS PREDECESSORS

Our rules framework attempts to be broad and comprehensive. Our focus is on identifying the rules and structures that perpetuate unequal racial outcomes in an attempt to identify solutions.[18]

We build on an extensive, related literature. Perhaps most closely related is john powell's concept of "racialization," which he defines as "harmful practices, cultural norms, and institutional arrangements" that "create and maintain racialized outcomes."[19] powell explains that "because racialization is a historical and cultural set of processes, it does not have one meaning. Instead, it is a set of conditions and norms that are constantly evolving and interacting with the socio-political environment, varying from location to location, as well as throughout different periods in history." This conflicts with how we traditionally think of race and racism, as a "well defined and a limited set of discrete practices that remain constant over time, in spite of social changes." We also borrow powell's concept of "targeted universalism" to propose a way forward to a more inclusive future. As powell explains, targeted universalism is:

An approach that supports the needs of the particular while reminding us that we are all part of the same social fabric. Targeted universalism rejects a blanket universal which is likely to be indifferent to the reality that different groups are situated differently relative to the institutions and resources of society. It also rejects the claim of formal equality that would treat all people the same as a way of denying difference.[20]

We also draw on many other scholars who advance historical and sociological explanations of persistent and durable racial inequality.[21] Of particular note is the work of William Darity, Jr., who counters traditional economics' focus on individual behavior with "stratification economics," which highlights the "structural and intentional processes generating hierarchy and, correspondingly, income and wealth inequality between ascriptively distinguished groups."[22] Institutions and rules are thus designed to protect privilege, Darity argues, and the deficit narrative utilized in American politics is itself is a tool to defend and perpetuate material benefits.

Our framework is slightly different, in that it does not attempt to identify the motive behind racial rules. We do not argue that racial inequality is simply a byproduct of efforts to secure material privilege or that material privilege is simply a byproduct of racism. But Darity and others have greatly influenced our thinking, and both Darity and powell have contributed chapters to this book in order to explain their theories in greater detail.

We also draw on a number of scholars who describe the cross-cutting dimensions of inequality based on class, gender, sexuality, and geography as they play out within black communities.[23] And we owe a debt to those who focus on structural transformations of the economy and the rise of concentrated urban poverty, including most prominently William Julius Wilson. Wilson highlights the importance of class in African American life chances and explores how deindustrialization and the disappearance of well-paying manufacturing jobs, racial residential segregation, and the pushback against fully enforced civil rights laws combined to create racialized urban poverty at the same time as mass incarceration accelerated.[24] Loic Waquant describes the current U.S. criminal justice system as one of our nation's four "peculiar" race-producing institutions, one of "forced confinement" built on years of racial subjugation and exclusion.[25] The other three are chattel slavery, Jim Crow, and the northern "ghetto" that corresponded with the Great Migration that ended in the 1960s.

A number of others have illustrated how our vast racial inequities – along with the specific penal system changes of the last three decades – have only deepened and reinforced the systemic social and economic exclusions experienced by black Americans, their families, and their communities. As Frederick Harris, Valeria Sinclair-Chapman, and Brian McKenzie show, these forces undercut the rise of black political power in the post–civil rights period.[26]

And finally, we draw on the work of those who show how geography and place are significant determinants of racial inequality.[27] To paraphrase sociologist Patrick Sharkey, African Americans are "stuck in place" in high-poverty and racially segregated neighborhoods, which constrain their life chances and outcomes much more than individual effort.[28] And it is a combination of racial rules we describe in this book that creates and perpetuates the conditions of "stuckness" for far too many black Americans.

## REWRITING THE RULES OF RACIAL INCLUSION: GOALS AND OBJECTIVES

Examining, at this level of breadth, the intersection of racial rules and economic and social outcomes entails a peculiar and specific set of challenges. Certainly, the literature around race and inequality is vast. However, at this particular juncture in American political life, we believe this effort can have particular value.

First, we hope to add to the theoretical conversation about racial disparities by challenging several different and still predominant schools of thought. By detailing the effects of the racial rules, we refute mainstream economic arguments to the effect that racial exclusion and discrimination will compete itself away, and show that assumptions about perfect markets and perfect rationality are insufficient to explain the outcomes we see around us. Just as bargaining power is affected by factors such as the strength of unions and firms' market power is determined by their ability to set prices, the political power of various groups determines their ability to have the rules of the market written and enforced in their favor.

We also argue that class-based economic policies alone will not improve racial inequities and that changing course requires a comprehensive agenda of racially targeted solutions. Our rules-based approach is an emergent one, bridging sectorial and historical analyses and showing the ways in which different kinds of rules reinforce each other over time and can have deeply problematic effects.

Second, we illustrate the cyclical and complex system of racial rules that lead to unequal opportunities and outcomes for black Americans. We aim to catalog and specify many of the rules that drive and contribute to economic inequality by race and by gender across a range of dimensions of life. The rules that drive this inequality are numerous, and their effects are compounding. Their sheer range and scope are impossible to document in a single book, but we strive to highlight the most egregious in order to demonstrate the ways in which they intersect and reinforce each other.

Third, cataloging the rules will make it clear that racial inequality, like economic inequality, is a choice. We can and must rewrite our current exclusionary and discriminatory rules – as we have twice before – to create a more inclusive economy and a more racially just society. Throughout this book, we make the case for a comprehensive policy overhaul, one with targeted solutions that will have universal benefits. We do not aim to provide a deep policy agenda, but we do set forth a framework for the kinds of policies we believe are required to improve the lives of all Americans, and specifically black Americans. We know that without proposals that policy makers and advocates can fight about and fight for, we will not see real change.

Finally, we hope this book will serve as a bridge between academics whose work has identified the racial rules driving and contributing to racial inequality, advocates who have called attention to the deeply unequal and unjust lived experiences of black Americans, and those in a position to rewrite the rules. In the 2016 presidential election, the demands of racial justice advocates pushed the Democratic candidates to acknowledge the impact of racial inequality and propose certain policy solutions for addressing it. However, progressive candidates and policy makers continue to lack a deep analysis of why we must tackle economic inequality and racial inequality simultaneously, and continue to lack a narrative that explains how neoliberal economic policies and the racial rules hurt not only black Americans but also poor and working-class whites. Rather than creating two diametrically opposed American realities divided by race, it is important to come to a shared understanding of the economic problems facing working and low-income people of all racial backgrounds, and of the polices that will benefit all Americans.

## WHY FOCUS ONLY ON BLACK AMERICANS?

We have chosen to focus specifically on the experiences of black Americans for a number of reasons. First, the United States' history and enduring legacy of black slavery is built into our current institutions, policies, programs, and practices and has multigenerational impacts on the life chances and outcomes of black Americans. Second, as we will describe throughout this book, black Americans face among the worst social and economic outcomes of all ethnic and racial groups, and the factors that drive those outcomes are often unique to the historic experience of black Americans and deserve an in-depth analysis. Third, the marginalization of black Americans also generates unequal outcomes for other racially marginalized groups, particularly Latinos and Asians, as well as poor and working-class whites. To paraphrase Lani Guinier and Gerald Torres, issues of race are the "miner's canary," warning of conditions in American democracy and the economy that pose a threat to us all.[29] Finally, the focus on black Americans is a response to the proliferation of and increased attention to police violence and mass incarceration and to the demand from grassroots movements for leaders at all levels to acknowledge our nation's long history of devaluing blackness and fostering black inequality in virtually every segment of American political, economic, and social life.

By focusing on black Americans, we do not suggest that racial rules do not touch the lives of other racial and ethnic groups in the United States. But racial rules are often particular to specific racial groups, and too often we refer to "people of color" as a monolithic group, without disaggregating data and understanding how racial rules impact groups under that umbrella in distinct ways. For example, the federal government relegated Indigenous Americans to reservations, and many Native children were forced into residential, segregated schools where they endured cultural genocide and physical, emotional, and sexual abuse. The Chinese Exclusion Act of 1882 prohibited only Chinese laborers from immigrating to the United States. Jim Crow laws targeted the comprehensive social and economic segregation of African Americans specifically. Our current failure to implement comprehensive immigration reform has left millions of families – many of them black immigrants – without access to fair-paying jobs, proper health care, quality education, or legal recourse in the face of human rights violations. The analysis in this book is just the beginning of the Roosevelt Institute's inquiry into how the racial rules of our economy and society have a unique impact on individuals across race, gender, and ethnicity.

## THE STRUCTURE OF THIS BOOK

We begin with three chapters that provide context for our analysis of the racial rules. Chapter 1, written by Roosevelt Institute president and CEO Felicia Wong, delves into the political, economic and social history that provides a backdrop for the racialized outcomes we observe today. In Chapter 2, William Darity provides an overview of stratification economics, and in Chapter 3, john powell discusses targeted universalism, as outlined above.

Chapters 4 through 9 examine the racial rules in practice across six different dimensions: wealth, income, education, criminal justice, health, and democratic participation. For each of these areas, we tease out causal mechanisms and mediating pathways that link rules to unequal outcomes. Of course, these mechanisms vary, and the ways in which the rules connect to different historical eras play out differently. But we also find common ground. Further, we know that the rules in these various sectors have compounding effects. Real people live in different neighborhoods and have varying levels of access to jobs and health care and fresh food, which are all related. But teasing out specific rules that drive outcomes in each of these areas of our society is also important and, we hope, valuable.

Against the backdrop of stark racial economic inequality dating back centuries, we make the case for pushing past both explicit and implicit exclusions, as well as ostensible race neutrality. In Chapter 10, we sketch out an agenda of positive rules and targeted universalism that we believe is a feasible – perhaps the *only* feasible – way to promote greater overall economic health and greater racial inclusion.

1

# American Politics and Economic Outcomes for African Americans

## A Brief Historical Overview

### INTRODUCTION

Throughout the history of the United States, dating back even before its official founding, unparalleled economic opportunity has been inextricably linked with deliberate racial exclusion. Race itself is in many ways not just a social but also a political construct. Before 1676 and Bacon's Rebellion[1] in colonial Virginia, individuals' primary political identification was based not on skin tone, but on religion ("Christians" or "heathens") or national origin (Germans, French, Irish, Scots, etc.). But after the rebellion, in which poor people of diverse backgrounds rose up together against oppressive oligarchic rule, British landowners realized that dividing working people by race could allow them to establish economic, social, and political dominance.[2] Thus, in the seventeenth century, American notions of race began to link skin color to power and powerlessness. This shaped the next three centuries of economic, political, and social rules and their outcomes.

This chapter situates the disparate social and economic outcomes we describe throughout the rest of this book in *political decisions* made over hundreds of years by elites, organizers and activists, and everyday people. We illustrate the repeated cycles of progress – or the promise of progress – and retrenchment over the course of the last 150 years, since the end of slavery. As we argue throughout this book, history matters. The past always weighs heavily on the present, and as twenty-first century calls for reparations to African Americans remind us, much of today's status quo is the product of racially exclusionary rules made long before our time.[3] At the same time, grassroots organizers, everyday people, political decision-makers, and academic experts have sometimes been able to work together to forge real progress and improve economic and social outcomes not only for African Americans but for all Americans. This push and pull is at the heart of America's racial story.

We begin by describing the cyclical relationship between economic trends, ideologies, and the political decisions that shape the racial rules. We then outline the history of racial rules and explain how they have shaped unequal outcomes over time, beginning with an overview of two important eras in our racial past: the First Reconstruction (1863–1877) and the Jim Crow retrenchment that followed (1877–1954). The main focus of the chapter will be on the mid-twentieth century, examining the modern civil rights movement and its complex aftermath. As we navigate extraordinarily difficult times in our politics and economy, it is necessary to recount and understand historical moments of progress as well as the backsliding that followed, the effects of which we continue to live with today.

### Complex Causality: Economics, Belief Systems, and Politics

The core of our argument is that economic outcomes cannot be considered in isolation from politics or belief systems. To understand economic outcomes for individuals and social groups, we must consider the interaction of three different factors (see Figure 1.1). The first is external, structural economic trends, such as the increased global mobility of capital or rapidly changing technology. The second is political belief systems, or ideologies. For more than a century, the ongoing debate has been between neoliberalism or laissez-faire fundamentalism, which privileges individuals and assumes that competitive markets work best without government intervention, versus an approach that includes a central role for the state, noting that markets and market outcomes are structured by political decisions. The third factor is political decisions, the choices that structure the regulatory and legal frameworks comprising the economy, including those that affect property ownership, corporate formation, labor law, copyright and antitrust policy, and monetary, tax, and expenditure policy. These choices create what we refer to as "the rules."[4] These rules are then embedded in and perpetuated through legal and political institutions – whether influential legal precedent, the structure of federal or state decision-making bodies, or the culture and practices of private-sector employers.

From a theoretical and methodological perspective, it would be preferable if we could say with confidence that one factor always influences the other in some linear chain. But it is never that simple; all three factors interact in multiple directions. In a historical overview, however, we can – as Karl Polanyi argues in his 1944 classic *The Great Transformation* – tease out

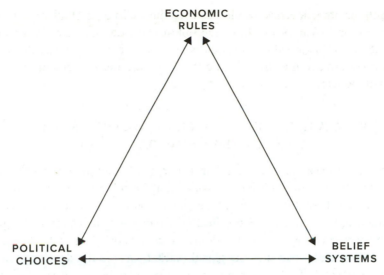

Figure 1.1. The reinforcing nature of economic rules, political choices and belief system.

those interactions to help explain various moments. In particular, we can show where human agency and political decisions could have been made differently, and can be made differently going forward, to promote better economic outcomes and greater racial inclusion.[5]

It is important to note that even the relatively basic points that history matters and that economics and politics are fundamentally intertwined are not universally or equally held. J. Phillip Thompson has argued that the notion that history matters, or perhaps more precisely how history matters, differs across racial groups in the United States:

The African American perspective has historical depth; an understanding that centuries of racism have led to endogenous forms of racism thoroughly embedded in institutions and culture. It is not unusual for African Americans to invoke slavery and segregation in contemporary debates on social policy …. On the other hand, white Americans tend to believe that equal opportunity is available for all. This is consistent with the core American values of individualism and egalitarianism. Within this framework, existing inequality is seen as fair, the inevitable result of the failure to avail oneself of opportunity.[6]

This difference in belief matters if we aim to create a more cohesive, collective set of understandings about the causes of and solutions to economic disparities. It is undeniable that inequality is racialized, but it is also true that in purely economic terms, far more inclusive growth is possible. Many of the solutions to economic inequality, whether measured by income, wealth, or other metrics, would improve the well-being of all Americans, not just black Americans. But deep political divides across racial groups, borne out of historical circumstances and exacerbated by social distance, will no doubt continue to make it difficult to pass and implement inclusive growth policies.

## PRE-CIVIL RIGHTS: THE FIRST RECONSTRUCTION AND THE JIM CROW BACKLASH

The first 250 years of the American experiment were defined by the formation and evolution of what was called that "peculiar institution"[7]: racialized slavery. Predating our country's official founding, and even protected in the original text of the Constitution, slavery was the economic engine of our young country. From the domestic expansion of agriculture, which sold cotton and tobacco to the global marketplace, to the development of infrastructure to facilitate domestic and global trade of slavery-produced commodities, to the growth and expansion of our entire financial system (banking, credit, and insurance) to expand domestic slavery once we forbade slave-trading in 1808,[8] our early economy and economic growth were deeply rooted in free labor from black slaves (and, early on, from white indentured servants). Later, the issue of slavery and its expansion to new territories in a rapidly growing United States came to a head in the bloodiest conflict ever fought on our shores, the American Civil War. After the North prevailed, the Radical Republicans, led by former general Ulysses Grant after Abraham Lincoln's assassination, initiated a program of Reconstruction to create inclusive racial rules for the former black slaves and unify the grossly divided country. Reconstruction always faced an uphill battle, as its success depended on the establishment of new institutions such as the Freedmen's Bureau that were opposed by many, including President Andrew Johnson, who empowered ex-Confederates and vetoed civil rights legislation proposed even by moderates.

The short-lived progress of the First Reconstruction and the immediate retrenchment that was Jim Crow exemplify recurring themes in American life, and demonstrate how political choices have constrained and shaped economic outcomes for black Americans throughout history. In this case, we see the economic importance of political choices made by Radical Republicans – a coalition of freed slaves and their white allies – versus those made by white "Redeemers" – led by wealthy pro-business interests in the South. The question of whether newly free black Americans would become full participants in American democracy and the U.S. system of free labor depended on both the economic interests and the racial attitudes of whites in power, as well as on the political and organizing levers available to the newly freed blacks themselves. This was all within the context of a Confederate defeat in the Civil War that was not only economically devastating (given that the South's economy was built around slave labor) but also politically, socially, and racially destabilizing.

## Racial Inclusion and Its Discontents: The First Reconstruction (1863–1877)

The First Reconstruction, which historian Eric Foner dates from the 1863 Emancipation Proclamation to the 1877 end of federal oversight in the South, was an era of far-reaching ambition in its attempts to reverse the social and economic effects of enslavement on newly freed African Americans.[9]

The core legal achievements of Reconstruction, which resonate to this day, are the Thirteenth, Fourteenth, and Fifteenth Amendments to the U.S. Constitution. The Thirteenth Amendment abolished slavery except as punishment for a crime, the Fourteenth Amendment ensured equal protection under the law and birthright citizenship for the formerly enslaved, and the Fifteenth Amendment prohibited racially discriminatory voting laws. These Reconstruction Amendments had a number of far-reaching ramifications and ultimately uprooted the bedrock of the U.S. economic, social, and political order.

But Congress, led by the Radical Republicans after the election of 1866, understood that passing the inclusive racial rules of these amendments would not fully guarantee the rights they espoused absent robust federal protection, both legislative and otherwise. Republican politicians took power in most of the southern states and utilized both the oversight of U.S. Army troops and the authority of the short-lived (1865–1872) Freedmen's Bureau (a federal agency established to provide assistance to former enslaved African Americans and impoverished whites in the South and District of Columbia),[10] in an attempt to truly develop a free labor economy for African Americans. Importantly, the Freedmen's Bureau, during its short tenure, attempted to distribute land – and thus wealth – to newly freed slaves. The opposition to this distribution, in particular, led directly to the racial wealth gap detailed in Chapter 4.

The additional inclusive racial rules passed during this period allowed federal officials to begin prosecuting violations of the foundational rights and inclusions afforded by the constitutional amendments. For example, the Civil Rights Acts of 1866, 1870, and 1875, as well as the Reconstruction Act of 1867, enabled federal supervision and enforcement against voter suppression, permitted blacks to serve on juries, guaranteed equal access to public accommodations, and more. These acts also expanded federal power and federal enforcement while curbing southern states' rights (which southern "Redeemers" sought to use to reassert white dominance). In doing so, they seeded a debate that roils even today around federal versus state power.

These legal and legislative successes did lead to real gains for newly freed black Americans. Across the South, black families were reunited, and they built schools and churches and other benevolent associations that became core social and political institutions in black communities. As James T. Campbell notes in his history of the African Methodist Episcopal Church, "For former slaves the right to assemble openly and without white supervision was a central dimension of freedom."[11]

Public school funding was equally distributed to black and white children, and black Americans had moderate access to legal protections. Indeed, it was the Reconstruction Era legislatures that introduced free, public schooling in the South. Freed blacks organized to increase political participation and representation; black leaders used the Declaration of Independence to argue for full equality before the law and for black suffrage. In the decades after the war, black leaders held political control at the local and state level, albeit briefly. Black elected representation in Congress in the late 1870s was among the highest it has been in American history.[12]

Economic empowerment was a major part of the Reconstruction agenda. As Foner describes, former slaves fought hard to "control the conditions under which they labored," organizing workers, bargaining collectively, and striking for better working conditions.[13] But political ideologies both inched them closer to – and pushed them further from – economic security and independence. Soon after Radical Republicans passed the 1866 Civil Rights Act, they enacted Senate Bill 60,[14] which would have made the Freedmen's Bureau a permanent national agency and also enabled freed blacks to own land. The bill would have authorized the federal government to purchase farmlands and resell to homesteading black Americans at low, long-term prices.[15] Andrew Johnson vetoed the bill, and the Senate failed by only two votes to override his veto.

The bill – which nearly two-thirds of both chambers of Congress supported – might have enabled freed blacks to escape the trap of tenant farming and finally become landowners. That base of economic security, paired with blacks' increased power in political offices and expanded civil society institutions, might have provided the necessary foundation for freed blacks to resist the backlash of politicians fighting to "redeem" the South. Unfortunately, as W. E. B. DuBois, Foner, and many others have noted, true economic equality – access to land ownership and to jobs – never materialized.[16] As Foner argues, "[T]he failure to respond to the former slaves' desire for land left most with no choice but to work for their former owners." The fate of S.B. 60 and the economic rules it determined was one of many political choices that fostered racial inequalities for generations.

In the end, the early successes of post–Civil War racial inclusion were both incomplete and short-lived. The mass mobilization of free blacks was met with fierce backlash and extreme violence as many southern whites attempted to preserve their social and economic domination. Newly freed slaves were threatened, assaulted, and killed for attempting to leave plantations, disputing contracts, attempting to buy or rent land, resisting whippings, and not working as their employers desired. Foner writes: "The pervasiveness of violence reflected whites' determination to define in their own way the meaning of freedom and to resist black efforts to establish their autonomy, whether in matters of family, church, labor, or personal demeanor."[17]

At the same time, in a series of high-profile cases, the Supreme Court systematically undermined the radical inclusionary reach of these pieces of civil rights legislation and of the Reconstruction Amendments themselves. The *Slaughterhouse Cases* (86 US 36, 1873)[18] and *Civil Rights Cases* (109 US 3, 1883) significantly narrowed the legal reach of the Fourteenth Amendment's guarantees of the "privileges and immunities" of citizenship and equal protection.[19] Even more glaringly, the Court in *U.S. v. Cruikshank* (92 US 542, 1876) essentially overturned the convictions of local white supremacists who massacred a crowd of African Americans in an effort to retain political control after several black candidates won power in local elections.[20]

The effect was immediate, with states across the South implementing laws aimed at overturning newly won rights for former slaves and their families.[21] Foner argues that, as bad as the economic situation for black Americans was, "It was not economic dependency … but widespread violence, coupled with a Northern retreat from the ideal of equality, that doomed Reconstruction."[22] Many forces were behind the political decisions of 1877, including the complexities required to resolve the hotly contested 1876 presidential election, but the outcome was the removal of federal troops tasked with monitoring inclusion in the South, the resurgence of white business-oriented political power, and the end of the First Reconstruction.

### Racial Exclusion and Jim Crow (1877–1954)

"Jim Crow" refers to one of the most pernicious periods of American history: a legalized racial caste system that required, throughout the American South, racial separation in all elements of public life. The hardening of Jim Crow laws by 1900[23] reflected the resurgent power of southern Democrats, whose ideology centered on white supremacy, and an agricultural economy that evolved to take advantage of African Americans as low-cost agricultural and domestic labor.

Of course, the political underpinnings and economic structure of Jim Crow were present as Reconstruction ended in 1877, and informal segregation was deeply woven into southern culture. However, the legalized caste system that made any kind of racial mixing – in public places, schools, or workplaces – illegal did not emerge immediately after the end of federal oversight, but instead took about twenty years to harden into law.

Between 1890 and 1910, a fierce response to Reconstruction gained ground throughout the South, with the passage of a number of voting laws, including poll taxes, literacy tests, and other restrictions. Federal lawmakers supported these efforts. As Richard Valelly notes, "A House report from the 53rd Congress (1893–1895) demanded that 'every trace of reconstruction measures be wiped from the books.' By 1911, this goal was effectively met. About 94 percent of a once-elaborate federal electoral regulatory code was repealed."[24] Voter registration and all black political and public participation dropped precipitously.[25]

These explicit racially exclusionary rules had clear political power effects, as well as a self-reinforcing effect on the ideology of white supremacy. As African Americans were restricted not only from voting but also from public life, the ideology of white supremacy was bolstered by the full force of political decision makers and the institutions they represented and controlled.

While less explicitly exclusionary than political restrictions, implicitly biased institutions circumscribed economic opportunity for black Americans in both the North and the South. While the South was still an agrarian economy, the North had far more factory jobs, especially for black men. This was the huge economic draw of the Great Migration, one of the most significant demographic shifts in American history, which saw 6 million African Americans move from the rural South to northern cities during and after the two World Wars.[26] The rise and subsequent fall of manufacturing jobs in all major American cities is one of the most important economic shifts undergirding the twentieth and twenty-first centuries.[27] These jobs could employ non-college-educated whites and black men alike (though differences in labor unions, worker organizing, and the racial dis-crimination of employers meant that black men and women were typically far worse off than similarly situated whites).

In the agrarian South, race-neutral land ownership rules were in fact on the books, but access to economic opportunity was not the same for black farmers as for white. Whites were more likely to own larger farms, more sophisticated farming implements, and other machinery and had more access to fertilizer. In short, they had more capital.

In the 1930s and 1940s, many of the social and economic advances of Franklin Roosevelt's New Deal rules – which aimed to provide worker protections and organizing rights, job creation, wage increases, and ultim-ately education and homeownership to middle-income Americans – were expressly not part of the social contract offered to blacks. And these implicit exclusions were nationwide, not just southern: African Americans, other people of color, and women were functionally excluded from the initial Social Security Act, critical labor law provisions, homeownership, and the G.I. Bill. As Dorian Warren notes:

Prima facie race-neutral occupational exclusions for domestic and agricultural workers in the [1935 National Labor Relations Act], identical to the exclusions in other New Deal social policies, had the racialized effect of excluding the vast majority of black workers, who found themselves at the bottom of the feudal-preindustrial and industrial racial and economic regimes. Southern political elites' material and social incentives to maintain these orders explain the com-promise between the Southern and Northern wings of the Democratic Party that led to this exclusion.[28]

In short, the federal decision to exclude domestic and agricultural workers was an explicit decision made in large part to win the support of southern congressional Democrats for a significant set of economic security rules. That political decision had disparate economic consequences that persist today.[29] New Deal provisions were a path to economic security and well-being for millions of Americans, and in fact many African Americans did ultimately support and benefit from the New Deal. But overall, the New Deal was a gateway to middle-class prosperity for whites that left many people of color behind. This was part of a larger pattern during the Jim Crow era, wherein both explicit and implicit rules, enabled by and ultim-ately enabling white supremacist beliefs held by both the voting public and political decision makers, led to backsliding and deep social and economic inequality.

## THE CIVIL RIGHTS ERA, 1954–1980: THE SECOND RECONSTRUCTION

In the mid-1950s, after decades of assiduous political organizing and intellectual ferment, the United States entered the most recent era of inclusion, and the one that bears most heavily on our contemporary consciousness: the Civil Rights era.

The popular cultural story of the Civil Rights Movement is tinged with nostalgia, with a multiracial cast of heroes marching toward social justice. And there is some truth to this version of the story. Between 1954 and the mid-1960s, legal victories – most famously *Brown v. Board of Education* in 1954, which ended legal racial segregation and thus formally ended Jim Crow – driven by smart organizing and dedicated movement building, did lead to a profound change in American social norms around race. Social movements, and especially the Civil Rights Movement, helped forge a common political identity for an entire generation of black and white Americans born postwar that resonates to this day. The black Civil Rights Movement also inspired a host of other movements around immigrants' rights, Asian and Latino rights, LGBTQ rights, and women's rights.

There is no doubt that contemporary history has been heavily influenced by the heroic version of this tale. But as we shall see, the ultimate narrative of this era is far more complex, as inclusive racial rules clashed with broader economic trends that resulted in fierce racial backlash. This historical overview, though brief, augments the economic theory we put forward in the book's first chapter and builds on the more distant history detailed earlier in this chapter. It suggests that the racial rules that shape today's economic and social outcomes have themselves been shaped by the beliefs and material outcomes of our recent past.

### The Civil Rights Movement: Legal and Political Victories and Lasting Consequences

One way to understand the levers and impact of the twentieth-century Civil Rights Movement is through a legal lens. The NAACP Legal Defense Fund innovated a strategic litigation strategy to win legal reforms around racial inclusion in a context where national political reforms were stymied.[30] Led by the Warren Court's landmark 1954 decision in *Brown v. Board of Education*, and then solidified by a range of subsequent legal decisions for the next several decades, the American legal system declared various forms of segregation – in schools and in housing – unconstitutional. In 1967's

*Loving v. Virginia*, the Court declared racial intermarriage legal. The impact of these laws was further strengthened by a series of hard-fought national legislative actions, most importantly the Civil Rights Act, the Voting Rights Act, and the Fair Housing Act, which collectively outlawed racial segregation of public spaces as well as discrimination in employment, voting, and housing.

These victories form the backbone of the Civil Rights era's accomplishments and in many ways continue to shape the legal norms around race in American politics. The court cases in particular have had at least three lasting consequences.

First, while these decisions certainly did not eradicate racism, research shows they did result in decreased social acceptability of explicit discrimination and racial intolerance.[31] Nondiscrimination and racial tolerance are not only the legal norm in the United States, but also the presumed social norm. As late as the mid-1960s, politicians could run on a platform of racial segregation, but ultimately the moral and legal practices of the Civil Rights Movement won out; for much of the next fifty years, outright and public racial disparagement were generally seen as professionally and politically disqualifying.

In its place, some have adopted the more implicitly racist "dog-whistle politics" described by Ian Haney López, in which speakers use rhetoric with coded messaging to signal more racially charged sentiments.[32] The success of Donald Trump's 2016 presidential campaign marks a shift from dog-whistle politics back to explicit racial rhetoric, and research shows that white Americans remain more likely to ascribe negative traits to blacks than to whites, less willing to support interventions to remedy persistent racial inequality, and highly resistant to "special favors" for blacks.[33] Still, equal treatment remains far more the American norm today than it was in 1950. We see this not only in the public sector but also in the private sector, with the 1964 Civil Rights Act in particular leading to a new norm of nondiscrimination among Fortune 500 companies and major employers.[34]

Second, the ending of formal legal segregation, especially in schools, has led to material gains. Clearly, this is not the case for all or even the majority of African Americans; this book is, after all, about the ongoing inequalities and inequities in outcomes for black and white Americans. As we will describe, there is unfortunately little evidence that blacks have gained in relative position on key economic indicators, and for one category, at least, things probably have gotten worse in relative terms: wealth. However, the benefits of desegregation and the Civil Rights Movement more broadly are worth noting and should be looked to as we strive to create policies that will lead to more equitable outcomes.

Finally, as CORE founder and March on Washington organizer Bayard Rustin hoped, the Civil Rights Movement ultimately did move from protest to politics.[35] By some measures, African Americans have gained significant political power since the middle of the twentieth century. In the wake of the March on Washington, 60 percent of the black electorate went to the polls in 1964 (and outside of the South, which saw vicious voter suppression the year before the Voting Rights Act of 1965, the rate was 72 percent).[36] Just as significantly, black political leaders began to win political office in the 1960s with astonishing rapidity. The year 1967 saw the election of the first black mayors in major American cities: Carl Stokes in Cleveland, Ohio, and Richard Hatcher in Gary, Indiana. Jeffrey Adler notes that this marked a sea change in American urban and political history:

After three and one-half centuries of complete or relative disenfranchisement, African Americans rapidly assumed the mayor's office in nearly every major city in the nation. Within sixteen years … three of the four largest urban centers in the United States had elected African-American mayors, and in 1990 the nation's biggest city, New York, followed suit. By 1993, African Americans had been elected mayor in sixty-seven cities with populations of more than fifty thousand residents, and most had majority-white populations. Nor was the trend restricted to major urban centers or to the liberal bastions of the North. Only a decade after Stokes's and Hatcher's victories, more than two hundred African-American mayors headed U.S. cities, and by 1990 the figure exceeded three hundred, generating one of the most important shifts in twentieth-century American politics.[37]

## Civil Rights: Where the Movement Fell Short

Changes in attitudes, material benefits, and political power: the Civil Rights Movement had real and deep impact. But why didn't we see more lasting gains? The reasons are multiple – and while racially motivated backlash on the part of both white citizens and politicians in power is clearly one answer, we must understand that retrenchment in a larger context.

The legal rules pioneered by civil rights advocates were vitally important, but ultimately uneven and incomplete.[38] Attempts to implement victories around school desegregation, housing desegregation, and the Voting Rights Act led to retrenchment. Moreover, as Warren argues, "greater democratic inclusion often occurs in the midst of structural changes in the economy and either precedes or accompanies greater economic inequality writ large, blunting the impact of advances in political rights."[39] This played out in the aforementioned case of the rise of black mayors in cities throughout the country, which occurred at the same time that deindustrialization led to employment and fiscal crises in those very locales.

The tectonic shift in the economy from primarily industrial and manufacturing work to service-focused work left many non-college-educated workers, both black and white, in a much more precarious position. And the common generational identity forged between the March on Washington and Freedom Summer, as important as it was, did not lead to truly diverse and integrated workplaces, schools, or neighborhoods. Instead, the interaction of key legal, economic, political, and social trends resulted in a racially fraught early twenty-first century. We will explore this retrenchment in greater detail in the next section.

## ECONOMIC WEAKNESS PERSISTS FOR AFRICAN AMERICANS: POLITICAL ROOTS AND STRUCTURAL FACTORS

Despite the midcentury victories for greater racial equality, political weakness and economic inequalities for black Americans have persisted. The following are just a few of many possible measures: The black unemployment rate has consistently been at least twice the rate of white unemployment since the 1960s. Black poverty (and poverty overall) did see real improvements in the 1960s, but since then the rate has mostly held steady at around 30 percent, approximately three times the recent white poverty rate.[40] A staggering racial wealth gap disadvantages black Americans in every sphere of their lives. And, as we describe in detail in subsequent chapters, neither education nor income seems able to ensure that black Americans have the wealth, homeownership, or health outcomes – or the freedom from discrimination by the criminal justice system – that similarly situated white Americans enjoy.

### Political Backlash and Prejudice

Among the factors holding African Americans back, the most readily apparent is social and political backlash. Anti-integration fights have been a major element in the American political landscape since the 1950s. Some have been explicit, from George Wallace's clear "Segregation now, segregation tomorrow, segregation forever" 1963 battle cry to Louise Day Hicks's antibusing organization, ROAR (Restore Our Alienated Rights), which became active in mid-1970s Boston. Others have been and continue to be implicit, from the ongoing political fight between the U.S. Department of Housing and Urban Development and Westchester County, New York, over affordable housing to the battle between voting rights advocates and those who would curtail legal protections for voters. The latter culminated in *Shelby County v. Holder*, a 2013 case in which the Supreme Court curtailed Voting Rights Act oversight in counties with a history of discrimination.[41] These are the political arguments that make headlines and are the basis of advocacy battles.

Backlash also includes policies that are clearly racially motivated but masquerade as either economic or values-based initiatives. Beginning in the 1970s, white suburbanites and their political representatives justified "white flight" based on economic freedom – specifically, the freedom to choose one's own property. Housing discrimination was justified on similar grounds.[42] Along the same lines, cuts to welfare often have been justified with veiled narratives about family values, work ethic, and fiscal austerity. However, at their core those policies have been shaped by centuries-old narratives about women of color, effectively using sexism and racism to promote divestment from the safety net that hurts poor women of color in particular and low-income Americans generally.[43] While these debates are often framed as color-blind political battles, the racial bias motivating the fight is rarely subtle or accidental.

### Structural Shifts: Deindustrialization and Demographic Changes in Cities and Suburbs

Major changes in the structure of the economy are often less clear, but they are no less a critical factor in the economic health of African Americans in the late twentieth century. As many scholars, most prominently William Julius Wilson, have noted, we must look to the overall trajectory and shape of the macroeconomy to understand the fortunes of black workers and black families. Clearly, the demise of the manufacturing industry (with its stable salaries, benefits, and protections) and the rise of the personal service economy (with its low wages, lack of benefits, and weak protections) are critical variables.

However, the rise of neoliberal ideology, which defunded public institutions that might have eased this economic transition, is itself a backlash against the inclusion of black Americans as beneficiaries of public investment. As Ira Katznelson outlines in *When Affirmative Action Was White*, public investment in education, benefits, infrastructure, and a range of institutions designed to support white Americans in the industrial economy was fairly noncontroversial before the Civil Rights Movement. The failure to adapt public institutions to the changing economy has had adverse consequences for both black and white Americans.

As we describe in Chapter 5, deindustrialization, meaning primarily the decline of manufacturing as a share of total employment, has been one of the defining features of twentieth century economic development. The phenomenon started early in the United States, with the share of manufacturing employment falling from a peak of 28 percent in 1965 to less than 15 percent in 2000, and 10 percent by 2012.[44]

This change in the fundamental structure of work coincided with a late twentieth-century American politics that was increasingly partisan and economically neoliberal, and which produced very little investment in infrastructure, K–12 public schooling, or other public goods. Thus a kind of slow-moving disaster befell millions of working men and women who, in the 1950s and 1960s, might have been able, with a high school education or some college, to obtain a job that paid enough to raise a family on.

This is a sadly familiar tale, but what is perhaps less well known is the extent to which deindustrialization had a disproportionate impact on black workers. As Wilson reported in his landmark 1990s research on joblessness in African American communities, "in 1950, a substantial portion of the urban black population in the United States was poor but they were working. ... However, as we entered the 1990s most poor adults were not working in a typical week in the ghetto neighborhoods of America's larger cities." Wilson goes on to note that by 1990, in three of Chicago's historic Black Belt neighborhoods, between 25 and 40 percent of adults reported working in any typical week. This lack of employment affects not just individuals and families but entire communities.[45]

Part of this is, no doubt, about education and skills. Fifty-five percent of black men in 1980 had completed high school, compared to 71 percent of white men, and only 12 percent of black men had completed four years of college or more, compared to 22 percent of white men.[46] This is in itself the result of political choices, given the relative educational opportunities made available to both groups historically. But the sociological research is clear that this is not the only factor in play. As the American Sociological Association (ASA) reports, "education and skills play a role but do not fully explain ... the historical disparities between whites and racial minorities with respect to earnings, labor force participation, training and promotion opportunities, and choice of occupation."[47] Furthermore, education and skills go no distance in explaining racial wealth differences.

In retrospect, the evidence suggests that black Americans were hit hardest due to the way that broader economic trends interacted with centuries of racialized rules. Those colliding forces resulted in residential segregation,

schooling segregation and educational inequality, and geographic disparities with respect to access to the labor market. But this was not always clear
to policy makers and activists in the moment. As Warren has argued, "most
policy makers and activists assumed that an industrial America was here
to stay and would continue to provide good jobs for working- and middle-
class Americans, especially black[s] and Latino American[s]."[48]

With the rise of the service economy, we have seen increased employer
bias toward hiring nonblacks for jobs that require "soft skills." The ASA
continued:

Relatively well-paying, unionized manufacturing jobs in the steel, auto, and durable
goods industries were eliminated. … [W]hite men without post-secondary education suffered the greatest wage losses (because their wages were higher to begin
with). But African American men were particularly hard hit by job losses; their
unemployment rate hit 20 percent during the recession in 1983.[49]

This also has long-term effects. Black workers who are unemployed go to
the back of the "job queue," which in many cases makes them seem undesirable and harder to hire.[50]

For decades, some of this private-sector job loss was offset by public-
sector employment, which, especially in the 1960s and 1970s, became a
very important source of steady, middle-class employment for blacks and
for women of all races. As we detail in Chapter 5, this was because government could hire directly and could also compel nondiscrimination and
affirmative action. But given austerity and budget cuts over the last several
decades, and the shrinking of government jobs at all levels – federal, state,
and local – this channel has become far less fruitful.[51] Here is yet another
example of an economic policy – in this case, the overall belief in spending austerity that drives government budget cuts at all levels – that has had
racially disparate consequences. Again, the root cause of job loss is often
hidden from public view.

The geography of deindustrialization also matters. Manufacturing
declined in a very location-specific way. From the late-nineteenth century through the first half of the twentieth, manufacturing plants anchored
city economies, providing factory work to millions, both black and white.
Starting in the 1940s, American business and manufacturing began to leave
the cities for the suburbs, in search of both cheaper land and more "tract-
able labor."[52] But from the 1950s through the 1970s, big American cities saw
their share of nonwhite residents grow considerably as blacks moved in and
stayed and whites left. The result was severe "spatial mismatch," a separation
of workers – particularly black and brown workers – from jobs and the job

market. Lack of public transportation linking suburban and urban areas only exacerbated that problem.[53]

Rules – in this case, economic incentives shaping markets both across U.S. states and internationally – played a major part in this structural shift. Anti-union laws in southern states, along with other state subsidies, encouraged manufacturing to move south, away from northern urban centers. Ultimately, neoliberal trade policy incentivized moving manufacturing out of the United States altogether. Employers decided that labor costs were too high, in part due to New Deal labor law and enforcement successes, and in part due to the "shareholder revolution," which held that the primary goal of company executives was to return short-term gains to stockholders – and when those employers were given the option to move their factories overseas, they did so. This hurt lower-income, less-educated workers of all races in ways that continue to play out politically even now.

"White flight" – the movement of whites to the suburbs that began in the middle of the century – was motivated and incentivized by a number of different factors, including a direct reaction to black in-migration. Functionally, it was a form of de facto resegregation in the face of post-*Brown* legal norms. Kevin Kruse writes:

Ultimately, the mass migration of whites from cities to the suburbs proved to be the most successful segregationist response to the moral demands of the civil rights movement and the legal authority of the courts. Although the suburbs were just as segregated as the city – and truthfully, often more so – white residents succeeded in convincing the courts, the nation, and even themselves that this phenomenon represented de facto segregation, something that stemmed not from the race-conscious actions of residents but instead from less offensive issues like class stratification and postwar sprawl.[54]

One major consequence of attempts to justify 1970s-era white flight as race-neutral and economically rational was the development of the 1980s-era language of neoliberal market freedom, which continues to dominate our politics. It made way for a new and still-pervasive meaning of freedom that could be summarized as, "I am not racist or motivated by bias, but it is my right to choose my neighbors, the schools for my kids."[55]

White flight was subsidized by all levels of government with neoliberal, promarket government austerity policies to reduce investments in public education and transportation and communications infrastructures. New suburban governments spent tax dollars on new infrastructure rather than on legacy upkeep of older systems. The federal government withheld maintenance capital mortgages and thus made inner cities far less physically desirable.

Local governments implemented restrictive zoning and redlining, while governments at all levels adopted policies concerning roads, public transportation, zoning laws, charter schools and school vouchers, among others, that actively aided the movement of more affluent – predominantly white – urban populations to the suburbs, while posing barriers to less affluent – predominantly African American and Latino – city residents. These are clear cases in which implicitly biased but seemingly neutral rules had the very racially disparate impact of exacerbating residential segregation and sense of cultural distance and stigma.[56]

In short, just as Civil Rights–era laws and subsequent policy developments such as affirmative action began to make educational and economic opportunity possible for blacks, and just as African Americans began to gain some power in the country's biggest cities, those cities became more and more financially unstable and thus worth ever less. Federal aid to cities fell rapidly in the 1980s: Between 1980 and 1990, federal aid to cities dropped from 18 percent of city budgets to just 6.4 percent.[57] All this took place as private companies that could meaningfully employ lower-skilled workers departed municipal centers. Joblessness grew, and the cycle of lower city tax bases and urban poverty continued. As Jon Teaford notes: "When blacks entered city hall to take the spoils of victory, they found that whites had carted away the wealth of the metropolis to suburban communities beyond central-city jurisdiction. The black-ruled fragments were little more than bankrupt relics of past greatness."[58]

The causal roots here lie in often opaque rules. It may or may not have been a coincidence that deindustrialization happened just as black political power was on the rise. (Whether blacks would have gained political power in a different municipal economy is an important counterfactual question.) But as a result, implicitly racialized decisions that further excluded blacks from resources and political participation perpetuated a vicious cycle. Joblessness and economic power, concentrated in urban core areas, exacerbated the criminalization of and underinvestment in black families. This rendered black political representation essentially powerless, and thus ever-fewer political resources went to black and other working-class citizens.

Truly powerful decision makers – whether federal policy makers advocating for government budget cuts or private-sector employers favoring executive compensation over investment in jobs and workers due to market incentives – were in many ways separated and insulated from this vicious cycle and thus helped perpetuate it. This echoes, in profound ways, the reaction of Jim Crow to Reconstruction-era efforts to create a true "free labor" economy and thus a healthier democracy.

## CONCLUSION: POLITICS, POLITICAL BELIEFS, AND THE ROLE OF NEOLIBERALISM IN DRIVING RETRENCHMENT

The interaction of these Civil Rights–era political repercussions and deindustrialization, which itself was shaped by a set of urban–suburban choices and decisions, all happened against the political backdrop of a new ideology that was gaining sway in the 1980s. Conservative neoliberalism held that market freedom should dominate; that public-sector solutions were, almost by definition, inefficient and ineffective; and thus that "free enterprise" should be given more credence and more power than any decisions that would come from courts or the federal government.

This was, and remains, the thinking that underlies the racial rules of today's stalled progress. Civil Rights–era inclusionary rules, including antidiscrimination, affirmative action, the drive for racially balanced schools, and voting rights laws, have been weakened and ultimately reversed. This backlash was predicated on a set of individualist, "pull-yourself-up-by-your-bootstraps" beliefs very closely related to Reagan-era supply-side, trickle-down economics.

The end result was at best ironic. The ability of black political authority – mayors such as Tom Bradley of Los Angeles and David Dinkins of New York – to bring about positive social and economic results for black individuals, families, and communities was curtailed by the falling industrial base, a radical expansion and harshening of the penal system, the rollback of inclusionary rules, and the public opinion shift against public investment.[59]

Sadly, early thinkers about rights for black Americans would not be surprised about the swing of the pendulum. Black leaders, from Reconstruction-era Republicans through W. E. B. Du Bois to the present day, always understood that political movements for black rights had, as a key goal, economic equality and economic strength. For Civil Rights Movement organizers, economic victory was always a major part of the prize.

Bayard Rustin, just months after the 1963 March on Washington, brought more than 250,000 people to the nation's capital protest, reminding the readers of *Liberation* magazine that "the roots of discrimination are economic, and since, in the long run, the Negro, like everyone else, cannot achieve even dignity without a job – economic issues were bound to emerge, with far-reaching implications."[60] Rustin, far earlier than most, was concerned about the effect of that technology on black economic advancement:

The civil rights movement alone cannot provide jobs for all. It cannot solve the problems raised by automation – and automation deprives more Negroes of jobs than any other single factor, including prejudice. Nor can it tackle alone the coalition of Dixiecrats and plutocrats which impairs the political and economic health of the country.[61]

Concern about rapidly changing technology and its impact on jobs, so central to twenty-first century economic anxiety, is actually an old story, and one recognized early on by our nation's racial rights leaders. Certainly Martin Luther King was, by the end of his life, leading not just a movement for civil rights, but, more fully, a poor people's movement. And Rustin and others could foresee something very important: the adverse effects of deindustrialization on blacks in particular.

Given the new – or is it old? – racial dynamics of twenty-first century American politics, we must recognize that the same economic rules that have disadvantaged blacks throughout our history have a real impact on working-class people of all races, including whites. The system that allowed plantation owners to own slaves and exploit free labor hurt white southern workers, who had less social and political capital than their upper-class white counterparts. Declines in unionization and the lack of a worker-centered manufacturing policy have led to lower wages, fewer benefits, and more precariousness for white workers in every region of the United States.

The question today is the same as it was during 1676 and Bacon's Rebellion: Will political leaders use racial anxieties and racial fears – ever-present, but exacerbated in times of overall economic decline – to garner support for an economic system that is bad for all workers and destructive to the true middle class? It is our sincere hope that by making plain the implicit and explicit racial rules – the belief systems and the political motivations behind them – that help support poor policy choices, we can, at minimum, clarify for voters and policy makers what is really at stake. As we illustrate in the following chapters, our nation's wealth, income, health, education, and very democracy depend on our ability to see things for what they really are.

# 2

# Stratification Economics

## A General Theory of Intergroup Inequality

William A. Darity Jr., Darrick Hamilton, Patrick L. Mason, Gregory N. Price, Alberto Dávila, Marie T. Mora, and Sue K. Stockly

## A THEORY OF GROUP IDENTITY AND GROUP ACTION

Research on happiness has established that, in general, human satisfaction is more strongly associated with a person's *comparative* position than with the individual's *absolute* position.[1] The key to this view of human happiness is establishing who is in the relevant comparison group. As the old cliché would have it: Who exactly are the "Joneses" (or perhaps the Kardashians) with whom someone is trying to keep up?

Stratification economics proposes that the key relevant comparison group will be an outside racial, ethnic, gender, caste, or religious group. Individuals' personal sense of well-being will be affected by how they feel their own social group is doing relative to another that they perceive as a rival.

In the more general case, in a world where comparative position matters, members of particular social groups will make both *between-* and *within*-group comparisons.[2] Typically, both the in-group and the out-group will have their own hierarchical pattern. Individuals in the subordinate or out-group may find themselves doing poorly in comparison with the average member of the in-group but doing well in comparison with members of their own (out-) group. Thus, dissatisfaction associated with a negative *between*-group position may be offset by satisfaction associated with a positive *within*-group position. It depends upon the degree of importance an individual assigns to each comparison.

The evidence deployed to make these comparisons might vary across individuals, time, and space. Primary concerns usually will be some combination of perceived comparative economic status and political power. The importance given to each category of perceived relative position also may vary. For example, some persons, both black and white, might view the relative position of black Americans vis-à-vis white Americans as having improved dramatically in the fifty years since the passage of the Civil Rights Act.

They might hold this belief despite little or no change in the relative position of blacks on a number of economic indicators, such as unemployment, per-capita income, or the proportion of the group that can be identified as middle class. Indeed, on some indicators such as wealth or net worth, the relative position of blacks may have worsened significantly since the 1960s; it definitely worsened over the course of the past decade. Nevertheless, for some, the election of a black president in 2008 might have trumped all other evidence in an assessment of relative group progress.

The phenomenon of *last place aversion*[3] – the intense desire to avoid being at the bottom of a social ranking – reinforces the importance for members of dominant social groups to preserve their group's comparative position. It also means that members of a subordinate group, a group with an "unsatisfactory social identity," may seek to "leave their existing group and join some more positively distinct groups and/or to make their existing group more positively distinct."[4]

If exiting from a particular group is feasible, given an individual's personal characteristics, it could mean attempting to "pass" as a member of the dominant group or constructing newer social groups with a less stigmatized status. Making one's "existing group more positively distinct" could involve the development of positive group images through group nationalism or a group pride movement, as well as efforts to reduce the gap that exists between the out-group (subordinate) and the in-group (dominant).

While placing intergroup differences front and center, stratification economics integrates insights from multiple disciplines to produce a distinctive mode of analysis of inequality across groups that are socially differentiated. It draws primarily from economics, sociology, and social psychology; it offers a frame for examining the role of *relative group position* and *group action* in determining individual life outcomes.

Stratification economics consciously rejects explanations for intergroup inequality on the grounds of collective dysfunction or self-defeating behaviors by the group experiencing comparatively negative outcomes. A substantial body of careful empirical research consistently undercuts both genetic and cultural-behavioral explanations for racial or ethnic inequality.[5]

In addition, stratification economics extracts the emphasis on self-interested behavior and *substantive* rationality from economics. It seeks the rational, *material* basis for group and personal identity formation, for membership in both dominant and subordinate groups. It takes the emphasis on the group, rather than the individual, as the fundamental unit of social analysis from sociology. Thus, stratification economics seeks to explore *processes* of identity formation, including both self and social classification with respect to group affiliation.[6]

At the "micro" level – that is, at the level of individual psychology – stratification economics utilizes the concepts of stereotype threat, stereotype boost, and stereotype lift from social psychology as foundational influences on individual productivity.[7] Thus, stratification economics pays close attention to the impact of widely held beliefs about one's group on an individual's task performance, because social prejudices can alter individual productivity.

Stereotype threat refers to the adverse effect that negative beliefs about a group can have on the performance of individuals within that group – for example, the stereotype that blacks are cognitively inferior to whites.[8] Socially held stereotypes affect individual productivity above and beyond an individual's stock of human capital: when negative beliefs prevail about the ability of one's social group, the determination not to confirm the stereotype can itself lead to reduced performance.

Steele, Spencer, and Aronson[9] find that stereotype threat can lead to a 13 percent lower SAT score for a black student. This is not a trivial reduction; a black student who might otherwise have scored 1,200 on the test scores 1,040 instead because of the impact of the widely held belief that "black students don't do well on standardized tests." The upshot of this depressive effect is that what might appear to be a fair measure of merit, such as a standardized test score, can be distorted, when comparisons are made at the intergroup level, by the effects of prevailing stereotypes about group ability.

Stereotype boost involves the upward push on performance of an (ostensibly) positive stereotype on members of a group who are "beneficiaries" of the belief,[10] such as "Asians are innately good at mathematics."[11] If an individual from such a positively stereotyped group does not have a prior history of success in that domain and lacks confidence in that domain, the existence of the "positive" stereotype might impair that person's performance; the individual may "choke" when confronted with the task.[12]

Finally, stereotype lift involves the increase in performance of members of a nonstigmatized group in a domain where members of a comparison group are stigmatized negatively. For example, whites might experience enhanced performance on a test of cognitive skills simply because they know that blacks are not expected to perform well.[13]

The more general point is that individual productivity is not solely a matter of personal characteristics, such as education, motivation, and training. It also is affected by the social context, whether it is widely held negative attitudes about the capability of members of one's social group or the hostility versus the receptiveness of the work environment.

Stratification economics investigates the processes that determine which group an individual sees as her own and which group (or groups) she sees as her rival.[14]

Significantly, it has evolved to provide a frame for understanding intergroup inequality *without* resort to explanations that invoke cultural differences. Instead, it emphasizes the struggle over relative position and control over real resources as the cornerstone of group formation, development, and continuity.[15] In stratification economics, an individual's group identification is necessarily a complex mix of ascription by others and personal choice. Stewart has demonstrated that this struggle is manifest even within an institution as highly regimented as the U.S. military.[16]

## THE THEORY OF PREJUDICE
## AND STRATIFICATION ECONOMICS

Stratification economics subscribes to a variant of *real conflict theory* as the basis for enduring group identity. Real conflict theory[17] proposes that competition over material resources lies at the heart of persistent group affiliation and attachment. Opposing claims to resources constitute the linchpin for the emergence of ethnocentrism or nationalistic sentiments about one's group. The group – ranging in scale from family to tribe to clan – develops a sense of kinship, fictive or otherwise, driven by the extent to which it is in competition with other groups over relative status.

Tajfel and Turner[18] have observed that "intergroup competition enhances intragroup morale, cohesiveness, and cooperation." Further, they write, "the more intense is an intergroup conflict, the more likely it is that individuals who are members of the opposing groups will behave toward each other as a function of their respective group memberships, rather than in terms of their individual characteristics or interindividual relationships."[19]

Experimental research has demonstrated that even minimal groups – groups formed on an entirely arbitrary basis in laboratory settings – quickly can develop within-group loyalties and preferences for other same-group members. But the same investigations indicate that "real groups" – those that are socially established – display greater salience and potency than minimal groups, the latter arbitrarily established *de novo*.[20]

The classic debate between social scientists Allport[21] and Blumer[22] over the sources of prejudicial beliefs provides another window into the theoretical foundations of stratification economics. In Allport's famous study, *The Nature of Prejudice*,[23] prejudice was treated as matter of individual or personal psychology. People with specific personality types – particularly those who were more likely to succumb to authoritarianism – were more susceptible to adopting and maintaining stereotypical beliefs about "the other"; this susceptibility was reinforced by sheer ignorance.

For Allport, the remedy was structured contact that could perform the therapeutic task of providing better information about "the other." In order to have the strongest effect in reducing prejudice, he argued that the members of the two groups should interact under conditions where they had equal status; common goals; a climate conducive to intergroup cooperation; and the sanction of authorities, law, or custom. Subsequently, Stuart Cook[24] said that the effectiveness of this contact would also be influenced by the proximity between the groups, the direction and strength of within-group norms about contact with "others," the direction and strength of expectations about authority figures' attitudes toward intergroup association, and the normal conditions of group interdependence – the predominance of competition or cooperation.

While research on the effectiveness of intergroup contact as a means of reducing prejudice suggests that there is a benefit when some of Allport's conditions are met, there is no definitive conclusion about which of his conditions are sufficient for a benefit to occur.[25] Still, there are some strong conclusions that have been reached about the *limitations* of intergroup contact.

Ridgeway and Smith-Lovin[26] have demonstrated that intergender contact does not consistently erase false beliefs about gender differences. Indeed, any observed inferior outcome on the part of the stigmatized group considered superficially can reinforce prior beliefs about the intrinsic inferiority of that group.

Ridgeway and Smith-Lovin speculate that a key reason for the failure of intergroup contact generally to reduce bias is the fact that the equal status condition is hard to meet, since individuals will carry attitudes prevailing in the wider social context into structured interactions. It is, perhaps, the inability (or failure) to produce the equal status condition that has led the greatest American "experiment" in intergroup contact, school desegregation, to have sharply inconsistent effects on students' racial beliefs.[27]

Tropp and Pettigrew[28] find that even in settings consistent with the optimal conditions for contact, intergroup contact is more effective in influencing *affective* rather than *cognitive* dimensions of prejudice. People can develop a liking for and friendships with members of the other group (affective); indeed, they can develop quite positive assessments about *individuals* from the other group. However, they will not necessarily alter their stereotypical beliefs about the group as a whole (cognitive). Their friends from the outsider group will be seen generally as exceptions.

The tenacity of prejudicial beliefs, even in the face of properly structured contact, would not have surprised Hebert Blumer. Blumer located the origins of prejudice not in the orbit of individual psychology but in a collective concern about *relative group position* among members of ethnic/racial groups. In Blumer's approach to prejudice, the "feelings" of one group about the members of another are grounded in comparative group status.[29]

Focusing on the group in the socially dominant position, Blumer identifies four major types of shared feelings among members of the in-group that constitute prejudice: (1) a feeling of superiority; (2) a belief that the "subordinate group is intrinsically different and alien"; (3) a sense of "proprietary claim"; and (4) a "fear and suspicion that the subordinate race harbors designs on the prerogatives of the dominant race." Blumer himself says that the third feeling, "proprietary claim," is of "crucial" importance. He elaborates as follows:

It is the feeling the part of the dominant group of being entitled to either exclusive or prior rights in many important areas of life. The image of such exclusive or prior claims may be wide, covering the ownership of property such as choice lands and sites; the right to certain jobs, occupations or professions; the claim to certain positions of control and decision-making as in government and law; the right to exclusive membership in given institutions such as schools, churches and recreational institutions; the claim to certain positions of social prestige and to the display of the symbols and accoutrements of these positions' and the claim to certain areas of intimacy and privacy.[30]

Stratification economics explicitly lines up with Blumer's view of the sources of prejudice. A signature feature of stratification economics is the critical role assigned to relative group position as a basis for the development and maintenance of prejudicial beliefs about the "other." The material benefits associated with group identity affect the dominant group's attitudes toward and treatment of the out-group. While both the dominant and subordinate group typically will have their respective patterns of internal hierarchy, comparative benefits of being part of the dominant group will span their entire membership and will be understood, at least implicitly, as such.[31]

Coalition stability has been a long-standing issue in the literature on collective action, and a key route to stability is a shared distribution of the benefits, although not necessarily on a uniform or equal basis.[32] In the later pages of his monumental study *Black Reconstruction*, W. E. B. Du Bois addressed the question of why lower-class whites stayed in the white racial coalition rather than joining blacks to challenge the white elite.[33] His answer begins with the suggestion that, in the immediate aftermath of Reconstruction, lower-class whites received a sheer "psychic benefit" from their racial status: "[T]he white laborers, while they received a low wage, were compensated in part by a sort of public and psychological wage." But Du Bois's discussion of the specifics of the "public and psychological wage" delineates tangible relative benefits that readily could be assigned monetary values:

They [the white laborers] were given public deference and titles of courtesy because they were white. They were admitted freely with all classes of white people to public functions, parks, and the best schools. The police were drawn from their ranks, and the courts, dependent upon their votes, treated them with such leniency as to encourage lawlessness. Their vote elected public officials, and while this had small effect upon the economic situation, it had great effect on their personal treatment and the deference shown them. White schoolhouses were the best in the community, and conspicuously placed and they cost anywhere from twice to ten times as much per capita as the colored schools. The newspapers specialized on news that flattered the poor whites and almost entirely ignored the Negro except for crime and ridicule.

On the other hand, in the same way, the Negro was subject to public insult; was afraid of mobs; was liable to the jibes of children and the unreasoning fears of white women; and was compelled almost continuously to submit to various badges of inferiority.[34]

Such an implicit intraracial contract – what Roithmayr refers to as a "racial cartel"[35] – continues to exist among whites in the United States.[36] As this book will explore in subsequent chapters, whites of all social classes and education levels have a much lower likelihood of exposure to unemployment; rarely become as asset-poor as blacks; experience better health outcomes and greater safety in encounters with the police and the criminal justice system; and, of course, are not subjected to racial microaggressions that erode emotional well-being and personal efficacy.[37]

Today's intraracial contract displays the long reach of an ideal explicitly articulated in a June 27, 1848, speech by John C. Calhoun, antebellum senator from South Carolina: "With us the two great divisions of society are not the rich and poor, but white and black, and all the former, the poor as well as the rich, belong to the upper class, and are respected and treated as equals."[38]

The evidence generated by studies on colorism expands the understanding of the advantages associated with white privilege. Colorism is a form of racism that allocates privilege or disadvantage on the basis of the lightness or darkness of one's skin shade. Greater proximity to white-identified norms of appearance and attractiveness carries benefits.

For example, using data from the Multi-City Study of Urban Inequality and after controlling for level of schooling, high school performance, work experience, health status, self-esteem, age, marital status, number of dependents, workplace characteristics, and parental socioeconomic status and neighborhood characteristics at age sixteen, Goldsmith et al. found lighter-complexioned black males experienced treatment in U.S. labor markets little different from white males.[39] On the other hand, using the same controls, black males with medium and dark skin tones incurred significant discriminatory penalties relative to white males.

In a companion study, they found that darker-complexioned black women suffered a significantly lower likelihood of marriage or remarriage than black women with lighter skin tones.[40] Having a darker complexion also is associated with greater odds of harsher sentences if convicted of comparable crimes, including greater odds of receiving the death penalty for similar capital crimes.[41] Clearly these findings also subvert an unqualified belief in the operation of an unvarnished "one drop rule" in the United States.

The advantages of whiteness and the disadvantages of blackness raise the more general question of why anyone ever would identify with a subaltern or subordinate group. Stratification economics points toward an answer that suggests, given the preexisting structure of intergroup inequality, members of the subordinate group incur net benefits from standing with the despised group. These net benefits can be associated with greater insulation from direct abuse and assault from the dominant group by the shelter provided by other members of the subordinate community and particular within-group possibilities for economic gain from which they are excluded by the dominant group.

The use of stratification economics will alter the way in which economists analyze a host of social phenomena. In the next three sections of this chapter, we consider how stratification economics affects the analysis of the provision of public goods, immigration, and employment discrimination.

## APPLICATION OF STRATIFICATION ECONOMICS
## 1: PUBLIC GOODS

Stratification economics posits that ascriptive markers such as race can serve as signals to provide privileged access to public goods/services.[42]

Given the nonexcludable nature of public goods, financing their provision requires some degree of cooperation and altruism among individuals. To the extent that there are at least some altruistic motives among contributors to public goods, own-group altruism among dominant groups can result in stratified public good provision. The dominant group's returns to own-group altruism can be an increasing function of their income and wealth relative to the racially subordinate group.[43]

In the absence of altruism, stratified public good provision can result if racially dominant groups are not willing to pay for public goods that will be consumed by subordinate groups.[44] This could occur when members of the dominant group assign positive weights to benefits only for members of their own race/ethnicity.[45]

While not explicitly identified as such, the theoretical model of redistribution considered by Alesina, Glaeser, and Sacerdote[46] captures some core insights and predictions of stratification economics with respect to public good provision. In their model, the demand for redistribution is determined by the extent to which individuals value the utility of private consumption enjoyed by others. The more altruistic individuals are, the more they value the consumption of others, and the greater the degree of redistribution.

Alesina et al. find that one empirical determinant of the level of redistribution appears to be race, as the level of redistribution in the United States is low relative to Europe, and the U.S. population is more racially heterogeneous. As such, an implication is that the relatively low level of redistribution in the United States possibly reflects a low level of interracial altruism based on whites possibly viewing nonwhites as being "undeserving" of income transfers or "handouts."

To the extent that public goods/services involve redistribution through the tax mechanism, the Alesina et al. model predicts that the provision of public goods/services also will be stratified, reflecting the preferences of a dominant group that views subordinate groups as being less worthy of benefiting from public goods financed by tax revenues. More sordidly, there is the possibility that relative to Europe, dominant groups in the U.S. view the misfortune of the non-white subordinate groups as being "their own fault,"[47] and thus may exclude subordinate groups from public good consumption. In the extreme, this can lead to death, since many public goods (e.g., clean water, pollution abatement, public health interventions) affect human mortality.[48] The provision of these goods is negotiated through voting, and voters may fail to prioritize the welfare of subordinate groups in a socially heterogeneous country.[49]

While stratified public good provision constitutes a departure from egalitarianism, it has particularly stark and vulgar implications for the distribution of casualties, fatalities, and recovery associated with natural disasters. Rescue and disaster relief are, if not pure public services, publicly provided services financed through taxes. In this context, stratification economics suggests that the population risks associated with natural disasters will not be distributed fairly or on a race-neutral basis.

Indeed, a violation of the egalitarian notion of equal environmental hazard risks for all individuals[50] appears to have occurred in the case of Hurricane Katrina. Price found that during Hurricane Katrina, the probability of dying in the city of New Orleans as a result of the hurricane increased if you were black and/or poor suggesting that the provision of publicly funded rescue services was stratified by race and class (measured by income).[51] Post–Hurricane Katrina, there is evidence suggesting that publicly funded relief remained racially stratified.[52] Banerjee also has detected a similar pattern of group-based stratification in relief provision in the aftermath of flooding in Bangladesh.[53]

The presence of huge deposits of lead in the water in Flint, Michigan, also is indicative of the stratified nature of the quality of public goods provision. Dominant social groups that capture the best public goods are engaged in a specific version of a more general practice that the sociologist Charles Tilly described as "opportunity hoarding."[54]

## APPLICATION OF STRATIFICATION ECONOMICS 2: IMMIGRATION

Immigration is another area in which stratification economics can provide distinctive insights about the nature of intergroup inequalities. In this context, we define socioeconomic "assimilation" as the process in which individual immigrants achieve levels of wealth, income, educational attainment, and other dimensions of well-being that are on par with the host country's dominant group. This form of assimilation is the most relevant to stratification economics compared against other assimilation dynamics involving norms, culture, intermarriage, and so on, because of its potential effect on intergenerational socioeconomic change correlated with race and ethnicity.

One would expect varying rates of socioeconomic assimilation as each immigrant arrives in the host country with personal characteristics that lead to temporary barriers to assimilation. Differences in language, education, skills, and social/cultural customs could initially affect labor market and other socioeconomic outcomes, including job performance, rates of adjustment to new social and job market circumstances, and expectations.

However, key determinants of socioeconomic assimilation also include immigrants' wealth and ethnic identifiers, especially their phenotypical characteristics. Dependent on human and financial resources, socioeconomic assimilation is typically viewed as a gradual but temporary process that usually does not extend beyond the first generation in immigrant families.

Darity describes "the master narrative about immigration" in the United States as one that "begins with the image of a nation of unbounded opportunity and freedom" where "newcomers were ... destined to enter their newly adopted country at the bottom of the urban social ladder."[55] He adds:

By dint of hard work, commitment to the value of education, acceptance of delayed gratification and a cultural orientation toward achievement, each new wave of ethnic immigrants would ride to the top of the urban escalator. Higher income, engagement in broad social and political participation, and assimilation into Americanness was available to all who entered the country if they had the desire and determination.

This "master narrative" and the belief that barriers to socioeconomic assimilation are temporary, malleable, and dependent on individual volition do not explain the emergence of immigrant enclaves whose residents face quantifiable disparities persisting across generations. Ignored are the experiences African Americans brought to this country by force through slavery. Also ignored are the similar experiences of descendants of Native American and Hispanic populations embedded in a web of violence and coercion directed against them, although their presence long preceded the establishment of the United States.

Immigrants to the United States within the last few decades do not appear to lack the will to assimilate in the broader context of the term. They frequently even prefer to identify with the dominant racial group in the United States. Evidence suggests that "regardless of their skin shade, two-thirds of recent immigrants to the United States choose the designation of white in their census responses."[56] But this *self-identification* presents measurement problems when studying immigrants' intergenerational socioeconomic mobility because some individuals (usually the more educated and affluent) stop identifying themselves as belonging to any racial or ethnic group except for the dominant one.[57]

An important implication of Darity, Mason, and Stewart[58] is that the intensity of self-identity of a subordinate group is a positive function of the identity penalty imposed on them by the dominant group. An increase in the intensity of social identification among the dominant group will be associated with an increase in the intensity of social identification among the subaltern group. For example, a rise in hate crimes against Islamic Americans after the attacks of September 11, 2001, was associated with a significant rise (9 percentage points) in the fraction of Arab and Islamic Americans who self-identified as "black" and "other-race" rather than "white."[59]

Antman and Duncan[60] demonstrate that evidence from the American Community Survey, where respondents report both their ancestry and race, reveals that identity making can be subject to a rational calculus given the situation at hand. Using a natural experiment created by some states adopting bans on affirmative action, they demonstrate that individuals from underrepresented groups (based upon their ancestry response) are less likely to identify with the corresponding racial group, while individuals from overrepresented groups (again, based upon their ancestry response) are more likely to identify with the corresponding racial group when affirmative action is prohibited.

It is worth noting, however, that an emerging literature that applies stratification economics to immigration indicates that skin tone (and other phenotypical features), rather than self-reported racial identity, is a significant determinant of immigrants' levels of wealth and income in the host country.[61]

Stratification economics offers multiple explanations of persistent inequality faced by immigrants; two of the most important will be mentioned here. First, individuals in the immigrant group may share characteristics, such as skin tone, that trigger discriminatory practices in the host country. Second, barriers to socioeconomic assimilation *within* an immigrant population may derive from stratification in the home country imported to the host country and possibly sustained over time through the flow of new immigrant arrivals into ethnic enclaves.[62] A paradigmatic example of *imported stratification* is evident in the replication of caste discrimination in the United Kingdom practiced there by members of the East Indian community.[63]

Stratification by skin tone is a major determinant of intergroup inequality in the United States. Persistent intergroup inequalities which may be explained by stratification economics are reported in many countries. Additional studies examine economic stratification by skin tone in Brazil and Mexico.[64] Discrimination by phenotype also seems to apply to immigrant populations. Darker citizens and immigrant residents and their descendants, whether the country of origin is in Africa, the Caribbean, or Latin America, do not seem to fare as well in the process of socioeconomic assimilation as their lighter-skinned counterparts.[65]

The concept of imported stratification offers support for Darity's (1989) *lateral mobility hypothesis*,[66] which links labor market outcomes to *premigration* resource attainment and to selection effects in migration decisions (for an excellent example, see Masao Suzuki's work on Japanese immigrants in the United States). The lateral mobility hypothesis proposes that the relative social position of the majority of members of an ethnic immigrant population in their country of origin will have a strong effect on the relative position achieved by their children and grandchildren in the receiving country. Indeed, their group is likely to reproduce the *relative* status held in their country of origin in the new country.

Preliminary studies point to empirically significant links between discrimination in the home and host countries and its effect on postmigration socioeconomic outcomes.[67] Tamara Nopper also cautions that attention must be given to which immigrant communities are recipients of significant state support to facilitate the transition to the receiving country and which are not.[68] As Nopper demonstrates, immigrant communities that receive the privileges of host country government support typically have superior outcomes compared to groups that do not.

## APPLICATION OF STRATIFICATION ECONOMICS 3: DISCRIMINATION

Propelled by Gary Becker's *Economics of Discrimination*,[69] the economic theory of discrimination has evolved into two principal approaches: Becker's own taste-based discrimination model and the statistical model of discrimination.[70] Taste-based models posit that agents discriminate against members of social group A because of their preference for members of social group B.

In the initial models examined by Becker, there were no productivity differential between members of groups A and B. Agents (employers, for example) simply "liked" members of group B more than they like members of group B. While Becker actually had some critical observations about Allport's approach to the theory of prejudice, Allport's foundation for stereotypical beliefs rooted in personal psychology is a convenient way to characterize the source of Becker's taste for discrimination as "exogenous" or given.

An intergroup wage gap in taste-based models arises from three potential mechanisms: employer discrimination, employee discrimination, and customer discrimination. Under employer discrimination, persons doing the hiring prefer members of group B over group A. They only will hire members of group A at a wage discount, thereby producing a wage wedge. Under employee discrimination, workers from group B – who, presumably, are first in – dislike working with members of group A and must receive a wage premium to work alongside members of A. Under customer discrimination, consumers prefer products or services made by members of group B, leading to a higher derived demand for B workers on the part of employers and a corresponding wage wedge in their favor.

Statistical models of discrimination posit that agents lack complete information regarding the true productivity of individual members of group A. As a cost-efficient measure, they assign what they believe to be the average productivity of the group as a whole to each member of group A. If they also believe A's average productivity is *lower* than the average for members of group B, then they will select members of group A for positions proportionately less often than members of group B. This can result in a wage gap.

The difficulty with both the taste-based discrimination and the statistical discrimination models is they are unstable. Ultimately, both approaches imply that non-productivity-based differentials in wages must evaporate over time; both approaches deny the persistence of discrimination.

Employer discrimination should be eliminated insofar as there are some employers who prefer pecuniary gain to prejudice and will take advantage of the lower cost, comparably efficient members of group A, to generate higher profits than the discriminators. Their success should drive the discriminators out of business, propel a rise in wages for members of A, and close the intergroup wage gap.

Employee discrimination is not sustainable if some employers simply hire work forces consisting exclusively of members of group A. Again, since they are lower cost and comparably efficient, those firms will experience a profit advantage until the relative growth in demand for A workers closes the wage gap. The standard conclusion is that employee discrimination will lead to a world of segregated work forces with equal wages.

Customer discrimination is the only one of Becker's three forms of taste-based discrimination that appears, in principle, to be sustainable. But this would require consumers to closely monitor the hiring practices of firms whose products appear in retail outlets without any explicit indication of whose hands made them. Customer discrimination seems to have greatest efficacy in the provision of face-to-face services, where consumers actually can see who is doing the work for them.

The statistical theory of discrimination also is subject to the instability problem. If employers are incorrect and the distributions of productivity for members of group A and B are the same, they should learn this over time and hire black and white workers at the same rate. Certainly they have a profit motive to improve the information they have about the potential of any job candidate, regardless whether they belong to group A or B. More cost-efficient methods for gauging the true productivity of any employee should evolve that will erode the information gap.

On the other hand, if employers are correct in their forecast that members of group A generally are less productive than members of group B, then there is no need for a theory of discrimination. While there may be inequitable outcomes for members of group A at the upper end of the distribution and members of group B at the lower end, strictly speaking, no economic discrimination is being exercised against members of group A. They are hired and paid at lower rates because their group collectively is not as productive. Human capital differences between the groups would fully explain the wage gap without resort to an explanation depending upon discriminatory behavior on the part of employees.

There are a number of weaknesses with all of these approaches. While both the taste-based model and the statistical model imply that employer discrimination cannot persist in a world where workers from two (or more) groups are equally productive, cross-national evidence does not indicate that workers from different social groups with similar productivity-linked characteristics progressively receive similar employment outcomes. Discrimination does not invariably decline, even in market-based economies; in some cases, such as Brazil, the degree of discrimination (against Afro-Brazilians) actually appears to have increased periodically.[71] A cross-section, intersectoral U.S. investigation by Agesa and Hamilton found that neither greater degrees of foreign nor domestic competition were linked to lower degrees of discrimination.[72]

The conclusion that the employee discrimination version of the taste-based model will lead to equal pay with segregated workforces assumes that the workers from the dominant group will accept an arrangement where they do not have to work side by side with members of the subordinate group. It overlooks the possibility of violent resistance to any conditions that create a greater measure of intergroup equality – in this case, greater equality in pay. During World War II, when the U.S. Navy attempted to hire black employees in all-black facilities, white workers even blocked the formation of the Jim Crow workplaces. White riots in shipyards from Mobile, Alabama, to Chester, Pennsylvania, prevented the Navy from establishing separate industrial worksites for black workers.[73]

The customer discrimination model fails to explain why black workers in the United States are disproportionately crowded into the low-wage personal services sector, where they necessarily have extensive face-to-face contact with white consumers.[74] A better explanation is that white consumers are not resistant to all contact with black service providers; they simply want black service providers to be "in places where they belong" – in comparatively subservient positions.

Finally, the statistical discrimination model does not explain the persistence of unequal outcomes when employers have greater knowledge about the characteristics of the job candidates. Particularly compelling are Devah Pager's urban field experiments, where she found that black men with no criminal records face lower odds of a call back for a job than white men with criminal records.[75] Bertrand and Mullainathan found that improved resumes for job candidates with black-sounding names did not increase their odds of receiving a call back.[76] These studies suggest that the failure to hire black workers at the same rate as white workers is not attributable to an informational deficiency about the individual black candidate.

The instability of discrimination is a conclusion wedded deeply to an imagined world in which discriminators act independently of one another, rather than as members of a coalition, tribe, team, or gang. Independent action makes virtually all economic theories of discrimination, including the statistical theory of discrimination, result in a condition where the discriminatory disparity logically cannot persist.[77]

Again, here is where stratification economics intervenes by offering a different vision. Intragroup alliances based upon common interest in preserving or extending the relative status of the group lead to a common understanding, on the part of dominant group members, of how to behave toward members of the subordinate group in arenas that affect material and political well-being.[78] This includes giving dominant group members a nepotistic advantage and subordinate group members a discriminatory disadvantage in employment opportunities.

If there is a cost to employers for subscribing to these principles, these can be offset by direct or indirect subsidies from the public sector.[79] Moreover, the potential cost of choosing employees from a group they prefer is lower if less-than-full employment conditions typically prevail. The goal, as Blumer argued, is turf preservation to maintain relative group position, with all the attendant benefits for the dominant social group. Within the purview of stratification economics, discrimination is both rational and functional, albeit unfair and inequitable.

## CONCLUSION

For far too long, conventional economics has overemphasized autonomous individual optimization and underemphasized the importance of group formation, group identification, and group action. In turn, that has led its practitioners to identify differences in individual attributes – such as human capital endowments, motivation, and tastes – as the key explanatory factors for intergroup differences in outcomes.

Simultaneously, conventional economics has overemphasized the significance of *absolute* levels of consumption, income, and wealth and underemphasized *relative* levels of consumption, income, and wealth as drivers of human satisfaction. Moreover, when attention has been drawn to relative values, conventional economics typically has limited the pertinent reference group to other similarly situated individuals, such as neighbors or classmates, rather than outsider racial, ethnic, caste, gender, or religious groups.

Instead, stratification economics calls for a reorientation of the analysis of intergroup differences. It calls for a foundation anchored in the analysis of the determinants of and the effects of relative group position. It calls for an alternative view of the social importance of the group and group affiliation with respect to individual's life outcomes. It calls for a rewrite of the rules for economic analysis.

3

# Creating Structural Changes

## The Role of Targeted Universalism

john a. powell and Wendy Ake

## INTRODUCING TARGETED UNIVERSALISM

In Europe and the United States, we have witnessed the ascendancy of two simultaneous political and popular movements that are ideologically contradictory.

On one side, there is popular support to explicitly marginalize specific groups of people and to assert a polarized political agenda. This explicit call emerges from the shadows of long-standing implicit support for their marginality. This is a clear move away from meaningful and influential democratic practice. There is a sorting out of who deserves rights and social protections. There is popular support to arrest the expansion of rights and destroy spheres of cultural reproduction. Building shared wealth is off the agenda.

On the other side, there is popular support for developing progressive politics and calling for policy to create inclusion and realize equity. There is an ongoing discussion of what redistributive policies could look like. The growing movements for creating safety and expanding the rights of marginalized groups is being embraced by traditionally narrowly focused agendas. Great attention is being paid to figuring out how democratic processes can be improved and be reformed. Large diverse cross-coalition groups are organizing for economic change, reclaiming community wealth and agency.

These two tendencies have been in the making for decades and are born out of two different solutions to shared social realities. And interventions, policy, rules, and legislation are all significant factors shaping these trajectories. These are usually sorted into two categories: those that target specific groups and those that are intended to serve everyone. These two categories have created inadequate policy and policy that may provide some measure of benefit. However, these strategies can deepen marginality or be vulnerable to political attack. These strategies have also sustained a discourse and practices that shape deeply and widely held values.

At this moment of divergent positions of popular support, it's important that the forces of equity shape the trajectory of our response. We have to rethink the frameworks that give rise to strategies for systemic change and intervention. And we need to create practices that support a new language of discourse – one that promotes equity, inclusion, and belonging. A great deal is at stake and is set in stark relief when we consider the accomplishments of ethno-religious nationalist extremists, many of whom are laying out a clear set of practices that can shape discourses and values for the worse.

Targeted universalism is a framework that is set apart from both targeted and universal strategies. It doesn't borrow from each category; it is its own unique approach.

## Targeted Strategies

Targeted policies can be justified by recognizing the extreme hardships and physical harm experienced by some people, including the harm experienced by black men and women, trans people, and trans people of color. This harm has been present for some time, but popular attention and urgency has been galvanized by the Black Lives Matter (BLM) movement. The BLM movement is catalyzed by recognition of the unique way people with these identities experience dysfunctional systems of public safety, the criminal justice system, and more. We will discuss in later sections how BLM robustly responds to the unique needs of black lives in their full diversity. We also highlight the ways in which attention is simultaneously drawn to both the very different experiences of other groups, and the ways in which others can be served by the changes the BLM platform advocates.

Targeted policies can foment resentment among those left out but still in need, even if their need is not as extreme as that of those who are targeted. These policies are also extremely vulnerable to political attack, especially if they are targeted to marginalized out-groups. If we combine these ideas, targeted policies can exacerbate inequality and sustain popular support for othering and marginality as a means for the excluded to experience relief.

## Universal Strategies

On the other hand, universal policies attempt to serve everyone. These types of policies might appeal to those who may object to targeted policies. However, universal policies often turn out to serve some groups more than others and end up looking like "targeted" policies when they play out on the ground. Universal policies assume that one solution will help everyone. However, different people have very different relationships with institutions, systems, and structures. All of these different relationships mean they need different tailored policies. In this way, a universal policy can actually accelerate inequality. While universal policies may seem like a fair way to get to equality, and while they may come from a well-intended impulse, they ignore difference, and in so doing, fail to serve everyone.

## Targeted Universal Strategies

In short, targeted universalism sets universal goals, then directs our attention to the systems, structures, and institutions that create the problems in need of transformative change. Doing this allows us to understand how different people are situated and have different experiences within those structures, systems, and institutions. We find the barriers, and we identify which people are similarly situated and can be served by strategies that remove those barriers. Failing that, we develop strategies to provide immediate emergency relief for those who are suffering while we work on removing the barriers, which may take time.

Targeted universalism is a powerful framework that accommodates difference and identities in all of their complexity and intersections. This abundance of difference is channeled into and fully informs change strategies. This is the "targeted" part of targeted universalism. And while honoring and attending to the very different immediate harms and different ways violence is experienced, targeted universalism also reflects the different ways everyone stands to benefit from structural, systemic, and institutional change. This is the "universal" piece of targeted universalism.

There are two conceptual distinctions that make targeted universalism a valuable framework for policy and intervention strategies, and one that acknowledges that we are all subjected to different institutional, systemic, and structural arrangements.

Firstly, targeted universalism uses systems as the unit of analysis: its foundation interrogates systems and structures – causes – that create the effects that draw us to the work. When we inspect structural roots, we find both the barriers different people experience and the practices that perpetuate barriers and marginality, which can then be targeted for change. In this way, targeted universalism creates strategies that address the very different ways a particular "group" is situated within institutions, systems, and structures.

Getting the "groups" right is very important, and they are not predetermined or uncritically inherited from the very power systems that we seek to change. Nor are they presumed or predetermined by what we know from popular media or prominent data presentations. For example, when gathering to work on a project using the targeted universal framework, we should not immediately dive into a specific strategy to address the high school achievement gap between black and white students. Addressing disparities data can often lock us into focusing on predetermined groups and analyzing effects rather than the systems that give us those effects.

The targeted universalism framework discovers a "group" only as a consequence of analyzing the system and the ways in which different people are affected and challenged by it. It embraces the full assemblage, fluidity, and constant construction of difference. Targeted universalism problematizes one distinction of groups and relies upon a structure of "similar people" that appropriately responds to the operation of difference.

The second key distinction of targeted universalism is the way in which universality is embraced as consistent with difference. While these may seem contradictory, the conceptual underpinnings demonstrate resonance and complementarity. This universality is embedded within a universal goal, an aspiration that, when realized, benefits everyone. This universality is not established through consensus; it is not derived by acknowledging the aspirations of people with unfair and brutal visions of society. Instead, it derives universal aspirations through the guiding principle of inclusion and belonging, which is realized through three metagoals – the universal goals of other universal goals: first, a government that serves the interests of people; second, an economy that serves a socially productive role; and third, a healthy public sector that creates meaningful access to influence and contestation.

Critically, the universal is such that a plurality of visions must be embraced. Within targeted universalism, a key distinction is that different people have to navigate very different paths to reach a "universal" goal. Universal goals are provisional; they serve a role that may only exist for a particular moment and may change later. If we are considering the goal for everyone to realize the opportunity to have a quality education, we must realize that opportunity for one person may look very different to another person. This is important because a universal goal cannot be imposed; it must be claimed in an inclusive, fair process.

This chapter discusses how the framework of targeted universalism can take us beyond accepting the terms of supposedly categorically different

groups – defined as groups that star in disparities data and popular coverage – while simultaneously embracing concepts of difference.

The chapter also details the ways in which the universal is uniquely
treated within targeted universalism, which is also a credit to the framework's potential to diagnose problems accurately and, in turn, calculate prescriptions for change. In describing these concepts, we show the potential
of the framework by considering specific applications that attempt to create
inclusive structures that diminish corporate control and limit public debate
and its influence.

## UNIVERSAL AND DIFFERENT: SIMULTANEITY IN TARGETED UNIVERSALISM

### Difference: Categorical or Contingent?

To say that targeted universalism does not uncritically accept categorical
differences as constituted within existing power structures is not at all to say
these currently very real differences are not profoundly important and meaningful. By rejecting "groups" as categorically different, we acknowledge that
there is not an immutable essence that determines patterns among people
who receive brutal or more fortunate experiences. Difference, as operation-
alized within targeted universalism, is not binding in all situations. Rather,
in line with much thinking on the topic and exploration of difference, it
is contingent on particular arrangements of power and experience within
specific contexts. Difference is not unconditional; quite the opposite, it is
entirely contingent, fluid, and undergoes constant constitution. The way
targeted universalism embraces this fluidity is the means through which
it accommodates intersectionality,[1] an important component of structural
change in which differences layer and combine to determine unique experiences of marginality and othering.

Difference is simultaneously incredibly meaningful, profoundly felt, and
a key part of the analysis in targeted universalism. Difference has very real
consequences in day-to-day life, realities that are of such substance and
importance that, operationally, it seems difference is constant. For example,
violence becomes state-sanctioned violence, including murder and physical violence, when exercised by police and against black cis-males and cis-
females, black, queer, and gay trans men and women, Native people, Middle
Eastern and Eastern people, and Muslims, as well as many other groups
marked as "other" and having multiple layers or dimensions of characteristics marked as "other" by our current systems of power.

Notably, consider the testament of this condition by the Black Lives Matter movement and the BLM platform. BLM was born out of an assertion that black people were very differently situated than white people within the system of public safety and the criminal justice system. It should be taken for granted that black lives matter – of course, the universal that *all lives matter* is true.[2] However, it's been demonstrably true that black lives do not systemically matter, and thus the deliberate focus on black lives is extremely justified and appropriate. Additionally, the BLM platform does not assume a "universal" black life. Rather, careful attention is paid to the full diversity and multiple differences that exist among people of color, including religion, immigration status, sexuality, gender identity, income, and many other markers of difference.

The BLM platform expands the avenues through which political and institutional systems can reflect a greater value. These include policy recommendations related to employment, education, housing, criminal justice, and more.[3]

Consider the policy recommendation related to education:

We seek complete open access for all to free public university, college, and technical education program (including technology, trade, and agricultural) as well as full-funding for lifelong learning programs that support communities and families. We also seek the forgiveness of all federal student loans. Policies shall apply to all and should focus on outreach to communities historically denied access to education including undocumented, incarcerated and formerly incarcerated people.

To this end, they suggest the passage of legislation:

[to] provide $165 billion per year to states to eliminate undergraduate tuition and fees at all public universities and colleges, and assist states to cover all related living costs for students. Additionally, the bill would allocate funding to lifelong learning and technical education programs and fund programs, educational support programs, and lifelong learning programs to every individual incarcerated in local, state, and federal correctional facilities. The bill would also increase work study programs and employment opportunities for students and expand eligibility to undocumented students and incarcerated adults.

What do we learn from this consideration of the BLM platform? We learn a very clear claim and observable fact that black people, incarcerated people, and undocumented students and people are situated very differently in the education system. Many of the institutional practices do not work on their behalf and further their opportunity and inclusion. This platform suggests strategies that could very well create changes and structures of inclusion.

The BLM platform is comprehensive and covers a great deal of policy contexts. This is an excellent example of an analysis that begins by examining structures. From this scrutiny of structures and their dysfunctions, it becomes clear that there are "groups" that will benefit from specific strategies. Simultaneously, after these structural flaws are revealed, there are policy recommendations and examples that reflect improved conditions for groups experiencing greater violence and harm, and policy that ends up having widespread benefits for all. And, importantly, structural flaws – in some cases, those that disadvantage everyone, and in other cases, almost everyone – are cast in stark relief when we analyze structures and the experience of marginalized people within them.

For example, the BLM platform has a specific platform on the education system; however, different aspects of educational practice and educational institutions appear throughout the platform in other sections. This is a comment on the constellation of power structures that are created through the interaction of multiple domains of society. Education matters are included in the context of currently and formerly incarcerated people, the discrimination and harassment of trans people in schools, students in states that still allow corporal punishment, school discipline, gender-based violence, the criminal justice system, physical safety on college campuses, and public safety.

## Universality: Hollow or Robust

Targeted universalism demands that we hold higher aspirations for everyone – that the goal for a particular strategy be one that will lift up the conditions of all of us. Immediately entangled with this universality, with the understanding that we are all mutually dependent on one another, is a profound assessment of our very different situations.

Note that, additionally, the remedies that BLM suggests also apply to the condition of many more groups. While there are different people who stand to benefit from these structural changes, these policies would apply to everyone. It is in this way that we can understand why it is important that the groups targeted for particular policy or change strategy are not defined by the litany of disparities data. They are not static groups of blacks, whites, non-Hispanic whites, and so on. Those groups will not always be the list of groups that can be targeted with particular change strategies.

Rather, goals are universal; the aspirations they reflect are ones shared by everyone. The strategies to "get there" – to realize changes such that structures and systems include rather than exclude – are based upon an analysis of barriers that keep people from the goals.

Targeted universalism does not take groups for granted or tick down the markers of difference that are derived from the system it seeks to change. Rather, it analyzes systems and structures of the pathways different people must traverse to realize a collective aspiration. If there are similarities between the structure and systemic challenges of those pathways, then we have a group. Thus, when we look at groups for which we must develop targeted strategies, we are not looking at a static laundry list predetermined by disparities data or societal neglect and hardship. We are looking for groups with shared interests in eliminating a particular barrier.

In this respect, we see that targeted universalism does not conceptually accommodate what's sometimes called "oppression Olympics" – the idea that, given limited resources, the strategy that helps the "worst-performing group" should take priority. Rather, when considering real-world resource limitations, strategies for change will target a particular barrier that affects a cluster of people with different "markers" of identity and difference.

The universal claim within targeted universalism is not that everyone is similarly advantaged or disadvantaged. Rather, the claim of universalism reflects that we are all subjected to similar structures, systems, and institutions of power. We can think of this subjection at many scales: local government, educational institutions, federal government, and more. At each of those scales, the first task of targeted universalism is to inspect the structures and systems of power that create the groups whose challenges we address.

## TARGETED UNIVERSALISM: FROM OTHERING TO BELONGING

Traditional power structures are withering. Corporate power has come to occupy the most privileged position, and a growing and diverse group of people are disadvantaged to different extremes. In this political environment, deeply held societal values are profoundly affected by extreme inequality, demographic changes, and migration in the United States and Europe. The rise of both progressivism and ethno-religious extremism is rooted in these realities.

As explored elsewhere in this book, inequality has reached historic levels. It is pervasive and exists across income, geography, wages, wealth, and physical health. Importantly, inequality of access to political representation has reached extreme levels. Furthermore, inequality is present if the data are cut in multiple dimensions of difference – within and across disability, race/ethnicity, gender identity, sex, and more. Not only do people experience inequality at the individual level, the places in which people live are extremely unequal in terms of public funding and fiscal stability, available resources, education quality, access to quality foods, public libraries, transportation systems, and more. When austerity policies are posited as a solution to inequality, even physical health is impacted.

Additionally, global migration is growing. Global migration has a number of drivers, including political turmoil, war, environmental degradation, urbanism, economic crisis or opportunity, and violence or violent forced displacement. In turn, data analysis of demographic changes explains that in the United States, nonwhite Hispanic people, such as European white people, will be a minority in the national population by 2065.[4] At the state level, California has already reached these demographic ratios.[5]

Extreme levels of inequality intertwined with the white majority's anxiety over demographic changes create fertile ground for explicit messages of othering. In fact, these two strands cannot be thought or examined separately. Whites may see their own immigrant forebears as having achieved success through hard work while perceiving current patterns of immigration as different and in competition with their own interests. This in turn leads to a desire to end or exile the problem factors, understood as migration, immigration, and demands for economic investment in those who have experienced the greatest disinvestment.

However, these trends have also created a tectonic shift in deeply held values of meritocracy and opportunity. It is increasingly acknowledged that economic hardship is not simply overcome by hard work.[6] The myth of meritocracy is being abandoned, and there is potential to build on this moment. Meritocracy can be understood as "structural blindness," in that it assumes that everyone has opportunity and ignores the ways different people do not access structures that we need for living healthy, meaningful lives. Nor does the current conception of democracy and meritocracy enable a diverse vision of what opportunity and success looks like. What we're looking for is a way to design society, through an incredibly large movement of change, so that structures work for everyone – so we have structural inclusion, rather than structural exclusion.

The myth of equality and evenly distributed political power, often simplistically understood as the condition that everyone can vote, is also undermined when there is an extreme need for groups to compete for policy solutions. In fact, the idea that everyone can vote is itself a form of structural blindness. Clearly, everyone does not have equal access to the voting booth: black and Latinx people, the homeless, formerly and currently incarcerated people, undocumented immigrants, older black seniors, students, and the poor all experience barriers to voting, some of them shared between groups.

An explicit turn to othering results in the practices of immigration policy, national defense, international relations, trade and economic policy, and more. This is creating a dominant public discourse, a political apparatus, and popular support for othering. This is the root of a full-fledged explicitly far-right ethno-nationalist religious extremism in formation.

It is up to advocates of structural inclusion to rise to the task of asserting a different set of values – that of inclusion and belonging. We suggest that targeted universalism also signals strategies for creating the means through which different deeply held, widely held values can emerge: values of inclusion and belonging.

## TARGETED UNIVERSALISM
## AS COMMUNICATION STRATEGY

A great deal of attention has been directed to the need to create a new narrative, to tell stories, and to reflect shared values in these narratives. This need is situated squarely in the attempt to create alternative values to othering; to disseminate and install deeply held values of belonging. When we have examined the systems, structures, and institutions that create and maintain othering – barriers that create out-groups – we see that the barriers persist not as concrete entities, but as a whole host of practices and activities that individuals and institutions enact on a daily basis. It is through these activities that marginality and othering are perpetuated. In turn, this pattern of marginality and othering creates a language of othering and belonging rooted in far-right ethno-nationalist religious extremism.

Targeted universalism is a communication strategy in addition to a policy framework. By this we do not mean that it is used to publicize the benefits that might accrue to everyone by taking up a targeted strategy, such as the economic growth that might be produced by creating a fast track to citizenship for undocumented people. Such an approach would have an overly narrow focus on the demand for targeted practices. It is a communication strategy that can appeal to shared goals while defending targeted strategies. But targeted universalism also encourages us to think more broadly: it starts by identifying barriers and the groups that they affect, then clarifies the ways in which those barriers are maintained. In order to develop distinct strategies to dissolve those barriers, it then identifies both the long-term strategies and day-to-day practices that will advance inclusion.

In order to advance change, it is not enough simply to talk differently about our demands or specific policies. It is not enough simply to discuss the idea of belonging. We need effective policy – policies as durable as the practices and behaviors that sustain structural change. We need to exercise practices of belonging from which new languages and discourse will arise. Together, these will create structural inclusion, or the power to belong.

# 4

# The Racial Rules of Wealth

## INTRODUCTION

Economists and policy makers have often looked to income disparities to explain deep and persistent racial wealth gaps, understating the extent to which disparities in wealth are the real bedrock of racialized economic inequality. We will address how the racial rules of the economy hamper black Americans' earnings and employment opportunities in Chapter 5. But as economists Darrick Hamilton and William A. Darity and their colleagues have written, wealth itself may be "one of the main mechanisms for perpetuating racial economic inequality by facilitating a lock-step intergenerational transmission of socioeconomic status."[1]

In this chapter, we argue that our current racial – and gendered – wealth gap is the result of racial rules that have constrained asset-building opportunities for black Americans and nonwhites more generally while simultaneously helping affluent white Americans accrue assets that are often passed down through generations. Both black Americans and poor white communities have suffered socially and economically from these rules, especially since the 1980s as the top 1 percent has broken away and eroded the middle class. The effects of de jure exclusion from wealth building have compounded over time, limiting black Americans access to a key form of asset building: intergenerational wealth transfers. Further, continued de facto practices of predatory lending and housing discrimination circumscribe opportunities to build wealth through homeownership.

Why does wealth matter? In many ways, it takes wealth to build wealth – to invest in homes, education, new businesses, and future generations – and to provide a buffer in times of economic strife. As Heather McCulloch writes, "Wealth is different than income. Wealth is a store of resources to be used for emergencies. It includes savings for college or a secure retirement;

resources to be leveraged into investments, like a home or a business; and it can be passed on to the next generation."[2] Current policy conversations about economic and racial inequality focus largely on closing gaps in education and income. However, wealth disparities are at the root of many other inequities, and unless they are addressed, other policy prescriptions will fall flat.

In this chapter, we describe the yawning gaps in wealth between black and white Americans – and also examine how those gaps differ along both race and gender lines. We describe various rules that limit wealth accumulation, illustrate how the rules have severely curtailed black homeownership from the mid-twentieth century to the present, and explain the multigenerational impact that the resulting wealth gaps have on black families and communities.

## Wealth Disparities and Inequities

The gulf between the wealth of white and black Americans is vast. In 2013, Thomas Shapiro and colleagues found that between 1984 and 2009, the racial wealth gap between white and black families nearly tripled from $85,000 to $236,500.[3] In a 2014 report, Rebecca Tippett and colleagues found that over two-thirds of African Americans could be considered "liquid asset poor," meaning they do not have financial assets (including retirement accounts) that can be used as a cushion during a crisis or to sustain themselves through retirement[4] (see Figure 4.1). Despite some gains in income relative to white earners between 1967 and 2013, the net worth for the typical black household in 2011 ($6,446) was lower than in 1984 ($7,150), while the net worth for white households was almost 11 percent higher.[5]

Substantial wealth disparities exist for black men and women. Mariko Chang's research shows that as of 2015, single black men had a median wealth of $300, compared to $950 and $28,900 for single Latino and single white men, respectively.[6] Black women are at an even greater disadvantage, with a median wealth of $100, compared to $120 and $15,640 for single Latina women and single white women, respectively. Single black mothers had a median net worth of zero.[7] The racial wealth gap was much larger before the 2008 recession, when single white women had a median net worth of $45,400. Amounts for women of color were essentially the same before and after the recession, a reflection of the fact that white women were able to accumulate – and therefore lose – more wealth.[8]

As we discuss in the next chapter, black women face a significant wage gap and are more often segregated in low-paying jobs that lack critical benefits

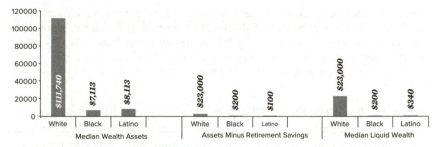

Figure 4.1. The racial wealth gap at a glance.
*Source*: Data courtesy of U.S. Census Bureau's Survey of Income and Program Participation; National Asset Scorecard in Communities of Color. Based on a chart originally published by the Center for Global Policy Solutions by Tippett, Rebecca, Avis, Jones-DeWeever, Maya Rockeymoore, Darrick Hamilton and William Darrity (2014).

such as paid sick and paid family leave and retirement benefits, all of which make wealth building exponentially more difficult. These challenges are compounded by the fact that black women are more likely than their white counterparts to be the sole income earners in their families, are more likely to run single-parent households, and bear the financial burden that results from the incarceration of a family member. As of 2014, 66 percent of black children live in single-parent households,[9] and in 2013, 46 percent of single mother–headed households lived at or below the poverty line.[10]

This lack of economic security is driven by a host of factors. Black women are less likely to have access to affordable financial services and products or business capital, and they are more likely to carry student debt.[11] They have fewer resources for retirement and less access to financial assets such as stock. Forty-five percent of single white women own stock, but only 23 percent of single black women and 14 percent of single Latinas own such assets.[12]

Black women also have less home equity than white women and are more likely to be targeted for subprime loans and other predatory financial products – and therefore are less economically secure throughout their lives.[13] According to Katherine Richard, in 2007 the average equity of a white woman's home was $74,000, compared to $35,000 and $47,000 for Latina and black women, respectively.[14]

The crash of the housing market during the 2008 recession took a devastating toll on older single black women. As the Institute for Women's Policy Research (IWPR) describes in its 2017 report on wealth inequality, among the Baby Boom generation, "older single black women who transitioned out of homeownership between 2006 and 2012 lost 96 percent of their total non-housing financial wealth," essentially depleting all of their financial assets as they approached retirement.[15] IWPR reported.

Among homeowners, single Boomer women of color saw their wealth decline by nearly half (48 percent) between 2006 and 2012, more than four times as much as the decline in wealth experienced by White women (11 percent). Among single Boomer male homeowners, men of color experienced a 77 percent decline in total wealth during the same time frame, 11 times as much wealth as White men lost (7 percent).

These trends mirror the broader growth of racial wealth disparities that occurred during and in the wake of the Great Recession. According to Pew Research Center, in 2013, white households held thirteen times the median wealth of black households, compared with eight times in 2010.[16] As Hamilton, Darity, and their fellow researchers have shown, the recession had a disproportionate impact on black Americans. Between 2005 and 2009, the average white family lost 16 percent of its wealth, while the average black family lost over half (53 percent) of its wealth.[17] Before the recession, the typical black family had a little less than 10 cents for every dollar in wealth owned by the typical white family. After the recession, that figure was down to a mere 5 cents.

Given these vast disparities in wealth, the high rate of poverty in black communities is not surprising. As of 2015, 24 percent of black Americans lived in poverty, compared to 21 percent of Latinos and 9 percent of white Americans. Almost 37 percent of black families headed by women live in poverty, and as of 2014, 37 percent of all black children lived below the federal poverty line.[18] As of 2014, 32 percent of black children lived in a neighborhood of concentrated poverty, defined as an area with a poverty rate of 30 percent or higher.[19] As we will discuss, living in poverty – especially for prolonged periods of time – impacts well-being on a multitude of levels, and only further reinforces socioeconomic and racial disparities.

## THE DRIVERS OF WEALTH INEQUALITY

Economists have identified a number of overlapping factors as drivers of wealth inequality; key among them are the often-interrelated factors of homeownership and intergenerational wealth transfers. One 2013 study by Shapiro and colleagues – which tracked the same group of families over a twenty-five-year period ending in 2009 – identified several factors that appear to strongly correlate with "policy and the configuration of both opportunities and barriers in workplaces, schools, and communities that reinforce deeply entrenched racial dynamics in how wealth is accumulated and that continue to permeate the most important spheres of everyday life."[20] Among the top factors they identified – years of homeownership, household income, unemployment, college education, and inheritance – years of homeownership was the most significant, accounting for 27 percent of the difference in wealth accumulation. Alternatively, Darity and Hamilton and coauthors argue that education, income, and employment disparities fail to explain racial wealth differences and that "by far, the largest factors explaining these differences are gifts and inheritances from older generations: a down payment on a first home, a debt-free college education, or a bequest from a parent."[21]

Scholars agree that the evidence counters a commonly pedaled "deficits" narrative that has long described the racial wealth gap as a product of individual failure. It is widely agreed that, because wealth inherently begets more and more wealth over time, America's racial wealth disparities are rooted in historical forces, and those forces shape current rules that further perpetuate the wealth gap.

## Pre–Civil Rights De Jure Exclusions

Understanding the root causes of the racial wealth gap – and devising policies to effectively address it – requires an examination of the racial rules and historical barriers to wealth building, such as slave codes, Jim Crow–era laws, and a range of racialized New Deal housing policies.

### Building White Wealth on Black Labor

The restrictions of slavery unequivocally prevented slaves from having independent economic lives, which also prevented them from building a base of economic assets upon which their families and future generations could ultimately build.[22] However, the history of American slavery is also a story of the creation of massive American (white) wealth on the backs of and at the expense of the enslaved. Various economists have calculated the amount of lost wages of enslaved black workers to be between $6.5 and $10 trillion in today's dollars.[23] The legacy of this expropriation of wages, which would have served as an asset-building platform that would have compounded over time, certainly explains some percentage of today's racial wealth gap. More recently, economic historians have identified this legacy of expropriation as a foundation for much of the wealth accumulated by whites.

For centuries, academics dismissed arguments that slavery and the slave trade were key to building U.S. national wealth, but recent research has linked capital from the slave trade and from slave-produced goods to the formation of early U.S. industries. Cheap labor, in the form of slavery, fueled the cotton industry, the engine of economic growth in both the agricultural

South and the manufacturing- and finance-dominated North.[24] By 1860, raw cotton comprised nearly 60 percent of U.S. exports and cotton manufacturing was the nation's top industry when measured by share of capital and labor employed and net value of the product.[25] This global cotton industry relied on a national infrastructure of banks who supplied credit, factories that produced goods for the South and its slaves, and merchants who linked the United States to the rest of the world. And this national infrastructure was embedded in a web of rules created by American political elites. Sven Beckert wrote about these interdependent relationships in his 2015 book *Empire of Cotton: A Global History*:

Slavery was just as present in the counting houses of Lower Manhattan, the spinning mills of New England, and the workshops of budding manufacturers in the Blackstone Valley in Massachusetts and Rhode Island as on the plantations in the Yazoo-Mississippi Delta. The slave economy of the Southern states had ripple effects throughout the entire economy, not just shaping but dominating it.[26]

New England merchants built fortunes through the trade of slaves and slave-produced goods.[27] Case studies of individual fortunes provide concrete examples of northern white capital accumulated through the slave trade and slave-grown cotton. Ronald Bailey provides a detailed account of how Moses Brown and James Brown, of Brown Bros. & Co., built their wealth and that of a key U.S. financial institution on investments in the slave trade and in the slaveholding South.[28] The capital accumulated by Lehman Brothers, Berkshire Hathaway, Aetna, Wachovia, and JPMorgan Chase can all be traced to slave labor, as historians Sven Beckert and Seth Rockman show us.[29]

### Implicit Exclusion from New Deal Housing Policies

During the transition from slavery to Emancipation and Reconstruction, and then soon after to "slavery by a different name" under the rise of Jim Crow, the Southern economy (undergirded by Northern finance) relied on the exploitation of black sharecropper labor and effectively prevented "free" blacks from acquiring wealth.[30] As discussed at length throughout this book, the racially exclusive and exhaustive rules of Jim Crow legislated de jure segregation in education and public accommodations and perpetuated political exclusion and the deprivation of full citizenry. Punitive measures such as vagrancy laws – combined with contract labor rules and a debt peonage system in which workers never got out of debt much less had the ability to build wealth – criminalized blacks' physical movements and lack of employment.

## New Deal Housing Policies

Often lauded as a model of broad-based, progressive social and economic reform, FDR's New Deal enabled millions of white Americans to amass wealth through homeownership but systematically excluded black Americans. As Katznelson argues, the New Deal exclusions were a painful ethical compromise that kept the Southern Democrats in the party coalition and kept liberal democracy in power during a time of rising fascism and socialism globally.[31] As a result, the twentieth-century white middle class was built explicitly on antiblack racism encoded into New Deal racial rules and policies.

Through the New Deal, President Roosevelt instituted a number of policies and programs meant to enable more Americans to purchase and keep their homes. In 1933, Roosevelt urged Congress to create the Home Owners Loan Corporation (HOLC) in an effort to reduce home foreclosures.[32] While refinancing thousands of mortgages, HOLC also created a standardized system of loan appraisals for properties and communities, which included an evaluation of the racial composition of communities. Under this system, neighborhoods were marked with different colors – green for those with homes that were new and more homogeneous, and red for predominantly low-income, black neighborhoods that were viewed as being in decline and thus the worst areas for lending. This practice became known as "redlining."[33]

The Federal Housing Administration (FHA), created in 1934 as part of the National Housing Act to stimulate and stabilize the housing industry, created a new mortgage system based on low interest rates and small down payments that made home buying affordable and accessible. But because of the way the administrative rules were set up, the growth in housing was channeled into suburbs at the expense of central cities. For example, financing was geared toward single-family detached homes and new homes over renovated ones.

The G.I. Bill – established in 1944 to provide a broad range of benefits for veterans returning from war – was also implemented in racially exclusionary ways. It established hospitals and provided funding for continued education, low-interest business loans, unemployment benefits, and low-cost mortgages for millions of vets. But the benefits were not shared equally across races. For example, in New York and northern New Jersey, "fewer than 100 of the 67,000 mortgages insured by the G.I. Bill supported home purchases by nonwhites."[34]

These types of racially exclusionary (yet implicit) rules, combined with the fact that HOLC's "residential security maps" made it hard for black

Americans to secure mortgages in redlined neighborhoods, laid the foundation for the neighborhood racial segregation that persists today.

Residential segregation constrains black middle-class households as well as poor and working-class ones. Research shows that black middle-class households making more than $100,000 per year live in and are ringed by communities with more disadvantages than white households that make less than $30,000 annually.[35] Middle-class neighborhoods of color typically have lower home values and price appreciation, fewer neighborhood amenities, lower-performing schools, and higher crime rates than white middle-class neighborhoods.[36]

We focus on residential segregation as an overarching impact of past and current rules because it is a significant barrier in shaping the socioeconomic determinants of the racial wealth gap. Multiple studies show that geographic concentration by race is linked to lower economic mobility stemming from problems such as concentrated poverty, limited access to jobs and quality education, and worse health outcomes.[37]

## Implicit Exclusions from Civil Rights to Today (1980–Present)

While the post–Civil Rights era certainly expanded the black middle class, there has yet to be sustained progress on reducing wealth inequality in America. Much of the progress made in the 1990s was undone in the wake of the financial crisis. Today's racial rules are less explicitly racist than slave codes or even New Deal housing policies, but they have been equally pernicious. We now look at how a lack of regulations – what we call racial "nonrules" – enabled the evolution of redlining policies, which morphed from their HOLC and FHA origins to become private mortgage discrimination practices, further entrenching residential segregation and the racial wealth gap. We also briefly discuss how the tax code reinforces these disparities.

### The Current Rules of Redlining

The Civil Rights Movement ushered in a series of rule changes to prevent historic racial exclusion and discrimination in housing markets. The 1968 Fair Housing Act and 1977 Community Reinvestment Act targeted racially discriminatory practices in the housing and lending industries. Redlining as a racial rule is no longer explicitly practiced by government agencies and is technically illegal. However, nonrules – a lack of regulations – have enabled new forms of redlining widely practiced by private banking institutions. Despite policy efforts to instill fairness in lending – such as the 1975 Home Mortgage Disclosure Act, which required disclosure of bank lending practices, or the 1977 Community Reinvestment Act, a racially inclusive policy to discourage discrimination – there is compelling evidence that mortgage discrimination by banking institutions toward African Americans still occurs. This discrimination occurs both through *exclusion* from mortgage loans and through unfavorable *inclusion* – or *reverse redlining* – into a more costly, toxic loan market, such as subprime mortgages.[38]

### Mortgage Exclusion

In the 1980s, there were news reports in various cities of banks rejecting black mortgage applicants at higher rates than whites who had identical economic profiles. The magnitude of this trend wasn't fully understood until 1992, when a groundbreaking study from the Boston Federal Reserve reported that black applicants were 80 percent more likely than whites to be rejected for a mortgage loan after controlling for the characteristics of applicants, properties, neighborhoods, and loans.[39] Multiple subsequent studies have confirmed the presence of discrimination in high denial rates for black families.[40]

### Predatory Lending: Reverse Redlining

Our history of predatory lending in a range of credit markets dates back more than three decades.[41] Predatory lending, often called "reverse redlining," is considered to be any lending practice that imposes abusive, unfair, or discriminatory loan terms on a borrower, often through coercive and deceptive techniques to lock them into an undesirable loan agreement. The unfortunate irony of predatory lending is that it developed as efforts were made to increase access to capital for people of color and low-income communities. This could be considered a byproduct of the broader trend toward the deregulation and financialization of our economy, which has produced a Wall Street with very little transparency and oversight, full of predatory tactics targeted at poor people of color.[42]

The opening up of credit markets in the 1980s and 1990s to long-excluded communities of color coincided with a set of new rules and practices that led to securitized mortgages. These new financial instruments of securitization – including credit default swaps and credit scoring, among others – expanded the pool of capital and credit available to borrowers and enabled lenders to determine the risks involved and drive up interest rates. By targeting previously excluded and thus untapped lending markets, this strategy ultimately led to reverse redlining.

The most familiar of these lending practices is subprime lending. Subprime mortgages carry higher interest rates and fees, making loans more expensive over their lifetime. They are marketed to people who can least afford them and often to people who could qualify for conventional mortgages at lower rates.[43] Subprime mortgage lending increased dramatically in the build-up to the financial crisis, from $20 billion in 1993 to $625 billion in 2005.[44]

Due to these lending practices, homeownership rates for blacks, other nonwhites, and low-income borrowers increased between 1993 and 2005. Combined, at least 40 percent of borrowers in these groups obtained mortgages from subprime lenders.[45] A study by economist Jim Campen found that while only 7 percent of white borrowers with annual incomes above $165,000 received high-interest loans, 55 percent of African Americans and 49 percent of Latinos in the same income bracket did.[46]

In the early 2000s, single women represented the fastest-growing group of homeowners in the United States, but they also experienced higher rates of risky lending than their male peers, even controlling for financial profile. A study from the National Council on Negro Women found that upper- and middle-income black women were at least twice as likely to receive high-cost loans as upper- and middle-income white women in more than 84 percent of the metropolitan areas examined.[47] Despite having higher credit scores, single female homeowners were overrepresented among subprime mortgage holders by 29.1 percent, and black women were 256 percent more likely to have a subprime mortgage than a white man with the same financial profile. Interestingly, the subprime disparity between women and men also increases as women's level of income rises, and upper-income black women are nearly five times more likely than white men to have high-cost mortgages.[48] This suggests that increased wealth does not function as a consistent protective factor in risky credit markets.

A number of reports have shown that the preponderance of subprime lending to communities of color was a result of bad rules, nonrules, and racial bias, not of the borrowers' creditworthiness. In her 2011 book, Anita Hill highlights a case brought against Wells Fargo by the city of Baltimore. In that case, former bank employees provided statements about "training they had received that helped them sell loans in poor, primarily African American neighborhoods throughout Maryland," and attested to "a consistent pattern of steering black loan applicants to subprime loans, even though they may have qualified for conventional loans at lower interest rates."[49] She also cites a lawsuit brought against Wells Fargo by the State of Illinois, in which employees reported a subprime loan-dominated culture that involved the bank setting quotas for the number of subprime or high-cost loans every area had to close and keeping score cards that recorded managers' subprime loan tallies.[50]

Implicitly exclusionary practices – brought on partly by deregulation in the 1990s – enabled subprime lenders to use a number of troubling predatory practices that stripped wealth from black Americans. Lenders used geographic and demographic data to target predominantly black and Latino neighborhoods, and often women of color specifically, for subprime loans.[51] They overvalued home appraisals, which led to higher-value loans, and ultimately to mortgages going "underwater" with loan balances that were above the market value of properties, even before the housing crisis set in. Subprime lenders would also charge excessive fees for late payments and impose large penalties in case of prepayment. It was not uncommon for lenders to structure loan payments that borrowers could not afford and then cajole those borrowers to refinance their mortgages, sometimes by proposing debt consolidation. This would incur additional loan origination fees and points, which accrue to the lender as income. It is not difficult to see how nonrules as well as seemingly race-neutral financial rules led to the preponderance of subprime loans among African Americans, nor how those loans and other predatory lending practices have fueled a vicious and almost inescapable cycle of indebtedness and lack of wealth.

The web of racial bias, changing rules that led to the financialization of the economy and shifting financial institution norms, and lack of regulation contributed to the 2007 housing market collapse and levied a devastating toll on communities of color. And, as the Great Recession painfully taught us, these lending abuses had a detrimental impact not only on the economic well-being of individuals, families, and communities, but also on the economy as a whole. According to the Center for Responsible Lending, "the recession cost 8.4 million jobs, and the U.S. economy lost an estimated $10 trillion in economic output."[52] Between 2005 and 2011, median home equity declined by more than a third for all racial and ethnic groups (36 percent for African Americans).[53] Given that home equity accounts for 92 percent of the personal net worth of African American homeowners (compared to 58 percent for white homeowners, 67 percent for Latino homeowners, and 72 percent for Asian homeowners), declines in housing values were especially devastating.[54] The consequences are now well known: massive black wealth loss and the persistence of racial residential segregation.

### The Implicitly Racialized Tax Code

While homeownership – and predatory lending's impact on homeownership for black communities – has helped to shape the racial wealth gap, other rules have played a major part. Our current regressive tax code also profoundly affects racial wealth inequality. Tax benefits – varying tax rates, tax credits, deferrals, and deductions – often favor asset holdings over income earned. We have, for example, a preferential treatment of capital gains and dividend income that disproportionately rewards a small number of mostly white wealth holders with lower tax rates.[55] In 2013, the federal government invested $384 billion in tax subsidies for retirement pensions and homeownership, of which more than two-thirds were allocated to the top income quintile, with the bottom quintile receiving only 1 percent.[56]

Considering Darity and Hamilton's argument that inheritance is the core driver of the racial wealth gap, the IRS "step-up" rule is particularly troubling. It essentially allows wealth holders to pass along assets that have grown in value without paying any taxes on that additional value. When someone inherits, for example, a stock option, they are allowed to "step up" their basis, meaning readjust the value of the option to the time of the inheritance, thereby allowing the recipient to avoid paying any capital gains or estate tax on the difference between the current market value and the value at the time of purchase.[57]

## IMPACTS OF RACIAL WEALTH GAP

The individual and household economic effects of the racial wealth gap in the United States can be understood in two categories: a weakened ability to absorb crises and a weakened ability to access opportunity.

### Absorbing Crises

A disproportionate number of black Americans suffer from economic insecurity and are therefore more susceptible to financial shocks.[58] Black families have many fewer assets to rely on to help them weather sudden employment gaps and hardships related to health care, housing payments, food security, utility and phone bills, or basic consumption needs.[59] Research shows that households with a minimum of $2,000 in liquid assets are less likely to forgo doctor visits or miss electric bill payments compared to those with fewer or zero assets, which potentially has negative iterative effects.[60] For example, foregoing doctor visits could escalate a health condition that becomes even more costly later.

Beyond black individuals' and families' own lack of assets, the systematic exclusion of black communities from wealth building means African Americans have limited access to assets within their social networks. Black households are 20 percent less likely than white households to be able to borrow $3,000 from a friend or family member in an emergency.[61] At the same time, they are also more likely to experience pressure to share economic resources with parents or other family members, further hampering wealth accumulation.[62]

With limited assets to draw on in times of crisis, black Americans are more likely to get stuck in a cycle of wealth stripping high-cost debt instruments and nontraditional financial products. A 2015 investigation by Pro Publica found black Americans in three metropolitan areas – St. Louis, Chicago, and Newark – were disproportionately likely to be sued and have wages garnished by debt collectors, even when controlling for income. The investigators write, "These findings could suggest racial bias by lenders or collectors. But we found that there is another explanation: That generations of discrimination have left black families with grossly fewer resources to draw on when they come under financial pressure."[63]

### Barriers to Opportunity

The racial wealth gap dramatically obstructs black families' ability to access opportunity. It makes it harder to start a business, finance a debt-free education, or purchase a home, all of which can generate further opportunities and wealth building. Studies suggest that even when controlling for income, family wealth is correlated with postsecondary success and college completion.[64] William Elliot III's research shows that family assets are an essential resource for translating educational success into higher income and earnings, stable employment, and greater levels of wealth.[65]

Combined, the web of racial rules – including historical racially exclusionary policies and practices, race-neutral deregulation of finance, and nonrules – has created contemporary and systemic racial wealth gaps.

### CONCLUSION

The massive disparity in black and white wealth provides one of the clearest examples of how historical institutions shape economic opportunities today. The effects of both individual and community wealth continue to compound over generations, and in twenty-first-century America, where a larger and larger share of the economic pie goes to capital holders as opposed to workers, and where privatization efforts reduce publicly available goods and services, the divide between asset-poor and asset-rich is only growing. Rule changes designed to increase opportunity or expand education are unlikely to close this yawning gap. Meanwhile, the role of family and community wealth in providing both a safety net and a springboard to success indicates a need for more direct redistribution in the form of investments in asset-poor communities and transfers to asset-poor individuals. This is a not an argument for wholesale equality in wealth distribution, but rather an argument for a minimum level of security and opportunity for all Americans.

# 5

# The Racial Rules of Income

## INTRODUCTION

In recent decades, major shifts in the structure of the economy have taken a significant toll on all U.S. workers, but given the way these structural shifts have intersected with a host of other racial rules, they have had a unique impact on black workers. As noted in Chapter 1, the predominant trends that characterize the twenty-first-century economy have been deindustrialization; declines in unionization; the fissuring of the workplace; and the growth of the caring economy and the rise of the service economy. The contemporary postindustrial economy is highly stratified, with the preponderance of job growth in low-wage retail and food service sectors and continued job loss in the public sector (especially at the state and local levels). There is also a significant lack of diversity in the highest-paying sectors, which include technology, finance, and banking. As David Weil describes, these shifts have resulted in declining wages, eroding benefits, a weakening of safety and health protections, and an overall growth in economic inequality.[1]

One result of these changes is that black workers now face a dual crisis of high unemployment rates and low wages, which intersect and reinforce one another.[2] The black American unemployment rate is twice that of white workers at nearly every level of education, and as of 2011 black households earn only 59 cents for every dollar of white median household income.[3] Between 1967 and 2014, the black–white income gap expanded from $19,000 to approximately $25,000.[4] White Americans of lower educational attainment are better positioned for higher-paying jobs than black Americans with higher educational status.

History teaches us that this cycle of inequality is neither intractable nor inevitable. In the mid-twentieth century, the racial wage gap improved,

Through mobilization and civil disobedience, thousands of ordinary people in the Civil Rights Movement challenged explicit racial inequality in American economic, social, and political institutions and demanded a rewriting of our economic rules to make them racially inclusive, ushering in black participation in both the public and private sectors. Local, state, and national political decisions and policies – changes in the rules – that led to better labor market outcomes often focused on explicit racial inclusion: affirmative action policies that increased black representation in public-sector and union jobs, enforcement of antidiscrimination policy, and desegregation of education, to name a few.

In this light, it is clear that our stalled progress on addressing the racial income gap has been a choice. Only by recalibrating employment and wage growth strategies for our changed and changing economy – with a specific focus on black American workers and other workers of color – will we be able to make progress again, for the good of all Americans and for the greater economy.

This chapter builds on the argument we set forth in Chapter 1 – namely, that racial rules and the racial implications of the very institutions that undergird our economy exclude black Americans from full participation in the labor market. Moreover, these rules interact with the changing economy in ways that are detrimental to black Americans. We begin by describing the vast income gaps between black and white workers, and describe the push-pull nature of progress for black Americans over the last 150 years. We explain some of the oft-cited explanations for these gaps, but argue that the real drivers of current earnings disparities are neoliberal rules – from "colorblind" approaches to employment policy to economic deregulation – in addition to a complex web of variables, including education, gender discrimination, and racial bias, that interact with and are shaped by those rules.

## EMPLOYMENT AND INCOME DISPARITIES AND INEQUITIES

By some measures, the income gap between rich and poor at the beginning of the twenty-first century is the highest it has been in the United States since 1928.[5] As with the wealth gap and so many other economic inequities, this disparity is not colorblind. At every level of education, earnings for black men and women lag behind those of their similarly skilled white counterparts (see Figure 5.1).

In 2008, among workers with a bachelor's degree or a high school degree, black men earned 74 percent of what white men earned, and among workers

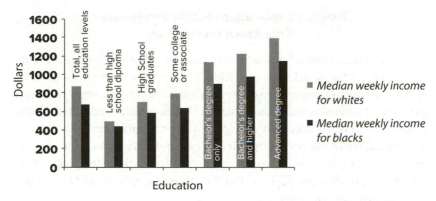

Figure 5.1. Median weekly income by race and education level, 2014.
*Source*: Data courtesy of the Bureau of Labor Statistics (2015).

with less than a high school degree, black men earned only 61 percent of what white men earned.[6] For younger black men, ages twenty-five to thirty-four, the pay gap often widens at higher levels of education.[7] While white women earn an average of 78 percent of what white men earn, black and Latina women earn an average of just 63 percent and 54 percent of white male wages, respectively.[8]

Women of color are often segregated into jobs that traditionally pay low wages, do not guarantee reliable schedules, and do not offer benefits such as paid sick leave or paid family leave, often making women choose between a paycheck or their family's health.[9] Black workers, especially black women, are disproportionately represented among minimum-wage earners. While the vast majority (76.3 percent) of the nearly 3 million hourly workers earning minimum wage or below are white, 3.5 percent of all black men and 5 percent of all black women earn at this level, compared to only 2.8 percent of white men.[10] Not only do women of color earn lower wages, but the wages they do earn do not go as far as they would for white workers, because a host of other racial rules that collide and drain resources out of black communities.

Occupational segregation refers to the trends that have pushed women and people of color into jobs and industries characterized by low wages and poor working conditions. The effects of occupational segregation became especially apparent during the Great Recession beginning in 2007. During the Great Recession, the unemployment rate for black Americans peaked at 16.7 percent, almost twice the peak 9.3 percent unemployment rate for white Americans. The effects of the recession hit black Americans particularly hard because black Americans – particularly black women – represent a disproportionate share of public-sector workers.

## Existing Explanations for the Persistence
## of the Racial Income Gap

Social scientists have offered a variety of alternative explanations for the persistence of the racial wage gap. Most often, researchers attribute differences in compensation to human capital differences in education, skills, and personal attributes, among other factors. While unequal educational outcomes and unequal access to educational opportunities certainly account for some share of the wage disparity, they do not fully explain the gap.[11] In terms of wages, even black college graduates fare little better than whites with two-year associate degrees, and they face unemployment rates similar to white high school dropouts.[12]

A second common explanation for the racial gap in household income is family structure. As of 2014, 67 percent of black children were born into single-parent households, compared to 25 percent of white children, 42 percent of Hispanic children, and 53 percent of Native American children.[*,13] For decades, black mothers – particularly black single mothers – have been blamed for high rates of poverty, for poor economic outcomes among black families, and for being a drag on the economy. Moreover, they have been used as scapegoats for ostensibly colorblind cuts to social and economic programs that disproportionately hurt people of color. But the focus on female-headed households ignores how economic forces – along with other dynamics such as the increasing incarceration of men of color, the hollowing out of the middle class, and decreasing investments in communities of color – have shaped family structure rather than the other way around. As Linda Harris of the Center for Law and Social Policy has written:

The over criminalization and disproportionate incarceration of young black men early in their adult life result in a sizable segment of the young male population in low-income, minority communities being marginalized in the labor force, with little prospect of earning a family-sustaining wage. This ultimately poses considerable barriers to successful family formation and positive civic engagement.[14]

These narratives about black single mothers ignore the stark discrimination that black women face in the labor market, which contributes to yawning gaps in income, wealth, and a broad range of socioeconomic opportunities between black and white female-headed households. Even putting aside these growing gaps, the rate of female-headed households has risen at the

---

* These data describe children under the age of eighteen who live with their own single parent and includes cohabitating couples that are not married.

same pace for all communities across race and ethnicity lines.[15] As such, the prevalence of black single mothers cannot explain away the household income gap between white and black communities.

How did we get here? To understand contemporary racial disparities in the labor market, we must consider how the historic racial rules of our economy have disadvantaged black workers from the earliest days of our country.

## PRE-CIVIL RIGHTS EXCLUSIONARY RULES

### Explicit Exclusion – Slavery and the Deprivation of Earnings

As noted in earlier chapters, from the earliest days of our nation, an ideology of white supremacy shaped notions of "race" and racial groups and was inextricably tied to the economic rules.[16] Relying on the exploitation of black indentured and slave labor, the American economy was de facto racially inclusive, but in the most pernicious way. In many ways, slavery was a "full employment" economy, although one defined by "unfreedom" for black slaves and their children.[17]

For a brief time following the Civil War, in the wake of the Thirteenth Amendment's abolition of slavery, blacks saw a short period of freedom and a shift toward racial equality. But, as early as 1865, the southern states' "Black Codes" gave rise to "slavery by another name," whereby the southern economy relied on the continued exploitation and control of black labor.[18] New racially explicit rules around vagrancy and contract labor criminalized blacks' physical movements and their lack of employment. The low wages of the post-Emancipation labor market evolved directly from the slave economy that deprived blacks of any earnings. The origins of tipped labor – work that today is highly racialized and gendered – can also be traced back to the late 1800s, when emancipated slaves were funneled into restaurant work and given no wages for their labor. This historic deprivation of earnings laid the foundation for the race and gender income and wealth gaps that are all too characteristic of the twenty-first-century American economy.

### Implicit Exclusion from New Deal Protections

Emerging from the economic collapse of the Great Depression, the rules and reforms of the New Deal created our uniquely "exceptional" American welfare state.[19] In addition, the postwar "labor accord" created a private welfare state of employer-provided health insurance, retirement security, and paid vacations for a newly emergent middle class. But, as noted in Chapter 4, scholarship shows that the New Deal also institutionalized race and gender exclusions in labor market and social policy rules, with long-term consequences for racial equity and wealth building.[20]

Ostensibly race-neutral rules excluding domestic and agricultural workers from New Deal provisions were far from colorblind in intent or outcome; rather, they were the result of southern political elites in the Democratic Party wielding their power to perpetuate white privilege and black subjugation.[21] In 1930, the legacy of slavery had perpetuated employment channels such that 41 percent of black workers were employed in agriculture (versus 26 percent of white men) and 63 percent of black women worked as domestics (versus 20 percent of white women).[22]

The New Deal's exclusionary rules were replicated in a number of critical policies such as the National Industrial Recovery Act of 1933, the 1935 Social Security Act and the National Labor Relations Act, and the Fair Labor Standards Act of 1938. All of these policies excluded domestic and/or agricultural workers from the important provisions guaranteed to other workers, ranging from unemployment benefits to a wide variety of labor protections such as a forty-hour work week and a national minimum wage. As a result of these critical pieces of legislation, racial exclusion was baked into the very building blocks of the white middle class that emerged in the 1940s and 1950s. Even today, domestic workers – nannies, housekeepers, and home health aides, who are disproportionately women of color – remain overwhelmingly unprotected thanks to exclusions that began with the New Deal.[23]

## CIVIL RIGHTS AND EXPLICIT INCLUSION (1955–1980)

The decades following the Civil Rights Act saw a steep decline in de jure labor market discrimination and led to a significant decrease in the wage gap between white and black men in the late 1960s and 1970s. Yet while the Civil Rights Act removed many rules that specifically excluded or segregated black Americans, an additional set of statues promoted explicitly racialized rules of inclusion. The range of policies and programs promoted in the post–Civil Rights Act era focused on increasing human capital through education and greater skill development and emphasized two key paths to the middle class for black Americans: unionized manufacturing jobs and public-sector employment.[24] The policy advance of this era had a positive impact on black workers. For example, the disparity in average weekly earnings fell to 25 percent in 1980, down from 40 percent in 1960 for men born in eighteen previously segregated southern states.[25]

## Affirmative Action and Unionization

New policies focused on not only access to education but also on direct intervention to promote the inclusion of black workers in public and private enterprises. Title VII of the 1964 Civil Rights Act provided legal tools to combat racism in employment and in labor unions, and the years following the passage of the Civil Rights Act saw an increase in private-sector employment.[26] Numerous studies of Fortune 500 firms during this period clearly illustrate that affirmative action worked in both hiring and promotion.[27]

The existing industrial economy transformed the cities of the Northeast and Midwest into bases for industrial capitalism during World War II and the postwar era and catalyzed the second Great Migration of southern black Americans to northern industrial cities.[28] Unionization of transport and manufacturing industries, in many cases led by black workers, produced stable employment, decent working conditions, greater racial equality in the workplace, and a path to the middle class for many black Americans.[29]

Indeed, while the Civil Rights era provided welcome inclusion for some, it did not deliver progress for all, as black Americans were never fully integrated into northern cities in the years after the Great Migration.[30] The "tragic irony of postwar African American history," writes Josh Sides, is that the "decline in industrial employment began just as the civil rights movement was finally making headway in America's largest industries."[31] The aim was to reduce racial and gender exclusion by focusing on changing the *composition* of employment rather than its underlying *structure*. The economic and political developments of the Civil Rights era took for granted the permanence of our postwar, middle-class industrial economy. That is, most policy makers and activists assumed that an industrial America was here to stay and would continue providing good jobs for working- and middle-class Americans.[32] The nation's nascent era of racial inclusion collided with dramatic changes in the economic rules: deindustrialization, the rise of the service sector economy, the fissuring of the workplace, and the rise of neoliberal economic policies all led to increasing numbers of low-wage jobs with greater insecurity, volatility, and reduced benefits and workplace standards.[33]

## Public-Sector Employment

The expansion of public-sector employment – and also public-sector unions – that emerged in the 1950s and exploded in the 1960s and 1970s enabled blacks to create an ethnic niche in local, state, and federal employment.[34] Executive Order 11246, signed by Lyndon Johnson, extended inclusion to the public sector by banning discrimination in federal government and among federal contractors and by requiring affirmative action policies. Government, in its role as a direct employer, has the ability to hire directly, advance inclusive racial and gender goals such as affirmative action more effectively than the private sector, and remain more accountable to pressure from constituents, especially insofar as voters can replace their "bosses" every two or four years.

Further, between 1965 and 1980, the Office of Federal Contract Compliance successfully drove a large increase in black employment by requiring affirmative action policies.[35] In one example, from 1969 to 1980, the percentage of federal procurement dollars going to minority-owned business rose from 0.03 percent to 3.20 percent.[36] As a causal mechanism and pathway for black economic mobility and security, public-sector employment was arguably as important in the late-twentieth century as manufacturing was from the 1940s through the 1970s.

Changes driven by the Civil Rights Movement ushered in the election of black officials at all levels of government. Black communities in large metropolitan areas were even able to elect black mayors (Atlanta, Cleveland, Gary, Chicago, Los Angeles, New York, Detroit, Newark, etc.). In the specific case of Chicago, Virginia Parks argues that "government, more so than manufacturing, served as black Chicagoans' most persistent and disproportionate sector of employment throughout the second half of the twentieth century – a singularly African American employment trend."[37]

The increased representation of black Americans in elected office and in other public-sector positions had a positive effect on black employment outcomes and fueled a new and expanded black middle class. The public sector's role as the sole remaining "ethnic niche" for upwardly mobile black workers became even more pronounced against the backdrop of the ravaging effects of deindustrialization on black communities that William Julius Wilson and others have long identified.[38] Unfortunately, as Adolph Reed and J. Phillip Thompson have shown in their work on the structural constraints and policy consequences of black urban regimes, black working-class and poor populations outside of the growing public-sector niche often saw little benefit.[39]

To make matters worse, the rise of neoliberal discourses and policies and the privatization of public goods and services, as well as conservative attacks on public-sector collective bargaining rights, have put this important ethnic niche at risk.

## War on Poverty

In his 1964 State of the Union Address, President Johnson proposed a "War on Poverty" as an explicit policy aimed at improving economic well-being in poor communities. Keeping in line with the fundamental ideals of the New Deal, the War on Poverty had similar negative externalities. Policies such as food stamps, Head Start, Job Corps, and Medicare and Medicaid came out of the War on Poverty. According to Sides, despite the good intentions of these approaches, "the great tragedy of the War on Poverty is not that it failed to eradicate poverty and unemployment among the black population but that it failed to recognize the new, as well as the old, causes."[40] In other words, like many policies that have been implemented to help poor communities and communities of color, the policies that came out of Johnson's War on Poverty did not recognize the explicitly and implicitly racialized backbone on which the policies were built.

## "RACE-NEUTRAL" RULES: COLORBLIND POLICIES AND TRICKLE-DOWN (1980–PRESENT)

We argue that by assuming away the rules and institutions that structure markets and shape opportunities, the neoliberal policies of the last thirty-five years have reinforced historical exclusions and continued individual bias. The move toward "colorblind" policies that fail to actively promote racial inclusion has furthered implicit exclusion from labor markets, perpetuating biased hiring, channeling, and more. The changing nature of the economy and neoliberal responses have destabilized the pathways to economic security first extended to black Americans in the middle of the twentieth century. The results have devastated the white middle class and halted much of the limited progress of black Americans. We will explore these trends in greater detail in the following sections.

## "Colorblind" Policies When Racial Bias Persists

Federal, state, and local governments, often assuming that personal bias no longer operates in labor markets, have haltingly enforced and at times gutted the antidiscrimination frameworks and affirmative action programs first promoted during the Civil Rights era. Public rhetoric suggests that because we have ended de jure segregation, colorblind policies now provide the most opportunity and justice for all.

In truth, our workplaces are still highly segregated by race, ethnicity, and gender.[41] What we know from social science research is that we made some progress for about fifteen years in terms of desegregation in the workplace by race and gender. However, after 1980, this desegregation progress plateaued, and in many firms and occupations resegregation has occurred.[42] Racial and gender occupational segregation at the workplace is particularly problematic because it is a causal factor in systemic and persistent racial and gender wage disparities.[43] As Darity and Hamilton explain, the higher proportion of white workers in a sector, the higher the wage. They illustrate that the average annual wages in occupations in which black men are underrepresented is $50,533, compared to $37,005 in occupations in which they are overrepresented – a difference of more than $13,000. "Indeed, a statistical analysis reveals that a $10,000 increase in the average annual wage of an occupation is associated with a seven percentage-point decrease in the proportion of black men in that occupation."[44] The relationship between wages and racial make-up of an occupation is true across all skill levels, which tell us that wage disparities cannot be explained away by education or training differentials. Bias does not just play out in individual hiring decisions then, but in aggregate cultural assumptions about what kind of work is valuable – assumptions that are informed by both racism and sexism.

Many workers also face significant barriers even gaining access to the labor market. One of the most significant problems of the twenty-first-century labor market is the incredibly high incarceration rate in the United States, which we discuss at length in Chapter 7. In recent decades, a spate of field studies comparing similarly skilled job candidates of different races and ethnicities has consistently identified barriers for nonwhite candidates. Researchers have argued that hiring in low-wage service work may, in fact, provide more room for discrimination and job channeling than hiring for manufacturing work. This is because positions that require "soft skills" such as customer service require a more subjective assessment of a job applicant's abilities than "hard skill" positions. In many ways, the transformation of the U.S. economy has facilitated discrimination and created barriers for nonwhite American workers.[45]

In a 2009 study, sociologists Devah Pager, Bruce Western, and Bart Bonikowski identify three distinct ways in which contemporary racial discrimination creates barriers to job market success for nonwhite workers: categorical exclusion, shifting standards, and job channeling.

- *Categorical exclusion* refers to circumstances in which job applicants are rejected without consideration of their qualifications simply due to race, ethnicity, or gender.[46] It is exemplified by field experiments that show examples of black job candidates being told positions had been filled while white candidates were offered opportunities to present resumes or to interview. A similar phenomenon is displayed in a much-cited experiment in which researchers submitted thousands of otherwise identical resumes that had been randomly assigned "white-sounding" names (like "Brendan") and "black-sounding" names (like "Jamal"). The latter elicited 50 percent fewer interview callbacks.[†, 47] Similar results were found in audit studies conducted in the 1990s, which paired white and black men who were trained to represent themselves in similar ways, and handed out equivalent credentials and correspondence tests. Young white men (ages nineteen to twenty-five) were three times more likely to get jobs as were young black men.[48]

- *Shifting standards* refers to a consistent trend of employers willingly overlooking missing qualifications in white job applicants and weighing qualifications differently depending on the applicants' race. In their field experiments, Pager et al. found "evidence that the same deficiencies of skill or experience appear to be more disqualifying for the minority job seekers."[49] In fact, Pager's previous research found that black applicants with no criminal record were offered jobs at a rate as low as white applicants who had criminal records.[50]

- *Channeling*, which has historic roots in slavery and the Jim Crow era, refers to ways in which bias affects employers' decisions to place workers in certain positions. Pager's research showed that employers were more likely to channel white workers "up" into more skilled or more client-facing positions, while black workers, by contrast, were more likely to be channeled down into back-office or assistant-level positions.

## Failure to Respond to the Transitioning Economy

While it is not possible to identify every factor driving the current earnings gap, we identify key sets of rules that have curbed progress. Here we focus on the twin trends of deindustrialization and declines in unionization; low-wage work and a lack of worker benefits and protections; the increasingly

---

† These and similar studies are not "double blind," and testers may thus act in ways that affect the results. The data generated by correspondence testing do not measure actual hiring decisions but only interview callbacks.

fissured nature of many workplaces; the rise of trickle-down economic policies; and the erosion of public-sector jobs.

The effects of globalization and structural changes in the economy in our postindustrial transition have adversely affected workers, especially workers of color, over last the forty years. Deindustrialization has coincided with cuts in government regulation, services, and public investment. While the impetus of antigovernment activism is debatable, the consequences for black workers have been clear. Specifically, the decline of unionization rates and – more recently – cuts in public-sector employment have eroded the two primary channels to middle-class incomes for black workers. It is important to recognize that these changes in the broader economy were shaped – at least in part – by long-standing racial rules. It is therefore not surprising that many of these seemingly unrelated changes in the economy disproportionately affect black Americans.

## Deindustrialization and Downward Trends in Unionization

These structural economic changes helped drive a devastating economic decline in many of the old Rust Belt cities due to the loss of hundreds of thousands of manufacturing jobs. These changes led directly to the deunionization of the workforce and increased unemployment, with the most pronounced impacts in black communities where the work has "disappeared."[51] By 1979, nearly one-quarter of black workers were in manufacturing; by 2007, that share had fallen to 9.8 percent.[52] Similarly, black unionization rates fell from 31.7 percent in 1983 to 15.7 percent in 2007.[53] The ladders to the middle class eroded before many black families were able to secure a place there.

One of the rungs on that ladder was unionized manufacturing jobs, once a concrete pathway to a middle-class life. However, the steady decline of those jobs has rapidly eroded pathways to a better future for many black Americans. Since at least the early 1970s, black workers have been unionized at higher rates than almost any other demographic group, and this had tangible effects: between 2008 and 2013, black union members earned nearly 30 percent more than nonunion members and were significantly more likely to have employer-provided health insurance.[54] The union advantage for black workers is especially pronounced among less educated workers, those who are the most vulnerable in the labor market. However, over the last three decades, rates of unionization among all workers have fallen, with a precipitous drop among black workers. In 1983, nearly 32 percent of black workers and 22 percent of white workers were members of a union or were covered by a union contract. In 2015, rates of union representation for black workers had fallen to 14.2 percent (a 55.2 percent decline) and for white workers 12.5 percent (a 43.6 percent decline).[55]

Research shows that the downward trends in unionization are directly linked to the decline of manufacturing jobs in the United States, which was driven by a number of causes, including the automation of labor; the manipulation of foreign currencies and, as a result, of imported goods; and the relocation of American companies spurred by international trade agreements and the lure of cheaper labor overseas. In sum, a combination of decisions by corporations about their production process – and by governments at home and abroad – helps explain why manufacturing is no longer the fount of job creation it once was.[56]

## Low-Wage Work and Weak Worker Protections

Meanwhile, in our transition to a service economy, we have failed to develop new rules or structures to expand and maintain the middle class. The legacy of New Deal discrimination is perpetuated through low wages and limited protections in sectors of the labor market in which women and people of color are most likely to work. At the same time that more and more workers have been funneled into low-wage work with fewer protections, the United States has failed to ensure that its minimum wage is a living wage. Between 1968 and 2016, the value of the federal minimum wage eroded from a real value of about $8.54 an hour to $7.25 an hour.[57] Cross-country comparisons would predict a U.S. minimum wage closer to $12.[58] The erosion of value not only hurts minimum-wage workers but also has spillover effects for all low-wage workers. While black workers are disproportionately represented among minimum- and low-wage workers, the vast majority of these workers are white. Fixing broken minimum-wage rules would have an outsized impact on communities of color but would lift all workers and have a positive impact on all U.S. families and communities.

## Fissured Workplaces

Similarly, the emerging fissured economy – in which large corporations outsource much of the work that was once done under one roof to small companies around the globe that compete with one another – has proven challenging to unionization efforts in the fast-growing retail and food service sectors. Walmart, the nation's largest private employer and the largest employer of blacks, Latinos, and women, is notorious for anti-union efforts in its stores and subcontracted warehouses.[59] And while the Fight for 15 movement that has targeted fast food corporations and their franchisees won many legislative victories to raise the wage floor for low-wage workers in cities around the country, successfully unionizing the thousands of fast food franchisees has proven difficult.

## The Rise of Trickle-Down Employment and Macroeconomic Policies

Deindustrialization was not only the result of apolitical economic processes such as "capital flight" and increased global competition. Local, state, and national political decisions and policies – changes in the rules – were also consequential. The hollowing out of the postwar industrial economy also coincided with increasing political polarization and a rightward shift in American politics. Efforts to retrench the racially inclusive economic rules won in the Civil Rights Movement began in the 1970s and gained momentum with the election of Ronald Reagan in 1980.[60] The ideological and political shift to the right in all branches of government chipped away at the effectiveness and legitimacy of these rules.[61]

Not only did policy makers roll back the racially inclusive rules of the Civil Rights era, they also rolled back rules and regulations designed to shape the market and ensure shared prosperity. The result has been weak and unenforced corporate regulations and the growth of "too-big-to-fail" financial institutions that receive a de facto public safety net from our tax dollars.[62] The [ongoing] "shareholder revolution," in which shareholders of large corporations demanded that the money that used to be spent on investing in the workforce of their companies be redirected to their soaring quarterly payouts, is representative of these rule changes. As a result, we have an economy in which the financial and corporate sector extracts "rents" from the rest of the economy where they once used to invest in and service it.[63] This broad web of rule changes increased the power and privilege of capital holders and CEOs – fueling the famed rise of the 1 percent – at the expense of median- and low-wage workers, thus disproportionately affecting black Americans.

One of these important rules changes relates to Federal Reserve monetary policy. Since the early 1980s, the Federal Reserve has focused on using monetary policy to keep inflation low at the expense of pursuing full employment. This seemingly technocratic policy is in fact a political choice to prioritize the interests of financial asset holders over workers. Indeed, estimates show that rising unemployment has a disproportionate impact on families in the twentieth percentile of the income distribution (disproportionately minority households), who see incomes fall 2.2 percent for each percentage increase in the unemployment rate. In comparison, median-income families see incomes fall by 1.4 percent and families in the ninety-fifth percentile see incomes fall just 0.7 percent. Moreover, workers of color face larger increases in unemployment in response to contractionary monetary policy.[64]

## Public-Sector Layoffs

With the decline of the manufacturing sector, the public sector has become the most significant source of good jobs for black Americans, particularly black women; between 2008 and 2010, 21.2 percent of all black workers and 23.6 percent of black women were public employees, compared to 16.3 percent of nonblack workers.[65] Significantly, these have been well-paying jobs, with a smaller wage differential between black and white workers than any other sector and a higher median wage for black workers than in any other sector.[66]

In the wake of the Great Recession and austerity measures, federal, state, and local governments laid off nearly 600,000 workers.[67] Not only were black workers disproportionately impacted simply due to higher rates of public-sector employment, but, in the wake of these layoffs, unemployment rates for black public-sector workers increased significantly more than for white public-sector workers.[68] Post–Great Recession public-sector cuts were especially devastating for women of color. Between 2007 and 2011, state and local governments shed about 765,000 jobs; of those losses, 70 percent were jobs held by women and 20 percent were held by black Americans.[69] Research from the University of Washington shows that in the years after the recession, the black–white public-sector employment gap for women increased almost sixfold, to 5.5 percentage points in 2011 from less than a percentage point in 2008.[70] By 2013, public-sector employment rates for black men had returned to prerecession levels, while rates for black women remained even lower than in 2008.[71]

## CONCLUSION

This brief survey of rules structuring black labor markets points to some positive directions for policy makers. It has been proven that policy has the power to greatly reduce income gaps and expand employment for black Americans. Inclusive rules that promoted unionization and full employment provided particular opportunity for black workers. Just as significantly, a combination of targeted investments in human capital, affirmative action, and rigorous antidiscrimination laws succeeded in boosting black wages and work. We know that the recent racial rules have not only been detrimental for black workers but for all workers, and that rewriting those rules would not only advance racial equity but would also improve economic opportunities and outcomes for all workers. In Chapter 10, we will examine some potential policy solutions in more detail. But first, we will turn from wealth and income, the most obvious manifestations of racialized inequality in the United States, to its less economically focused dimensions, including education, health care, experience with the criminal justice system, and access to full democratic participation.

6

# The Racial Rules of Education

## INTRODUCTION

Perhaps no other aspect of American racial inequality has been more studied than education and schooling, from the effects of explicit legal segregation under Jim Crow through the continuing black–white achievement gap. By no measure – racial integration, academic achievement, economic outcomes – is America's education system serving black students acceptably. In this chapter, we focus on the rules that drive educational inequalities and argue that we cannot begin to meaningfully address these inequities without stopping – and reversing – the resegregation of America's schools.

We begin by describing the persistent educational disparities between black and white children and explain the roots of those disparities in the explicit racially exclusive rules of the nineteenth and early-twentieth centuries. We note that the racially inclusive rules of the Civil Rights era drove meaningful improvements in educational attainment, health, and labor market outcomes, and that desegregation seems to have no negative outcomes for white students who have attended desegregated schools.[1]

We then describe how the backlash to Civil Rights era resulted in the racially implicit rules of the last thirty years, which have led to resegregation and racial isolation and to trends such as high-stakes testing and school choice that have had a disproportionately negative impact on students of color. Next we describe how the narrowing of the black–white achievement gap, a goal toward which there had been real progress after *Brown v. Board of Education*, has now stalled, and why this not only has negative impacts on black students, families, and communities, but on all students and on our economy more broadly.

While we primarily focus on the evolution of school segregation, we acknowledge that a number of other explanations account for the difference in achievement between black and white students. Family socioeconomic

93

status, which is itself a product of racial rules, has been cited as a driver of educational inequality as early as 1966, in the Coleman Report, published by the U.S. Department of Education.[2] Other factors often mentioned as important in school success are parental attitudes and expectations, conditions in homes and neighborhoods, the quality of early childhood interventions, and how children spend their time outside of school.[3]

A number of factors at the school and school district levels are also deeply important to student achievement. Educational and economic outcomes depend on the ways in which we organize and govern our educational systems. We argue here that a number of school-based racial rules have made getting a high-quality education far more difficult for African American (and Latino) students than for whites and Asians. The most important include the following:

- Concentrated poverty, especially when it overlaps with racial homogeneity in schools and districts
- The quality of teaching, which tends to be far worse in poor schools serving students of color
- School financing and lower per-pupil spending in poorer schools
- School discipline policies for children of color

These elements are all deeply connected to trends in resegregation, and improving any of these components will require tackling all of them with targeted policies that will change the racial composition of schools in order to improve opportunities and outcomes for students of color.

Race-specific policies have historically been both politically and legally difficult to adopt and implement and are even tougher in an environment perceived as zero-sum, in which a black student's gain – which can be as simple as a seat in a mixed-race or predominantly white school – is viewed as imposing costs elsewhere. We conclude that these perceptions are at odds with the evidence that desegregation can bring with it stronger teaching, better financing, a more genuinely diverse group of student backgrounds and abilities, and therefore better outcomes for all students.[4]

## EDUCATIONAL DISPARITIES AND INEQUITIES

### Barriers to Racial Achievement

Barriers to educational achievement persist for black Americans on all educational levels, from pre-K through postsecondary schooling. These create a cumulative disadvantage and persistent inequality for black students and other students of color. Studies show that the differences in cognitive skills for preschool-aged children create significant disparities between black and white students at the start of schooling and continue to widen substantially as children move up through grade levels.[5]

Racial disparities in education access begin with early childhood education. At the prekindergarten level, racialized poverty reinforces achievement gaps and gaps in school readiness among young children, as African American and Hispanic children are more likely to be raised in poverty.[6] According to 2011 data, more than 50 percent of African American children and 63 percent of Hispanic children ages three to four do not attend preschool, likely due to lack of resources and access.[7] This disparity is meaningful, as pre-K education has a significant impact not only on achievement at the K–12 level but also on lifetime earnings and outcomes.[8] Research from 2013 by Cascio and Schanzenbach estimates that early childhood education programs increase lifetime earnings from 1.3 to 3.5 percent, reduce crime rates, and save on education costs in later years.[9]

As students move through high school, educational inequalities persist and can be measured in achievement, graduation rates, and dropout rates. African American high school dropout rates have narrowed in recent years, but as of 2012, black students still had the lowest graduation rate – 68 percent – across groups, along with Native American students, also at 68 percent. Graduation rates among Asians, whites, and Hispanics were 93 percent, 85 percent, and 76 percent, respectively.[10] Achievement gaps and graduation rates are significantly impacted by the recent trend toward resegregation of American schools.

While earnings for college-educated African Americans still remain lower than for their white counterparts with equivalent educational attainment, the earnings gap does begin to close among individuals with college education, which suggests that inequitable access to college is one barrier to more equal earnings in the labor market. However, the disparities between black and white students completing education beyond high school have been *widening* over the past decade despite increasing overall enrollment. The National Center for Educational Statistics reported that the bachelor's degree attainment gap grew from 1990 to 2014. During that time period, degree attainment among blacks increased from 13 to 22 percent and among whites from 25 to 41 percent, which translates to the black–white degree attainment gap in this period increasing from 13 to 18 percent.[11] Put simply, though more black students are enrolling in college, the pace at which they are enrolling still is not keeping up with the pace of white students.

## Racial Isolation

Black and Latino students continue to be highly segregated and isolated by race, with the average black student attending a school that is 49 percent black; Latino students attend schools that are 57 percent Latino; and the typical white student attends a school that is almost 75 percent white.[12] In 2014, 48 percent of all black children attended high-poverty schools, as compared to only 8 percent of white children.[13] The most recent research suggests that this segregation and isolation, which has increased since the 1980s, has real consequences. Poverty and race are so highly correlated that if we want to lessen achievement disparities and thereby increase school attainment, income, and other long-term outcomes – including health and overall well-being – for African Americans, we must end racial isolation.

## THE RACIAL RULES OF EDUCATION

### Pre–Civil Rights: Explicit Exclusion

The story of race and education in the nineteenth and twentieth centuries has both driven and mirrored the story of American race relations writ large. Explicitly exclusionary rules served as the backdrop and legacy of this era, with the most obvious being Jim Crow laws. Legally required school and residential segregation throughout the American South and de facto segregation throughout the country made it exceedingly difficult for African Americans to break into upper-middle-class employment or amass wealth. For the last century, the story of reform has been recurring attempts to rewrite engrained rules and replace them with newer policies and behaviors that would promote black student achievement and ultimately better economic outcomes for African Americans.

In the early part of the twentieth century, more than 80 percent of all African Americans lived in Jim Crow states, which mandated separate schooling for blacks. The curriculum offered little beyond basic literacy and numeracy, primarily preparing students for domestic or agricultural work. Per-pupil spending was very unequal, with disparities of up to ten to one in some of the states in the Deep South. Similarly, the monthly salary of black teachers in 1930 was about 60 percent of that of white teachers. Across the United States, one out of eight black adults had completed high school, compared to four out of ten whites.[14]

### The Civil Rights Era: Landmark Legislation and Inclusionary Rules

*Legal Victory and Expanded Federal Role*
In 1954, after decades of legal organizing, *Brown v. Board* ushered in an era of desegregation. The clear declaration by a unanimous Supreme Court

that "separate is inherently unequal" was one of the watershed moments in American history. The implementation, of course, played out in fits and starts, but nonetheless *Brown* was a sea change in American politics.

After the ruling, the NAACP drove strategic litigation designed to make the Supreme Court's ruling a reality. But carrying out the edict of *Brown* – desegregating schools "with all deliberate speed" – became harder as local districts asserted control and fought back. Thus the role of the federal government, which increased dramatically under President Lyndon Johnson's landmark 1965 Elementary and Secondary Education Act (ESEA), loomed ever larger in the fight to improve education for children in poverty and children of color. Under President Johnson, federal funding to local schools increased from several hundred million to nearly one billion dollars annually.[15] The combination of the ESEA and the Civil Rights Act, which outlawed the use of federal funds in schools segregated by race, radically increased federal leverage in the fight to integrate schools.[16]

Despite significant political opposition from organized and well-funded citizens groups, and after much federal support, the push for desegregation actually worked. Racial concentration in schools decreased. By the early 1970s, southern schools, once the most racially separate, had become the most integrated in the country.[17] Some of these gains persisted for a decade or more. In southern states, the percentage of black children in traditionally white schools went from essentially zero to 44 percent in 1988.[18]

### Desegregation Has Positive and Lasting Effects

Desegregation, as contentious and complex as it has been, had several positive effects in the decades immediately following *Brown*. Longitudinal evidence suggests that changing the racial composition of schools seems not only to have improved educational outcomes, but also to have improved economic and other long-range impacts for individuals.

First, desegregation drives educational outcomes and is correlated with a shrinking of the racial achievement gap.[*, 19] A 2004 study showed that desegregation had an impact on decreasing dropout rates among African American high school students during the 1970s and 1980s.[†, 20] Earlier work

---

* Barton and Coley identify sixteen different correlates for achievement, and survey a wide range of literature in additional to looking at National Assessment of Education Progress (NAEP) results, suggesting the complexity of the issue.
† Jonathan Guryan used census data from 1970 and 1980 to measure changes in black and white high school dropout rates. The analysis focuses on a sample of large school districts,

suggests that movements toward desegregation and reductions in class size, as well as the advent of the Civil Rights–era War on Poverty policies, which included increases in per-pupil expenditures and early childhood programs such as Head Start, can largely be credited with reducing barriers to K–12 achievement relative to white students.[21]

More recent work also documents significant effects of desegregation. Rucker Johnson's 2015 study of four thousand subjects born between 1950 and 1975 (including sibling pairs) noted the following outcomes:

- *Educational Attainment.* For African Americans, a five-year increase in attending a desegregated school correlates with a 14.5 percentage point increase in the likelihood of graduating from high school and roughly a 0.6 percent increase in years of education for blacks. Overall, Johnson estimates that the desegregation effect on graduation rates is comparable to the impact of having college-educated parents.[22]
- *Health Effects.* Subjects who attended a desegregated school for five years had the health of those seven years younger.
- *Criminal Justice and Safety Effects.* Black men attending a desegregated school were almost 15 percent less likely to be incarcerated by age thirty.
- *Labor market and wage effects.* Workers with five years of exposure to a desegregated school had a 15 percent increase in wages and roughly 165 additional work hours per year, with a combined result of a 30 percent increase in annual earnings.

Johnson controlled for a number of different potential independent variables, including desegregation itself (e.g., exposure of black children to white peers).[23] His results suggest that the achievement gains for African Americans reflect improved school inputs in desegregated schools. Students who went to desegregated schools attended classes that were smaller by three to four students. Most strikingly, per-pupil spending increased by almost 23 percent annually for black students who went to desegregated schools throughout their K–12 career. As Johnson notes, "a political economy explanation for these results is that state legislatures were under pressure to ensure that the level of school resources available to whites would not be negatively affected by integration."[24] The point is that desegregated schools were better resourced and presumably higher quality.

---

86 percent of which implemented desegregation plans between 1961 and 1982. He compared changes in black and white dropout rates during the 1970s in districts that integrated during the decade to changes in the same outcomes in districts that integrated both earlier and later.

Sean Reardon and colleagues at Stanford have also conducted a significant number of recent studies on segregation, finding that "the data clearly show an association between racial school segregation and achievement gaps, net of many socioeconomic differences between white and minority families." They suggest that socioeconomic integration is insufficient. As Reardon argues:

The greater the difference in poverty rates in white and black students' schools, the larger the achievement gap, on average. That is not to say, however, that having poor classmates impacts students' achievement directly. Rather, exposure to poor classmates is perhaps best understood as a proxy for general school quality – quality of instruction and opportunities to learn. High-poverty schools may have fewer resources, a harder time attracting and retaining skilled teachers, more violence and disruption, and poorer facilities.[25]

One important and related finding has to do with school funding. Experts, of course, debate the degree to which school funding matters to student achievement.[26] But Johnson's historical data suggest that integrated schools enjoy greater per-pupil funding, and that school funding matters. A 2014 paper by Johnson and colleagues shows that a 20 percent increase in per-pupil spending each year for twelve years of public schooling correlates with almost one additional year of education completed, 25 percent greater earnings, and a 20 percent reduction in the annual incidence of adult poverty. The paper argues that "the magnitudes of these effects are sufficiently large to eliminate between two-thirds and all of the gaps in these adult outcomes between those raised in poor families and those raised in non-poor families."[27]

Other research has demonstrated that students who attend integrated schools do better psychologically and socially.[28] Erica Frankenberg argues that children who attend integrated schools are less likely to develop racial stereotypes and are better able to breach color lines to work with people from different backgrounds. There is also evidence that being exposed to different viewpoints in classrooms helps students develop more critical thinking skills.[29]

Despite the virulent political pushback that desegregation generated in the decades after *Brown*, the evidence seems clear: attending a racially balanced school has lasting positive effects on economic and social well-being for black and nonblack students alike.[30]

## The Current Rules: Implicit Exclusion (1980–Present)

### Resegregating Schools
American schools today are resegregating such that nearly 25 percent of students in some states now attend what Jonathan Kozol calls "apartheid

schools," meaning that 99 percent or more of their student bodies are students of color.[31] The era of resegregation began almost as soon as desegregation began. The first significant marker was the Supreme Court's 1974 *Milliken v Bradley* ruling, which determined that de facto segregation was, in fact, lawful. In the early 1990s, a series of court decisions – *Board of Education v Dowell, Freeman v Pitts*, and *Missouri v Jenkins* – reinforced the *Milliken* ruling by releasing school districts from court oversight. In more than two hundred medium-sized and large districts, this reversal of legal requirements drove a significant increase in the racial segregation of schools.[32]

Unraveling the rules that drove and maintained racial balance in schools has incurred a significant cost. After significant progress in the 1960s and 1970s, almost half of all African American children and a similar number of Latino children now attend schools that have racially concentrated poverty. Research from John Kuscera and Gary Orfield illustrates resegregation in the New York City school system, the largest in the United States and also the most racially segregated. In 1968, 68 percent of black students were in majority-minority schools. By 1980, that number had climbed to 77 percent, and by 2010, 85 percent of black students (and 75 percent of Latino students) attended schools that were majority-minority. More than half attended "intensely segregated schools," defined as those with less than 10 percent white enrollment.[33] It is clear that in the absence of a proactive and consistent push for desegregation via court orders, our schools will mirror our racially separate neighborhoods.

### Racial Isolation

School resegregation is not a problem limited to schooling, narrowly defined: school resegregation concentrates neighborhood social disadvantage and thus has profound impacts on both individuals and communities. At home, students who experience school resegregation and the geographical concentration of disadvantage are less likely to have literate parents, adequate housing, or quiet places to study, and their families have fewer resources to dedicate to education. Resegregated schools have difficulty retaining quality teachers and administrators, and teachers in such schools must focus more on remediation and less on excellent student achievement.[34] In neighborhoods and communities, resegregation is associated with increased crime. Economic studies show that group segregation in neighborhoods, including segregation along racial and ethnic lines, is correlated with disparities in human capital investment at the neighborhood level.[35] All of these factors have important implications for broader inequality in the economy and individual economic outcomes for students, and increasingly we are seeing these dynamics reproduced over generations.[36]

In the absence of explicit desegregation efforts, school segregation is largely driven by geographic segregation, which in turn is shaped by a series of racialized rules. We discuss private redlining and other drivers of residential segregation in this book's chapter on wealth. Most school funding is based on local property taxes, endowing areas with higher housing prices (and higher property tax bases) with better school systems and creating school districts that are racially and economically homogeneous. As Carey Hawkins Ash and Chaneé Anderson write, "Where one resides has become the 'new' proxy for race in distributing quality educational opportunities in this 'colorblind' American society."[37] There is little question that neighborhoods with concentrated and racialized poverty have poor schools, as measured by spending, teacher quality, and educational outcomes, for children of color. Research shows that schools with 90 percent or more students of color spend $733 less annually per student than schools with 90 percent or more white students. If a typical high-minority school (with an average of 605 students, according to research by the Center for American Progress) were to receive the same per-pupil funding as predominantly white schools, they would see an annual increase of $443,000 in state and local spending – enough to fund the average salary for nine veteran teachers or twelve additional first-year teachers.[38]

### *The Rise of "Accountability" and High-Stakes Testing*

In the midst of the legal changes that fueled resegregation, an education reform movement focused on standards began to develop. In the 1980s and continuing through the 1990s and beyond, reformers stressed school accountability, clear goals, and clear standards for teaching and learning – standards applied to both students and teachers and measured primarily by testing. These were the themes of education reform from Ronald Reagan through George W. Bush. Reagan's *A Nation At Risk* report was in many ways the clarion call and catalyst; it provided a new frame for education reform and emphasized the economic importance (as opposed to civic, moral, or any other rationale) of education and schooling and drove a focus on standards and back-to-basics. *A Nation At Risk* also placed an individual focus on schools as key to educational and economic improvement rather than looking at schools in the context of a larger society in which poverty and broader inequality existed.

The shift in focus set the foundation for Clinton's Goals 2000 and Improving America's Schools Acts, the latter of which reauthorized ESEA, and later for Bush's 2001 No Child Left Behind Act (NCLB), which ushered in an era of high-stakes testing. In 2000, in a speech to the NAACP, Bush laid the groundwork for NCLB:

There's reason for optimism in this land. A great movement of education reform has begun in this country built on clear principles: to raise the bar of standards, expect every child can learn; to give schools the flexibility to meet those standards; to measure progress and insist upon results; to blow the whistle on failure; to provide parents with options to increase their option, like charters and choice; and also remember the role of education is to leave no child behind.[39]

In his remarks, Bush also addressed race and poverty: "Some say it is unfair to hold disadvantaged children to rigorous standards. I say it is discrimination to require anything less – the soft bigotry of low expectations." Goals 2000 and NCLB focused on reducing achievement gaps, including both the gap between American schoolchildren and their international counterparts and the black–white achievement gap, and improving teaching and learning by focusing on common high standards across all states, testing to achieve those goals, and improving teacher quality overall. Schools would face sanctions if they did not make "adequate yearly progress" on test scores and graduation rates, especially for low-achieving children, and did not make progress in closing the racial achievement gap.

The era of accountability lingers on with continued high-stakes testing, but the value of testing is increasingly questioned in school districts across the country. However, there is limited national conversation about revisiting race as central to the equation. As Gary Orfield and Erika Frankenberg note:

Educational policy since the 1980s has largely ignored issues of race and has focused attention on harsh accountability policies. These policies are premised on the assumptions that equal opportunity can be universally achieved in separate schools through the application of uniform standards and sanctions and that racial segregation can be ignored.[40]

Whether this shift in rules has been good for students, and good for their long-term economic prospects, is the question to which we now turn.

## IMPACTS OF EDUCATION GAPS

Throughout almost three-quarters of a century of changes in our educational politics and rule making, the black–white achievement gap has for the most part persisted. Beyond resegregation itself, it is important to ask whether the push for accountability has actually improved educational results or eliminated racialized barriers to achievement.

A wide range of studies suggests that the answer is mixed and our efforts over the last several decades to improve test scores for children of color have been uneven. A study by Sean Reardon and colleagues found "no support for the hypothesis that No Child Left Behind has led, on average, to a narrowing of racial achievement gaps," although there has been some variation across states. It is notable that the most segregated schools with the biggest achievement gaps have seen the most improved scores, and it may be that real pressure on the most segregated schools does lead to improvements.[41]

Similarly, a large-scale overview conducted by McKinsey and Company shows that the performance of schools – even within the overall standards and accountability framework – varies widely among states, among districts within states, among schools within districts, and among classrooms within schools.[42] As McKinsey reports, Texas students are, on average, one to two years of learning ahead of California students of the same age, even though Texas has less income per capita and spends less per pupil than California." Evidence from McKinsey and others continues to suggest that investments in teaching and in school site leadership – that is, in the role of school principals as educational leaders, and not just managers – is vital to high-performing schools. This echoes the work of Linda Darling-Hammond, who has conducted groundbreaking research on the effects of excellent teaching, as measured by preparation and certification.[43] But overall, surveys of achievement gap results over the past several decades show very modest progress.

Our understanding of causal mechanisms is limited, though school financing as well as quality teaching and educational leadership seem to matter most. These are, of course, related; schools with more resources can attract more experienced teachers and administrators. Most strikingly, very little if any of the recent literature on the black–white achievement gap makes mention of changing the racial distribution of students in schools.[‡, 44]

Additionally, the accountability movement has had many unintended consequences, including incentives to "push out" low-performing students from schools to improve overall scores.[45] This trend is especially prevalent in charter schools.[46] Research shows that, in addition to pushing students

---

‡   The McKinsey report does acknowledge that "school-level segregation may play a role in influencing outcomes." State variations in the racial achievement gap cannot be explained by the proportion of blacks and Latinos in a state's educational system, although school-level segregation may play a role in influencing outcomes. And a few cities, including Cambridge, Massachusetts, have continued to advocate for "Controlled Choice," wherein socioeconomic status has replaced race as a way to think about creating more integrated schools, but where race is clearly still important to many decision makers.

out, charter schools present stark racial disparities in punishments for black and white students. A 2014 report from the Department of Education illustrated how students of color in public schools are more likely to be suspended and receive referrals to law enforcement. In fact, at all age levels, black children are three times as likely as white children to face suspensions. These hold even for the youngest students. At the preschool levels, black students represent 18 percent of enrollment but 48 percent of suspensions. Further, while boys receive the majority of suspensions, African American girls receive suspensions at a higher rate – approximately 12 percent – than girls of any other background. Black students represent about 16 percent of enrollment nationwide but 27 percent of students referred to law enforcement and roughly a third of those subjected to school-related arrests.[47] A report by the Civil Rights Project at UCLA finds that more than five hundred charter schools suspended black students at a rate that was at least 10 percentage points higher than white students. The same report found that charter schools suspended disabled students at extremely high rates: 235 charter schools suspended more than 50 percent of their students with disabilities.[48] This increase, which is the result of both the rewards structure of the accountability movement as well as personal bias, has been a central concern of the Movement for Black Lives. As we develop a complete education and economics policy agenda for African Americans, we must address zero-tolerance policies, school discipline, and the "school-to-prison pipeline."

## Economic and Educational Inequality

There is a vigorous debate about the degree to which black–white economic inequality can be attributed to educational inequality. One prevailing argument is that education, as important as it is, is not a silver bullet. Much evidence now suggests that improving education alone would not eliminate the earnings and wealth gap between African Americans and whites. In fact, the typical white high school dropout holds more wealth than the typical black college graduate.[49] Eliminating disparities in college graduation rates would only increase black wealth by $1,313 and close the racial wealth gap by 1 percent.[50]

The numbers make clear a painful reality: Even with significant educational achievement, black Americans still face enormous discriminatory barriers – in job opportunities and earnings; in access to credit and other modes of wealth building; in equal access to justice, health care, housing, and safe communities; and in so many other realms. It is the systemic and intersecting nature of these barriers, not educational attainment alone, that prevents far too many individuals from pursuing and attaining the economic opportunity that Americans hold so sacred. As William Darity and Darrick Hamilton have written:

> Education is not the great equalizer when it comes to race and wealth .... Conventional wisdom proclaims a college education is the primary vehicle for economic mobility and the "great equalizer" when it comes to black–white disparity. In reality, a college degree does little to undo the massive difference in wealth across race.[51]

This is a critical point. But despite the debate about the relationship between wealth and education, most would argue that lessening barriers to higher achievement for black students would be a win-win: better for individuals and families and better for economic output and growth.

Over the last several decades, some have tried to ameliorate these inequalities with privatizing schools and supporting an increased number of charter schools. As Diane Ravitch points out, this movement is a natural consequence of No Child Left Behind, which called for privatization or charter schools where public schools have not made progress. But neither privatization nor charters are addressing the deeper issue. These schools have proven to be overly selective, often have high attrition rates, and overall are, at most, a patchwork solution to a much larger structural problem.[52] In short, these interventions, which have now been embraced by elite decision makers in both political parties, are workarounds that do not actually change the rules that disadvantage students of color.

The growing trend of "school choice" is also a driver of school segregation. Not long after the *Brown* ruling, school vouchers first emerged as a "free-market" policy prescription championed by University of Chicago economist Milton Friedman, but they were embraced in the South as a strategic means to preserve segregation.[53] While school vouchers have often been billed as a ticket for low-income and minority parents out of low-performing schools, in many ways they can be seen as a Trojan horse, leading to inconsistent outcomes for students of color and contributing to "white flight" as white families are able to send their children to predominantly white schools. The cases of Wisconsin, Georgia, and Florida are prime examples: school vouchers programs that were initially framed as helping advance black and Latino families were rapidly expanded to include families that were solidly middle class, shifting funding to from low-income families to families with greater economic resources. In Milwaukee, school vouchers were initially limited to students whose family incomes were less than 175 percent of the federal poverty level, but policy makers later raised the cap to 300 percent of the federal poverty level.[54]

These programs entrenched and subsidized segregated schools and segregated systems. In a 2006 study, researchers found that households where children attend schools with a large nonwhite population are significantly more likely to support school vouchers. Tellingly, this effect is absent in nonwhite households and households without children.[55] Historian Diane Ravitch notes, "for many years school choice was widely understood by the courts and the public as a strategy to preserve school segregation."[56] Kuscera and Orfield have written about the segregating impacts of school choice in the absence of targeted policies meant to prevent such outcomes: "We learned in the South a half-century ago that choice plans without civil rights standards increase stratification of schools and leave almost all the children of color still segregated."[57]

Together, the trends that we have seen over the last thirty years – resegregation, the rise of the standards movement, and the charter movement – have, however unintentionally, led to a stalling out. Overall, we see more concentrated poverty by race and less educational progress for African American children than we did a generation ago. This will very likely lead to worsened economic prospects, and therefore is not only bad for individuals and their ability to fully participate in the labor market but also bad for the American economy as a whole. The lack of progress in the realm of education represents an enormous lost opportunity.

## ECONOMIC IMPACTS

As detailed, school desegregation has positive long-term economic, labor market, and well-being effects for individuals. McKinsey has projected positive effects, including increased earnings, increased high school and college graduation rates, improved health, and decreased rates of incarceration from closing the racial academic achievement gap.

More speculatively, and perhaps most provocatively, McKinsey makes a number of macroeconomic projections about the effects of improving student achievement, including closing the black–white achievement gap:

If the gap between black and Latino student performance and white student performance had been … narrowed, GDP in 2008 would have been between $310 billion and $525 billion higher, or 2 to 4 percent of GDP. The magnitude of this impact will rise in the years ahead as demographic shifts result in blacks and Latinos becoming a larger proportion of the population and workforce.[58]

## CONCLUSION

The arc of history is becoming clear. African Americans educated in desegregated schools experience much better economic outcomes as adults. In contrast, the standards and accountability movement has showed some lessening of the black–white achievement gap at certain grade levels but has had little to no educational or economic effect overall. Combined with the fact that more black and Latino children now attend schools with 90 percent or more children in poverty and with more densely segregated black and Latino populations than at any time since the 1980s, it seems clear that recent accountability measures, despite best intentions, have had at best no impact and in some cases negative impacts on students of color.

This points strongly to the need for a significantly different approach to improving schooling, and economic outcomes, for black Americans. It is time that we look again at what has worked in our past. We must rediscover and redouble our efforts to create schools that are racially balanced, well-financed, well-staffed, and high-achieving – schools that prepare our children and our society for the economy ahead.

# 7

# The Racial Rules of Criminal Justice

## INTRODUCTION

We have already explored how a wide range of racial rules has shaped opportunities and outcomes for black Americans. But as numerous grassroots efforts have reminded us in recent decades – particularly those such as the Movement for Black Lives, which arose in response to unchecked violence against black men and women at the hands of the police – any conversation about the well-being of black Americans must address the overarching and inescapable influence of the criminal justice system on nearly every aspect of black life.

The radical scope and impact of the U.S. penal system is not an accident of history but rather a direct result of the increasingly harsh incarceration policies implemented over the last three decades. These in turn are deeply connected to the racially explicit rules rooted in the founding of the nation. The racial rules around criminal justice and mass incarceration have predictably and effectively resulted in the permanent social and economic exclusion of black Americans, their families, and their communities.[1] As Todd Clear explains, "Imprisonment has grown to the point that it now produces the very social problems on which it feeds. It is the perfect storm."[2] Our current and historic racial rules have thrust black Americans – more than any other racial or ethnic group – into the eye of that storm without any clear path out of it.

A number of scholars describe our current criminal justice system as an outgrowth of the explicitly racially exclusionary policies that came before it. Sociologist Loïc Wacquant describes the U.S. criminal justice system as one of four "peculiar institutions" – including chattel slavery, the Jim Crow era, and the northern "ghetto" that corresponded with the Great Migration that ended in the 1960s – which have "operated to define, confine, and control" black Americans.[3] While the successes of the Civil Rights Movement dismantled many of Jim Crow's explicitly discriminatory legal rules, the new set of penal rules that began to take shape in the 1980s provided the foundation for what Michelle Alexander has called a "new Jim Crow."[4] Alexander notes that the rules accompanying the mass incarceration and criminalization of black Americans also legalize discrimination in employment, housing, education, public benefits, and voting. In this chapter, we do not aim to uncover the intent of the current rules, but rather to illustrate that those rules are derived from an explicitly racist system and have shaped a new system that is rife with – and replicates – racial inequity.

As the ACLU describes in its 2014 report on racism in the U.S. criminal justice system, racism and racial disparities exist at every level of the U.S. criminal justice system, "including stops and searches, arrests, prosecutions and plea negotiations, trials, and sentencing."[5] A 2015 high-profile Department of Justice (DOJ) report on the Ferguson, Missouri, police department in the wake of the shooting of Michael Brown illustrated the omnipresence of racial injustice in the U.S. criminal justice system. The report found that black Americans – who represent fewer than seven in ten Ferguson residents – account for roughly nine out of ten vehicle stops, citations, and arrests. The DOJ concluded:

Our investigation indicates that this disproportionate burden on African Americans cannot be explained by any difference in the rate at which people of different races violate the law. Rather, our investigation has revealed that these disparities occur, at least in part, because of unlawful bias against and stereotypes about African Americans. We have found substantial evidence of racial bias among police and court staff in Ferguson.[6]

In this chapter, we first highlight some of the vast racial disparities we see in the criminal justice system. We then identify the historical arc of this persistent racism, beginning with the explicitly exclusionary rules of slavery and Jim Crow and concluding with a range of current racial rules that shape the criminal justice system. We illustrate the web of socioeconomic factors and outcomes that shape – and are shaped by – black Americans' interactions with the criminal justice system. And we again seek to demonstrate the deep and intersectional roots of systemic racism and the vast inequities it has brought forth, making the case that we must fix our broken criminal justice and economic systems simultaneously if we are to correct the injustices they foster.

## DISPARITIES AND INEQUITIES IN THE CRIMINAL JUSTICE SYSTEM

It is possible that nothing makes the United States more exceptional than the trends in incarceration that have characterized the last thirty years. With only 5 percent of the global population, we have 25 percent of the world's prisoners.[7] The prison population has quintupled since 1980.[8] As of 2016, 1.3 million individuals were being held in state prisons, 646,000 in local jails, and 211,000 in federal prisons, and there were an additional 4.6 million individuals on probation or parole.[9] In other words, one of every thirty-five adults is under some type of correctional control within our criminal justice system.[10] Black Americans bear a disproportionate and undue burden from the rules that have driven these statistics.

The majority of people currently in prison in the United States – over 60 percent – are racial and ethnic minorities.[11] In 2016, one in every ten black males in their thirties were in prison and over half of all black men without a high school diploma spend time in prison at some point in their lives.[12] Black men spend more time incarcerated over their lifetimes than do Hispanic or white men: 3.09 years in prison or jail compared to 1.06 and 0.5 years for Hispanic and white men, respectively.[13] On average, they can expect to spend nearly sixty-two times longer in prison or jail as compared to the group at lowest risk, white women.[14]

Black women are also more likely to spend time in prison compared to other women. Overall, one in fifty-six women face imprisonment during their lifetime, but the likelihood of imprisonment for black women is one in nineteen; for Hispanic and white women it is one in forty-five and one in 118, respectively.[15] Black women spend on average 0.23 years incarcerated, compared to 0.09 and 0.05 years for Hispanic and white women.[16]

The charges and sentences levied against black defendants also tend to be disproportionately severe. Black Americans comprise only 13 percent of the U.S. population but represent 42 percent of defendants facing a death sentence. One 2000 study found that 89 percent of defendants prosecuted for capital crimes were people of color.[17] Too often these stark racial disparities are blamed on a "culture of violence," but as we will explain, this is simply not the case. In fact, while prison populations were rising in recent decades, both violent and property crime rates were falling and are now below earlier levels (see Figure 7.1).[18] At every stage of the criminal justice system, the rules are stacked against black Americans, making it more likely they will come in contact with law enforcement in the first place and essentially guaranteeing that when they do, they will be treated more harshly than whites.[19]

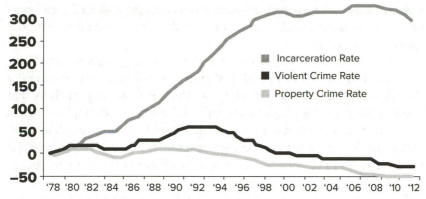

Figure 7.1. Incarceration rose even as crime fell.
*Source*: Data courtesy of U.S. Department of Justice, Bureau of Justice Statistics and FBI, Uniform Crime Reports. Based on a chart originally published by the Center on Budget and Policy Priorities by Mitchell, Michael (2014).

## Black Women and Black LGBTQ People: Invisible Victims of Mass Incarceration

Conversations about mass incarceration in the United States primarily focus on black men, but black women are increasingly impacted by the criminal justice system. The percentage of women in state and federal prisons has grown exponentially in recent decades, in many ways an unintended consequence of a rapidly expanding criminal justice system.[20] Women represent only 7 percent of the population in state and federal prisons, but between 1980 and 2010, the number of women in prison increased by 646 percent from 15,118 to 112,797.[21] As of 2012, including local jails, there were more than two hundred thousand women incarcerated, with black women being far more likely to be incarcerated than white and Hispanic women. Approximately half of the women who are incarcerated have never been convicted of a violent offense.[22]

A combination of factors has made black women more vulnerable to the racial rules that drove mass incarceration and has subjected them to a system originally designed for male offenders with little thought given to its effect on women. Meda Chesney-Lind describes this phenomenon as "vengeful equity" and explains that the increase in women's imprisonment is not a reflection of the "seriousness of women's crime" but is instead a result of the racial rules of the penal system, and particularly the increasingly harsh penalties implemented through the War on Drugs.[23] Black women's unique experiences – sexual and physical trauma, domestic violence, low-paying and low-status jobs, changes in welfare policies, and a lack of social supports – increase the likelihood that they will come into contact with the system in the first place.

Nearly 60 percent of women serving time in state prisons reported having been either sexually or physically abused at least once before spending time in prison, and for approximately one-third of all women in prison, that abuse began when they were young girls and continued throughout adulthood. Such victimization patterns are significant because research on girl's and women's crime often exposes significant links between these traumatic experiences and behavior that later involves them in the criminal justice system.[24]

In many ways, the very system that claims to protect women from violence has only exposed them to more of it. The growing trend of criminalization of domestic violence survivors who defend themselves from their abusers is just one illustration. In 2012, Marissa Alexander fired a warning shot into the ceiling to fend off her abusive husband. She lived in Florida, a Stand Your Ground state, and despite the fact that no one was injured or killed, Alexander (a black woman who had given birth days earlier) faced a mandatory minimum sentence of twenty years in prison. As a result of massive organizing and advocacy efforts, Alexander's lawyers struck a plea deal that reduced her sentence to a two-year house arrest. But Alexander's experience is not unique, particularly for black women. In fact, because of mandatory arrest policies, which require police to make an arrest when responding to a domestic violence call, domestic violence survivors – rather than abusers – are often arrested. Women of color and low-income women are particularly vulnerable to these trends. The organization INCITE found that in cases of arrests against domestic violence survivors in New York City, 66 percent of the women arrested were African American or Latina, 43 percent were living below the poverty line, and 19 percent were receiving public assistance at the time of their arrest.[25]

Once imprisoned, women face unique challenges, particularly related to health care. They are more likely than men to have chronic medical problems (59 percent compared to 43 percent), and nearly three out of every four women battle with mental health illnesses, compared to just over half of male prisoners.[26] Additionally, many women enter the prison system while they are pregnant (one in twenty-five women in state prisons and one in thirty-three in federal prisons). A study by the Correctional Association of New York found that pregnant women often receive substandard reproductive health care and face serious delays accessing obstetric and gynecological services, and that women are "routinely denied basic reproductive health items, including contraception and sufficient sanitary supplies." Pregnant women often face poor living conditions, including confinement, insufficient nutrients, and harmful childbirth experiences, such as shackling during labor.[27] In fact, in all but thirteen states, women can be shackled during labor and delivery, and even in states where it is outlawed many women still experience such treatment. These racialized and gender rules hit black women the hardest.

Even though women are imprisoned at lower rates than their male counterparts, the impact of their imprisonment has an outsized impact on their communities and their families. Todd Clear explains:

The smaller number of women who cycle in and out of prison from these same neighborhoods does not mean that their *impact* is as small as their numbers. The role women play in their social networks, social capital, and informal social controls, especially in very poor urban neighborhoods, is thought to be more important, per person, than men.[28]

Thus, the increased criminalization of black women reinforces – and exacerbates the impact of – the very racial rules that brought them into contact with the criminal justice system in the first place.

Along with cisgender black women, the black transgender population is at the nexus of several of these criminal justice rules. Transgender people – those who identify as a gender other than the one assigned to them at birth – are disproportionately incarcerated. Among black transgender people, nearly half (47 percent) have been incarcerated at some point in their lives.[29] In addition to frequently being denied hormones and other vital transition-related health care, many black trans people are incarcerated in prisons that do not correspond with their gender identity. Once incarcerated, black trans people are often placed in solitary confinement (or "protective custody"),[30] which has devastating effects on their mental health.[31] CeCe MacDonald, a black trans woman who was attacked by street harassers and used the fabric scissors she had in her purse to retaliate in self-defense, was arrested and immediately placed in solitary confinement in two separate men's prisons for five months.

Additionally, policies such as the 2003 Prison Rape Elimination Act (PREA), which was ostensibly implemented to decrease the staggering rates of sexual assault in prison, has – according to many advocates – had the effect of criminalizing consensual sex between bisexual, queer, and lesbian women in prisons rather than preventing assaults.[32] Queer and trans people in prison already face rates of sexual violence that are ten times higher than the rest of the prison population,[33] and sexual violence in prison has overall increased, not decreased, since PREA was instituted.[34] These rules add multiple targets to the backs of black people in prison who are women, queer, transgender, or any combination thereof.

## THE RACIAL RULES OF THE CRIMINAL JUSTICE SYSTEM

### Pre–Civil Rights: A Long Era of Brutality and Explicit Exclusion

As we have described, Reconstruction resulted in a brief period of progress for black Americans, with the passage of laws that established public schools, paved the way for voting rights, and ushered in a wave of black elected officials. However, this progress occurred against the backdrop of intense resistance to the shifting social order, and ultimately met fierce backlash that resulted in what Douglas Blackmon has calls "neoslavery," or "slavery by another name."[35]

During this period, southern states enacted an "array of interlocking laws" meant to criminalize black life, and white southerners organized gangs and militias to monitor, terrorize, and imprison freed blacks. Forced labor camps run by state and local governments, large corporations, farmers, and entrepreneurs were set up across the South. In the late 1800s, hundreds of cities and municipalities began selling the rights to and leasing out their prisoners to employers looking for cheap labor, a practice that became known as convict leasing. White northerners were relatively indifferent to the new systems that replicated old injustices.

Historic narratives often describe the criminalization of blacks during this time as an inevitable way to control increasing crime rates among the newly freed population. But, as Blackmon describes, this was not the case:

Instead of evidence showing black crime waves, the original records of county jails indicated thousands of arrests for inconsequential charges or for violations of laws specifically written to intimidate blacks – changing employers without permission, vagrancy, riding freight cars without a ticket, engaging in sexual activity – or loud talk – with white women. Repeatedly, the timing and scale of surges in arrests appeared more attuned to the rises and dips in the need for cheap labor than any demonstrable acts of crime.[36]

Convict leasing was an implicitly racial rule that could not have more closely mirrored the institution of slavery from which it emerged. It was fueled by continued racism at both the individual and institutional levels – terrorizing black communities into complying with the social order of white supremacy – and by the economic needs of southern states, counties, and individual employers who were looking to regain their economic power.[37]

At the end of Reconstruction, every formerly Confederate state, with the exception of Virginia, had adopted the practice of convict leasing, and as the 1880s came to a close, approximately ten thousand black men were forced to work in labor mines, fields, and work camps across the South.[38] As Blackmon explains, the conditions for convict laborers were even worse than under slavery:

Slaves of the earlier era were at least minimally insulated from physical harm by their intrinsic financial value. Their owners could borrow money with slaves as collateral, pay debts with them, sell them at a profit, or extend the investment through production of more slave children. But the convicts of the new system were of value only as long as their sentences or physical strength lasted. If they died while in custody, there was no financial penalty to the company leasing them.[39]

As such, employers frequently pushed laborers to the brink of illness and death. Ironically, this new labor regime was rendered legal by a clause in the Thirteenth Amendment that said, "Neither slavery nor involuntary servitude, except as a punishment for a crime whereof the party shall have been duly convicted, shall exist in the United States."

It would be nearly fifty years until convict leasing was phased out, thanks to public opposition to the violence and torture that characterized the system. In its place, new form of forced labor – the chain gang – took over, and was tied to the economic and infrastructure needs in the South. Under this system, chains were shackled to prisoners, binding together men as they slept, ate, and worked. While this system was created to rectify the injustices of convict leasing, it simply recreated them. Men were chronically undernourished, abused, and even killed while being forced to build roads, dig ditches, and clear land, among other tasks. The brutality of this system eventually attracted public outrage, and it was abolished nationwide in the 1950s, making way for the modern prison system.

### An Era of Civil Rights and Inclusion

As a spirit of social reform began to take hold across the country in response to the vast racial injustices that characterized the Jim Crow era, a series of inclusive rules were written that had the potential to – and for a time did – move the American criminal justice system closer to one of justice and fairness.[40] As early as 1955, the National Council on Crime and Delinquency proposed that the civil rights of offenders should be restored upon completion of criminal sentence. In 1967, the President's Crime Commission called for a reevaluation of the penalties associated with criminal convictions, and the Bail Reform Act of 1967 reduced pretrial detention for low-income individuals.[41] In the early 1970s, the Advisory Commission on Corrections recommended overturning voter disqualification statutes, arguing, "If corrections is to reintegrate an offender into free society, the offender must retain all attributes of citizenship."[42] The reform spirit that moved these federal initiatives also spread to many of the states, and during the 1960s and 1970s the number of punitive state laws declined while the number of laws that required the restoration of civil rights to offenders increased.[43]

In these decades, indeterminate sentencing allowed for greater variability in prison terms for offenders; when an individual was convicted, he was given a sentence with a minimum and maximum term and was then eligible for parole after serving the minimum term minus any credits for "good time." In some ways, this was more equitable than the harsh penalty guidelines that would follow, but it also resulted in disparate outcomes for people of color and drew the ire of civil rights advocates who were pushing for racial equity across a range of institutions, motivating them to call for "colorblind" policies that would be applied equitably. The flames of the "rehabilitative ideal" that were lit during the civil rights movement would be swiftly extinguished as more conservative social and economic ideologies took hold.[44] The era that would follow gave rise to "race-neutral" policies that were hardly race-neutral in practice.

### Post–Civil Rights: From Rehabilitation to Social Exclusion

A series of shifts in socioeconomic circumstances, public opinion, and political discourse laid the groundwork for the dramatic changes that still characterize our criminal justice system. During the 1960s and 1970s, unemployment among unskilled men rose as urban labor markets collapsed in the wake of industrial job losses. Poverty and "chronic joblessness" became commonplace in the Northeast and Midwest, leaving black neighborhoods increasingly under the scrutiny of police.[45] Black Americans, who had not been fully or meaningfully incorporated into northern cities over the course of migration, were particularly vulnerable to the effects of these economic changes.[46] Yet even before the rise of urban deindustrialization, race and notions of "criminality" requiring overpolicing and incarceration were already well established. As Khalil Gibran Muhammad argues, during the height of our industrial economy, blacks in northern cities were still overrepresented in terms of arrest rates and incarceration in both northern and southern prisons.[47]

The 1960s and 1970s brought rising crime rates that ignited concern across the political spectrum, and for conservatives that concern was fueled by backlash against the inclusionary social movements of the time. As Marc Mauer of the Sentencing Project posits, social activism and disorder fueled the anxieties and resentments of working-class whites, driving them to conservative politicians who were increasingly promising tough-on-crime measures. Todd Clear explains further:

This concern about crime also served as a symbol for other, less easily voiced worries about civil-rights unrest, antiwar disturbances, and bubbling reaction to the underlying principles of the welfare state and Lyndon Johnson's Great Society. In the public mind, the social fabric of American society had broken down and disorder and disruption were rampant. A strong response – law and order – was required.[48]

## THE WAR ON DRUGS: HARSHER TREATMENT AND COLLATERAL PUNISHMENT

A strong response is precisely what followed, as new racial rules around crime and punishment were enacted with devastating consequences for black Americans. In 1971, responding to and reinforcing public perceptions about the crack epidemic, Nixon declared the "War on Drugs." This laid the groundwork for a series of penal changes that would drive up incarceration rates for all Americans, but particularly for black Americans. These include the following:

- *Mandatory minimum sentences*, a departure from indeterminate sentencing, essentially presets prison terms for certain violations, limits the discretion of judges in the sentencing process, and are credited with keeping many offenders, even those of low-level crimes, in prison longer.[49]
- *Truth in sentencing* guidelines established at the federal level require states to imprison individuals for 85 percent of their sentences in order to receive certain funding streams.
- *Three-strikes laws* levy automatic lengthy sentences – in many cases life sentences and sometimes life without parole (LWOP) – against individuals with two previous felonies. Black Americans make up 28.3 percent of all prisoners serving life sentences, but represent 56.4 percent of those serving LWOP and 56.1 percent of those sentenced to LWOP as juveniles (the United States is the only country in the world that sentences youth to life in prison without parole, despite a wealth of cognitive science research that demonstrates young people's brain development makes them more likely to suffer from impeded judgment).[50] Black youth serve LWOP sentences at a rate ten times higher than that of white youth.[51]

At the end of the 1970s, states began to turn away from parole release in favor of minimum required sentences, and by the end of the decade there was hardly a state that had not made major changes to its penal structure.[52] New York's Rockefeller drug laws of the mid-1970s paved the way for the wave of federal sentencing changes for drug-related crimes during the Reagan and Bush eras. Harsher policing rules were also key tools for expanding mass incarceration. In 1982, a landmark article by George Kelling and James Wilson called "Broken Windows" laid the groundwork for official policy in the country's largest cities and their police departments.[53] The theory of broken windows policing posited that low levels of nonviolent crime and disorder, like the symbol of broken windows, leads to increased fear and social withdrawal that creates the conditions for more serious, violent crime to take place. Among others, New York City mayor Rudy Giuliani codified this theory into practice, appointing police commissioner Bill Bratton to enact rules like stop and frisk policies in line with the broken windows framework.[54] But in 2016, the New York City government issued its own investigative report of the practice, finding that contrary to the broken windows theory, there was in fact neither correlation nor causation linking low-level crimes with more serious violence.[55]

In the 1980s and 1990s, a number of vicious crimes committed by former prisoners fueled the push for harsher penalties as political leaders seized on public shock and fear and portrayed opponents as weak on crime. The 1988 Willie Horton ad from the George H. W. Bush campaign to defeat Michael Dukakis is a prime example of this.[56] The ad painted Dukakis as weak on crime because of his support for furloughs (a common practice in the 1980s, in which inmates were permitted brief passes to visit family, apply for jobs, attend religious services, and begin to readjust to society), which the ad juxtaposes with a stark account of Horton's charges of a violent home invasion. The Marshall Project credits the ad with shaping much of the political discourse about criminal justice in the years that followed.[57]

In 1994, President Bill Clinton oversaw the passage of the Violent Crime Control and Law Enforcement Act, which put more cops on the streets, expanded the use of the death penalty, increased prison sentences, restricted educational opportunities for prisoners, and invested significantly in the expansion of the U.S. prison system.

When the legacy of President Clinton's 1994 crime bill came into sharper focus during the 2016 presidential campaign, some suggested that the bill was, at least in part, a response to the concerns of black communities about threats of violence in their neighborhoods. But as Elizabeth Hinton, Julilly

Kohler-Hausman, and Vesla Weaver explained, while black Americans were concerned about crime, violence, and drugs in their neighborhoods, they were not asking simply for tough-on-crime measures to address them: "Calls for tough sentencing and police protection were paired with calls for full employment, quality education and drug treatment, and criticism of police brutality."[58] Policy makers ignored the calls for more holistic interventions and investments and selectively focused on stricter surveillance and harsher punishments. "When blacks ask for *better* policing, legislators tend to hear *more* instead."[59]

One of the hallmark rules of the War on Drugs was the sentencing disparity for using crack cocaine (whose users are more often poorer and black) compared to powder cocaine (whose users are often wealthier and white). Despite the fact that the substances are virtually identical in composition, sentences for using crack cocaine are one hundred times longer than for powder cocaine. As of 2004, two decades after the original mandatory minimum sentencing rules for crack cocaine were enacted, black Americans served nearly as much time in prison on average for nonviolent drug offences (58.7 months) as whites did on average for violent offenses (61.7 months).[60] In 2010, thirty thousand people were sentenced for crack cocaine offenses under the harsher rules regime; 85 percent of them were black.[61] Research has shown that more than 80 percent of defendants sentenced for crack offenses are African American, despite the fact that more than 66 percent of crack users are white or Hispanic.[62] In 2010, Congress passed the Fair Sentencing Act, which reduced the sentencing disparities from 100:1 to 18:1. Despite this improvement in the law, disparities persist, perpetuating "outdated and discredited assumptions about crack cocaine that gave rise to the unwarranted 100-to-1 disparity in the first place."[63]

The War on Drugs increased arrests among African Americans, but those arrests were not reflective of drug use in black communities. Research shows that African Americans comprise only 15 percent of the country's drug users, yet they make up 37 percent of those arrested for drug violations, 59 percent of those convicted, and 74 percent of those sentenced to prison for a drug offense.[64] Black high school seniors report using drugs at a rate that is three-quarters that of white high school seniors, and white students have three times the number of emergency room visits for drug overdose.[65]

## COLLATERAL PUNISHMENTS

A series of new rules enacted in the mid-1980s and the 1990s expanded punishment beyond prisons and paved the way for a wide range of "collateral punishments": denying convicted felons the right to vote, encouraging the termination of parental rights, restricting the right to hold public office, enacting occupational exclusions, and barring formerly incarcerated individuals from a wide range of public safety benefits.[66] The federal government gave states financial incentives to abide by these measures.[67]

Worse, the Personal Responsibility and Work Opportunity Reconciliation Act (also known as "welfare reform") required states to permanently bar individuals with drug-related felony convictions from receiving assistance and food stamps. States were given the option to opt out of these bans but had to do so proactively, and many did not. The U.S. penal system quickly became one of "wholesale exclusion."[68] Individuals who violated probation or parole temporarily lost access to food stamps, public housing benefits, Temporary Assistance for Needy Families (TANF), and Social Security insurance. The Higher Education Act of 1998 made drug offenders ineligible to receive publicly funded student loans for at least one year. As Jeremy Travis, president of John Jay College of Criminal Justice, explains, these developments "heightened the vulnerability of poor people to the negative effects of invisible punishment."[69] The state had erected barriers to the very systems and opportunities that would promote reintegration and prevent recidivism, instead ensuring permanent exclusion.

These penalties were theoretically race-neutral, but given the disproportionate representation of black Americans in the criminal justice system and the vast disparities in wealth, income, and education – just to name a few critical indicators – that make black Americans more likely to rely on these social programs, it was inevitable that collateral punishments would have a disproportionate impact on black communities.

## PROSECUTORIAL DISCRETION

The rules of public defense and prosecutorial discretion also allow for bias to be reinforced by institutions and result in elevated charges and longer sentences for black Americans. Angela Davis has documented how the proliferation and overlapping of drug war rules allow for individual – often unconscious – bias to shape unequal prison sentences: "Race ... may affect the existence of a prior criminal record even in the absence of recidivist tendencies on the part of the suspect."[70] Among the factors prosecutors are recommended to consider are previous convictions and likelihood of conviction – factors largely shaped by socioeconomic circumstances and which reinforce institutionalized biases. A 2014 report from National Academies Press indicates that black and Hispanic defendants are more likely than whites to be detained before trial, which increases the likelihood of a prison sentence, and that race and ethnicity affect charging and plea bargaining decisions. In other words, there is no strong evidence of racial bias at the sentencing stage per se, but bias that occurs earlier in the justice and trial process paves the way for unwarranted incarceration differences.[71]

## NONINCARCERATION PENALTIES

The detrimental effects of our criminal justice system on people of color are not confined to prisons and incarceration. The noncustodial justice system – which encompasses fines, fees, and other economic penalties that can result in loss of property and sometimes liberty – affects far more individuals, families, and communities. As the 2015 DOJ report explains, these penalties are often driven by budgetary needs that have little to do with public safety. They have driven "a pattern of unconstitutional policing" and led to court procedures "that raise due process concerns and inflict unnecessary harm on members of the Ferguson community."[72] Municipal courts issue arrest warrants "as a routine response to missed court appearances and required fine payments." In fact, in 2013, the court issued more than nine thousand warrants on cases related to minor offenses such as traffic tickets, parking infractions, or housing code violations.[73] These violations are not unique to Ferguson. In California, where blacks are two to four times more likely to get pulled over for a traffic stop than whites, a host of policies turn minor citations into a poverty sentence for many African Americans. In San Francisco, over 70 percent of individuals seeking legal assistance for driver's license suspensions were black, even though they comprised a mere 6 percent of the city's population. Over 4 million individuals in California have suspended licenses for failure to appear or pay.[74]

The current rules in our criminal justice system exacerbate historical disparities and reinforce the other deep racial, social, and economic inequities described in this book.[75] Racial gaps in wealth and income make it less likely that black Americans will have access to capital needed to pay for alternatives to incarceration and for minor fines and fees that the criminal justice system disproportionately levies on them.[76] Living in poverty increases the likelihood of falling prey to incarceration or one of the abovementioned civil violations, which only further fuels the cycle of poverty. According to the Prison Policy Initiative, in 2014 the median annual income for incarcerated black men and women was $17,625 and $12,735 respectively, nearly half of the median annual income for nonincarcerated black men and women.[77] Violations that lead to arrests or license suspensions disrupt employment, schooling, health, and familial and community responsibilities, and they pull money out of communities that are already reeling from the state's overinvestment in the criminal justice system and divestment from communities of color.

## THE COLLATERAL CONSEQUENCES OF INCARCERATION

Much of the research on the collateral consequences of incarceration does not focus specifically on race, but given what we know about the disproportionate impact of the criminal justice system on black Americans, it is clear how the cascading costs of incarceration are particularly detrimental to black individuals, families, and communities. The effects of incarceration transcend an inmate's time within the correctional system and have life-long, even intergenerational impacts on economic security and mobility for families and communities. Like the Jim Crow laws, the prevalence of criminal records banishes African Americans to second-class status.[78] This in turn fuels a vicious cycle of racial inequities in income, wealth, health, education, and democratic access.

### Incarceration's Impact on Individuals

Incarceration has staggering economic and health impacts. Individuals who have been incarcerated find it harder to retain employment, earn less money over their lifetimes, are less likely to marry, and report an array of medical and psychological problems.[79]

Several studies illustrate the dismal job market prospects for ex-prisoners.[80] An Urban Institute study of 740 males exiting prisons in Illinois, Ohio, and Texas found that only 45 percent were employed eight months after their release. Another study of 2000 ex-prisoners from Ohio found that 42.5 percent remained without work one year after their release.[81] It is estimated that the earnings loss associated with incarceration ranges from 10 to 30 percent.[82] There are numerous additional rules, such as those that deny ex-prisoners access to education and housing safety net programs, which further impede the ability of ex-prisoners to secure employment and achieve economic security. The American Bar Association (ABA) uncovered thirty-eight thousand statutes with a collateral consequence for a conviction; 84 percent of these are related to employment, and 82 percent of them have no end date. The ABA notes, "a crime committed at age 18 can ostensibly deny a former offender the ability to be a licensed barber or stylist when he or she is 65 years old."[83]

Another factor is stigma against formerly incarcerated job applicants. In a series of studies, employers showed they would rather hire a high school dropout, a welfare recipient, or someone with little work experience than a former convict.[84] Pager's research shows that having a prison record reduces the success rate of a black job applicant by one-half to two-thirds.[85] Given that employers have been shown to prefer white male applicants with a felony conviction over black men without one, it is not hard to imagine how the double burden of race and incarceration status impedes the job prospects of black men.[86]

Research shows there are also significant health consequences for individuals who have been incarcerated. It is estimated that half of incarcerated individuals have drug and/or alcohol addiction before they enter prison, and more than half suffer from serious mental illness.[87] The lack of rehabilitative or substantial mental health services causes health conditions to worsen, leaving individuals less equipped to successfully navigate personal, social, and economic challenges than they were before imprisonment.[88]

## Family

As the Annie E. Casey Foundation explains, incarceration is a sentence prisoners share with their entire family:

They feel it when their refrigerator is bare because their family has lost a source of income or child support. They feel it when they have to move, sometimes repeatedly, because their families can no longer afford the rent or mortgage. And they feel it when they hear the whispers in school, at church or in their neighborhood about where their mother or father has gone.[89]

A number of studies have linked parental incarceration with a "cascade" of negative outcomes, from mental and behavioral health problems to early substance use and abuse to poor educational outcomes and social exclusion more broadly.[90] As Wakefield and Wildeman explain, incarceration has the effect of "piling disadvantage on vulnerable families, delivering a 'serious and sometimes lethal blow to an already weakened family structure.'"[91]

Incarceration takes a toll on the economic security of families, many of whom were living in poverty long before incarceration touched their lives. In the years after a father's incarceration, average family income is 22 percent lower than the year before incarceration, and in the year following the father's release, family income is still 15 percent lower.[92] Nearly two-thirds of families with an incarcerated individual were unable to meet their family's basic needs.[93]

Women – already struggling with gendered wealth and income gaps – often shoulder the financial and emotional burden of their family member's incarceration. The Ella Baker Center found that in 63 percent of cases, family members of the incarcerated were responsible for court-related costs associated with conviction, and 83 percent of those family members were women.[94] Women represent 87 percent of family members responsible for call and visitation costs, which are often prohibitive. In 2013, the Federal Communications Commission responded to pressure from prisoner advocacy groups and implemented an interstate rate cap on phone companies, reducing the cost of fifteen-minute calls to $3.75, and banned additional fees for connecting calls. Before that, the cost of such a call was $17.[95] It is not hard to see how the long-term costs of incarceration can amount to a year's total household income and force a family into debt.

Children also bear a unique and heavy burden of incarceration. From 1980 to 2000, the number of children with a father in prison or jail rose by 500 percent, and today more than 5 million children have had a parent incarcerated at some point in their lives.[96] Pew Trusts reports that one in nine African American children (11.4 percent), one in twenty-eight Hispanic children (3.5 percent), and one in fifty-seven white children (1.8 percent) have a parent who is incarcerated.[97] Sixty-two percent of women in state prison have children who are minors, and nearly 75 percent of incarcerated women are the primary – and sometimes only – caretakers of their children prior to arrest.[98] It is not unusual for a mother's arrest to result in her children's entry into the foster care system.[99] Research has shown that children with parents in prison are more likely to experience social and emotional problems, more likely to have trouble in school, more likely to have trauma-related stress, and more likely to have experienced homelessness than children without incarcerated parents.[100] As Wakefield and Wildeman show, incarceration "not only increases the risk all children contend with, but also increases their risk of an untimely demise." They show that parental incarceration is associated with a 40 percent increase in the odds of infant mortality, nearly as strong as the association between maternal smoking and infant mortality, and that is as important in shaping risk of infant mortality as is getting adequate prenatal care compared to inadequate care.[101]

## Community

Incarceration permeates beyond the individual level and dramatically impacts the economic and social fabric of entire communities.

Despite strong economic growth, for the past few decades the United States has continued to experience high poverty rates while incarceration rates have grown by more than 300 percent. One study by Robert DeFina and Lance Hannon, measuring the impact of incarceration on three different poverty indices, examines a possible relationship between the increased incarceration of the past thirty years and impeded progress toward poverty reduction. The results suggest that growing incarceration has dramatically increased poverty, and that the official poverty rate would have fallen considerably during the past three decades had it not been for mass incarceration.[102]

As scholars Robert DeFina and Lance Hannon point out:

Many are mired in poverty and contend with crime, poor quality housing, low-performing schools and a dearth of resources that further prevent families from creating a safe and nurturing home environment. The effects of incarceration exacerbate the situation. One study found that if incarceration rates hadn't increased during a 24-year period, the U.S. poverty rate would have fallen by 20 percent, rather than remaining relatively steady.[103]

Clear argues that high incarceration rates in poor communities destabilize social relationships and end up causing crime instead of preventing it.[104]

A number of researchers have illustrated how mass incarceration disrupts a neighborhood's informal mechanisms of social control and social support by breaking apart families, extracting purchasing power from the community, and building even greater barriers to economic security. "The detrimental effects of mass incarceration on a community's collective efficacy may ultimately lead to a type of 'durable inequality' where residents cannot escape what might otherwise be only episodic poverty."[105]

As the 2009 Annie E. Casey report explains, in neighborhoods where a significant percentage of residents are incarcerated, the effect is cumulative: "The sheer number of absent people depletes available workers and providers, while constraining the entire community's access to opportunity – including individuals who have never been incarcerated."[106] Research has shown that living in a community with high rates of incarceration increases the likelihood that residents will experience depression and anxiety, and even for those who do not have personal experiences with the penal system, "heightened police vigilance can cast a shadow over their children, families and homes."[107]

## CONCLUSION

In this chapter, we have described the historic roots and current drivers of today's criminal justice system. We have illustrated the vicious and cyclical nature of our current penal system: the racial rules contribute to racial, social, and economic inequities that disproportionately expose black Americans to the criminal justice system. Experience with that system – be it in the form of probation, incarceration, or other penalties – makes it even more difficult for individuals to escape from the vortex of inequities.

Research tells us that harsher criminal justice policies and increased incarceration rates do not, contrary to popular belief, make people safer. What does make communities safer are the very programs that are deprived of funding by investments in the criminal justice system. Those include education programs for youth from preschool age through high school; jobs programs and lower unemployment rates; an increase in real wages; access to quality, affordable mental health and substance abuse programs; and community-supported policing strategies.[108] But as we have detailed, investments in these areas remain woefully inadequate while investments in the prison system have soared. Achieving equity and justice for black Americans will require dramatically reforming our current criminal justice system; it will also require reckoning with historic and current injustices and investing in all aspects of black communities.

# 8

# The Racial Rules of Health

## INTRODUCTION

So far, we have discussed how a complex web of racial rules impacts the social and economic well-being of black Americans, but we also know that these rules penetrate beyond the social and economic level and physically affect individuals and their families. We argue that the racial rules are "fundamental causes" of a range of negative health outcomes, and that those causes have multigenerational impacts on black communities.[1] Any analysis of racial inequities would be incomplete without an examination of the relationship between the racial rules and health outcomes; after all, health care access and good health are essential preconditions for well-being in all other areas of life, and as such are considered fundamental human rights.[2]

Economic status is known to be a strong predictor of health status. However, we also know that race itself is a factor, so much so that even black Americans at higher income and education levels experience negative health outcomes that closely resemble the outcomes of lower-income and less educated white Americans. Indeed, research shows that at all educational levels, black Americans face worse health outcomes than white Americans with similar educational backgrounds.[3]

In this chapter, we describe the stark health disparities between black and white Americans and illustrate how the racially implicit current rules contributing to those disparities are linked to the racially explicit rules rooted in the founding of the country. Our focus includes the rules – and the effects of those rules – in five areas: health coverage, residential segregation, educational outcomes, racial bias in the medical profession, and toxic stress.

We also illustrate the cyclical relationship between the racial rules and the health outcomes of black Americans: racial rules lead to social and economic inequities that drive health disparities, and those disparities only further reinforce unequal socioeconomic outcomes. Throughout this chapter, we highlight the extensive impact these rules have on black women and note the central role that reproductive justice plays in the overall well-being of black women and their families.

## HEALTH DISPARITIES AND INEQUITIES

By most measures, black Americans experience worse health outcomes than any other racial or ethnic group.[4] They are twice as likely to die from asthma and prostate cancer and have a higher prevalence of – and are 30 percent more likely to die from – heart disease than are white Americans.[5] They are 40 percent more likely to be obese and 60 percent more likely to be diabetic, both health conditions that are often precursors to more serious health issues.[6] Black Americans make up approximately 14 percent of the U.S. population but accounted for 40 percent of tuberculosis cases in U.S.-born persons and approximately 44 percent of all new HIV infections in 2014.[7] The Centers for Disease Control and Prevention (CDC) reports that of the nearly two hundred thousand new HIV infections between 2008 and 2011, black Americans accounted for just under half of the total and represented 64 percent of diagnoses among women and 67 percent among children under thirteen. In 2010, the mortality rate for blacks with HIV was twenty-five per one hundred thousand, compared with three per one hundred thousand for whites.[8] The statistics related to other sexually transmitted infections, such as gonorrhea and chlamydia, are equally staggering.[9]

Black women and children experience a unique set of health disparities. When compared with white women, they are more than twice as likely to die from cervical cancer,[10] about 40 percent more likely to die from breast cancer, and are three to four times as likely to die from pregnancy-related causes.[11] In some parts of the United States, maternal mortality rates among black women are higher than those in certain parts of sub-Saharan Africa.[12] There have been significant declines in infant mortality for all groups over time, but racial disparities persist.[13] Children born to black women are more than twice as likely to die in infancy, twice as likely to die of sudden unexpected deaths, and more than twice as likely to die from asthma as white children.[14]

Health disparities are particularly acute for transgender people of color. A 2011 study by the National LGBTQ Task Force found that "the combination of anti-transgender bias with structural and interpersonal racism meant that transgender and gender non-conforming people of color, including those who are multiracial, experience particularly devastating levels of discrimination." Health outcomes for multiracial transgender and gender nonconforming individuals – including high rates of smoking, drug and alcohol use, suicide attempts, and HIV infection – are evidence of stark social and economic marginalization compared to the general population. Fifty-four percent of multiracial respondents in the Task Force's study reported having attempted suicide, compared to the already high 41 percent of all study respondents and 1.6 percent of the general U.S. population.[15]

The disparate health outcomes experienced by all black communities in the United States are shaped by a number of racial rules, many of which have deep historic roots.

## THE RULES OF RACIAL HEALTH INEQUITIES

### Pre–Civil Rights: The Deep Roots of Health Inequities

As with the many other topics we have examined in this book, the explicit racial rules that once regulated black bodies are no longer "on the books" as they were during slavery and Jim Crow, but the arc of those historic policies is long and has shaped the current rules that impact the health and economic lives of black Americans.

In the earliest days of our nation's history, the medical establishment used "scientific racism" to justify the enslavement of blacks and the exploitation of the black body in countless other ways.[16] Scientific racism defined "blackness" in different and contradictory ways that suited the social and economic needs of whites at the time. Scientists argued that blacks had physical and mental defects that made them incapable of caring for themselves and therefore needed to be under white supervision and control. At the same time, however, they argued that blacks' "primitive nervous systems" made them immune to emotional and physical pain, which justified the subjugation of black bodies for labor and economic gain, and also for medical experimentation."[17] The most notable of those experiments was the Tuskegee syphilis study, a study conducted between 1932 and 1972 in which six hundred black men and their families were "deceived into participating in a research study that denied them treatment, so that [U.S. Public Health Service] scientists could trace the progress of the disease in blacks."[18]

Studies supporting these race theories were printed in and validated by the premier medical journals of the time, cementing the racist rules of medicine and health into the very foundation of our nation's medical system. As Harriet Washington writes, "The dearly held precepts of scientific racism sound nakedly racist, absurd, or both today, but in the eighteenth and nineteenth centuries scientific racism was simply science, and it was promulgated by the very best minds at the most prestigious institutions of the nation."[19] Physicians routinely used slaves for medical experiments, and the mistrust of doctors among slaves was so pervasive that it caused many to hide their – and their children's – illnesses and prevented them from seeking medical attention.[20] These were the roots of the fear and distrust of the medical system that still exist in many black communities today.

Since the earliest days of slavery in America, black women have fought for control over their own reproductive lives. Scientific racism fed – and was fueled by – early tropes about the hypersexuality of black men and women, theories used to justify the rape and sexual assault of black women and girls. Black women were considered important assets because of their ability to bear children and produce more property – future labor – for their owners. Thomas Jefferson once said, "I consider a slave woman who breeds once every two years as profitable as the best worker on the farm."[21]

Later, when black women's fertility was no longer deemed an asset to white economic interests, the state controlled it with involuntary sterilization. By the early 1920s, a number of states had involuntary sterilization laws on the books, and in 1927 the Supreme Court confirmed the states' right to sterilize "unfit" individuals in its *Buck v. Bell* decision. Speaking for the eight-to-one majority in that decision, Oliver Wendell Holmes said, "It is better for all the world if, instead of waiting to execute degenerate offspring for crime, or to let them starve for their imbecility, society can prevent those who are manifestly unfit from continuing their kind," concluding, "three generations of imbeciles are enough." The decision codified the explicitly racist and gendered rules of slavery and Jim Crow and unleashed a wave of state-based sterilization efforts.[22] The number of procedures increased tenfold in the two decades that followed. By 1961, more than 62,000 eugenic sterilizations had taken place in the United States, 61 percent of which involved women. As Rebecca Kluchin points out, men were also sterilized as punishment for criminal behavior and to treat "aggression."[23] A third of those sterilizations took place in California alone.

This history of forced sterilization is not only a distant one. Between 2006 and 2010, doctors contracted with the California Department of Corrections and Rehabilitation forcibly coerced nearly 150 female inmates to become sterilized, and it is believed that 100 more such sterilizations took place dating back to the late 1990s. The Center for Investigative Reporting found that at least 148 women inmates received tubal ligations between 2006 and 2010 – in direct violation of prison rules.[24] Over the last

decade, North Carolina and Virginia granted reparations to some sterilization victims, but there are many more women in states across the country
for whom abuses have not been recognized.[25]

In the years that followed slavery, the health system was characterized
by the same racial segregation and discrimination that defined the majority of U.S. social and economic systems. This was especially true in the Jim
Crow South (where in 1946 only 9.6 percent of black births took place in a
hospital, compared to 69.3 percent of white births), but also in the North,
where black physicians were denied admitting privileges to historically
white hospitals. Even black individuals who had good health insurance
were relegated to county hospitals and denied referral or admission to better facilities or those closer to their homes.[26]

## The Civil Rights Era: A Push for a More Inclusive Health System

Between the mid-1940s and 1960s, a series of inclusive rules began to
address vast racial inequities in health access and outcomes. President
Truman's executive orders prohibiting discrimination in the federal
workforce and desegregating the armed forces were also applied to hospitals run by the Department of Veterans Affairs. Those orders initiated progress that expanded when civil rights efforts pushed President
Kennedy to make desegregation in medical schools and hospitals a pre-
requisite for federal grants and contracts. After the 1954 *Brown v. Board*
decision, the Hill–Burton legislation that allowed for racial exclusion in
publicly funded facilities was successfully challenged, which set the stage
for the inclusion of Title VI in the 1964 Civil Rights Act. That provision prohibited "the provision of any federal funds to organizations or
programs that engage in racial segregation or other forms of discrimination."[27] A series of legal decisions and continued pressure from the
Civil Rights Movement set the stage for the 1965 passage of Medicare,
which prompted the largest sea change in the desegregation of the medical system. Medicaid was enacted at the same time, but the refusal of
many physicians to see Medicaid patients perpetuated the long history
of discrimination against black Americans.[28]

Current black–white health disparities in access and outcomes emanate
from this long history of racial rules. There are a number of pathways that
link the racial rules to negative health outcomes, and providing an exhaustive list of those causal pathways is beyond the scope of this book. Here we
include a number of pathways that have a clear relationship with the racial
rules we have described elsewhere.

## THE CURRENT RULES: PROGRESS STALLED
## AND ACHIEVED

### Health Coverage

Research has long shown that having health insurance is associated with significant health benefits and that lacking such coverage can have a detrimental impact on individual and community health. Adults without health insurance are more likely to die or suffer poor outcomes after an event such as a stroke, heart attack, or severe injury or trauma. They are more likely to be diagnosed with cancer at advanced stages and less likely to be aware of hypertension and to have inadequate control of blood pressure.[29] Studies have also shown that when parents are insured, their children are more likely to be insured and to have more continuous preventive care and better health outcomes.[30] For much of U.S. history, the quality and status of one's health coverage has largely been dependent on their income and employment status, which is affected by race. Given the previously described disadvantages black Americans face in the labor market and their disproportionate representation in jobs that do not guarantee health coverage, it follows that they would be uninsured at higher rates and also experience greater health disparities.

In 2013, before the major coverage expansions of the Affordable Care Act (ACA) took effect, more than one in five black adults – and one in three Hispanics – were uninsured, compared with one in seven whites.[31] Fewer than 50 percent of black nonelderly Americans have private insurance, compared to more than 70 percent of white Americans.[32] Adults with low incomes are more likely than other adults to be uninsured, and in 2013 nearly half of black Americans had incomes below 200 percent of the federal poverty level, compared to less than one-quarter of whites.[33] At that time, almost 30 percent of black adults reported not having a usual source of care, compared to just 21 percent of whites, and black adults reported forgoing care because of costs at a rate nearly double that of whites (Figure 8.1).[34]

The ACA, which expanded coverage to more than 16 million individuals and led to a precipitous drop in the uninsured rate among black Americans, was one of the most inclusive pieces of legislation in recent decades.[35] It enabled 3.1 million young adults to gain coverage through their parents' insurance plans.[36] It also expanded access to care for low-income individuals by establishing tax credits and health subsidies for individuals with incomes up to 400 percent of the federal poverty level (FPL) to purchase private insurance on the exchanges.[37] And it raised Medicaid eligibility

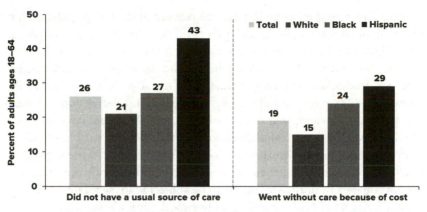

Notes: Black and white refer to black and white non-Hispanic populations. Hispanics may identify as any race.

Figure 8.1. Blacks and Hispanics are more likely than whites to lack a usual source of care and go without care because of cost.
*Source*: Data courtesy of the 2012 and 2013 Behavioral Risk Factor Surveillance Survey. Based on a chart originally published by the Commonwealth Fund by Hayes, Susan L., Pamela Riley, David C. Radley, and Douglas McCarthy (2015).

from 133 percent to 138 percent of FPL and expanded access to adults who were not pregnant, disabled, or elderly (categories that previously excluded many adults).[38] In addition to expanding coverage, it also raised the floor of coverage for all individuals, especially women, by prohibiting discrimination based on gender and preexisting conditions, mandating no-cost contraceptive coverage, and requiring full coverage for a wide array of preventive services. It also provided for an investment of more than $11 billion in community health centers.[39]

These vast expansions were meant to provide a path to coverage for all individuals and promised to have an outsized impact on black Americans. But in 2012, the Supreme Court decided the federal government could not force states to expand Medicaid, essentially making that component of the law optional and leaving low-income families in nineteen states without coverage. In states with low Medicaid eligibility levels, the coverage gap is particularly large and has a disproportionate impact on people of color. As the Kaiser Family Foundation explains, "Medicaid eligibility for adults in states not expanding their programs is quite limited: the median income limit for parents in 2016 is just 44% of poverty, or an annual income of $8,840 a year for a family of three, and in nearly all states not expanding, childless adults remain ineligible."[40] By January 2015, 55 percent of black Americans resided in states that had refused the Medicaid expansion; and as of early 2017, nearly one-quarter of uninsured black adults fell into the coverage gap.[41]

Black Americans make up just over 13 percent of the U.S. population but represent nearly one-in-five individuals covered by Medicaid, a fact that can be attributed to the high poverty rates among black Americans, particularly those in the South.[42] And while having public coverage is certainly better than not having any coverage, Medicaid is not a perfect system. Health access and outcomes for individuals with Medicaid varies across states, many private providers will not see patients with Medicaid coverage, and Medicaid patients have complained about being treated poorly in medical settings.[43] Additionally, because of Medicaid's low reimbursement rates for doctors and hospitals, beneficiaries – who are predominantly poor and disproportionately minority – continue to be subjected to "separate, often segregated systems of hospital and neighborhood clinics."[44] Additionally, the Hyde Amendment prevents low-income women from using their Medicaid coverage for abortion services in nearly all circumstances, which is particularly burdensome in states where regulations have closed clinics and made abortion increasingly difficult to access.[45]

At many points in recent years, conservatives have proposed converting Medicaid into a block grant, meaning the federal government would provide states with a fixed dollar amount that would be considerably less than what they receive under the current program. A number of analyses have shown that this neoliberal policy change would lead to a dramatic increase in the numbers of un- and underinsured; likely eliminate the current guarantee that all eligible applicants receive coverage; and enable states to restrict eligibility, curtail benefits, and make it more difficult for individuals to enroll.[46] As states took on additional funding burdens, they would likely be inclined – for either budgetary or ideological reasons, or both – to charge fees that would be a significant barrier to care for low-income individuals. As the Center for Budget and Policy Priorities has noted, under a block-grant system, states would have the ability to impose work requirements and end coverage for individuals they deem noncompliant:

This could result in people with various serious barriers to employment – such as people with mental health or substance use disorders, people who have difficulty coping with basic tasks or have very limited education or skills, and people without access to child care or transportation – going without health coverage.[47]

Given the various obstacles that black Americans already face as a result of discrimination in education, the criminal justice system, and the labor market, and the historic and lasting gaps in wealth, modifying Medicaid would have a disproportionately negative impact on them.

Such changes would also have a distinct impact on women, and particularly black women and other women of color, who are more likely to rely on Medicaid for medical coverage and also on publicly funded providers for their health care. This is particularly true for reproductive health care. Medicaid currently matches 90 percent of states' costs for family planning services and supplies and requires that states allow patients to visit the provider of their choosing. Block-granting the program would eliminate the family planning match and could give states the option to restrict providers. Between 2011 and 2016, a number of states attempted to prevent individuals from using Medicaid coverage at providers that also perform abortions; Texas went through with such a plan and lost the matching funds as a result. In the wake of that decision, eighty-two family planning clinics across that state closed and the birth rate among women who relied on publicly funded services increased.[48]

## Residential Segregation

As we illustrated previously, black Americans are more likely than whites to live in racially and economically segregated neighborhoods, and this segregation has a cascading impact on the their socioeconomic well-being. In 2001, David R. Williams and Chiquita Collins wrote, "Segregation is a fundamental cause of differences in health status between black Americans and whites because it shapes socioeconomic conditions for blacks not only at the individual and household levels but also at the neighborhood and community levels."[49] One 2009 study by Margery Austin Turner and Karina Fortuny showed that more than 30 percent of black low-income working families lived in high-poverty neighborhoods, compared with only 3 percent of whites. As the researchers explain:

Segregated housing patterns not only separate white and minority neighborhoods, but also help create and perpetuate the stubborn disparities in employment, education, income, and wealth. More specifically, residential segregation distances minority jobseekers (particularly blacks) from areas of employment growth.[50]

In 2012, the Joint Center for Political and Economic Studies released a report on Cook County, Illinois, where communities are deeply segregated by race and class.[51] That report illustrates the devastating toll levied by racial and economic segregation. Areas with higher concentrations of communities of color had lower educational attainment and less food access, and residents in the quintiles with the least access to chain

supermarkets and independent grocers had an average life expectancy
roughly eleven years shorter than residents in the quintile with the best
access to such food providers. In 2007, the premature death rate for black
residents in Cook County was 445.9 per 100,000; for white residents, it
was only 179.5. The report also found that areas with median annual
income greater than $53,000 had a life expectancy nearly fourteen years
longer than that of individuals residing in areas with an annual median
income below $25,000.

Individuals who reside in segregated neighborhoods – particularly those
with high levels of concentrated poverty – are less likely to have access to
quality-of-life goods that are necessary for and conducive to positive health
outcomes. They are also much more likely to be exposed to conditions that
lead to negative health outcomes. For example, segregated neighborhoods
often have fewer healthy food options and greater air pollutions, along with
health conditions such as cancer, cardiovascular disease, sexually transmitted
infections, obesity, and low birthweight.[52] A 2009 study by Hope Landrine
and Irma Corral showed that segregated black neighborhoods had two to
three times as many fast food outlets as white neighborhoods of comparable economic status, and they also had two to three times fewer supermarkets than comparable white neighborhoods. Such neighborhoods are often
referred to as "food deserts," where unhealthy foods are much more affordable and accessible than healthy food options.[53] In these neighborhoods,
environmental exposure to toxins and air pollutants are five to twenty times
higher than in white neighborhoods with comparable incomes thanks to the
"deliberate placement" of toxic waste sites and polluting factories.[54] The lack
of green space and public recreation areas in black neighborhoods further
reduces quality of life and health.[55] Making matters worse, black Americans
often seek health services from medical facilities located in their own communities, which tend to have less advanced technology and fewer specialists.[56]

## Educational Attainment

As we described in the previous chapter, America's schools are becoming
increasingly resegregated, and educational disparities between black and
white Americans remain vast. We know that educational attainment is correlated with health outcomes. Americans with lower education levels face
higher rates of illness, higher rates of disability, and shorter life expect-
ancies. In the United States, twenty-five-year-olds without a high school

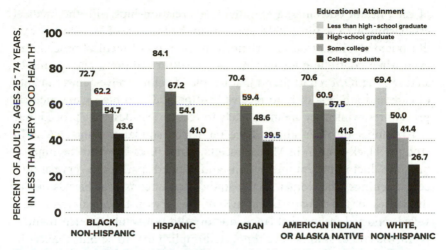

Figure 8.2. Less education is linked with worse health. Across racial or ethnic groups, adults with greater educational attainment are less likely to rate their health as less than very good.
*Source*: Data courtesy of Behavioral Risk Factor Surveillance System Survey Data, 2005-2007. Based on a chart originally published by the Robert Wood Johnson Foundation by Egerter, Susan, Paula Braveman, Tabashir Sadegh-Nobari, Rebecca Grossman-Kahn, and Mercedes Dekker (2009).

diploma can expect to die nine years sooner than college graduates.[57] However, research also shows that black Americans at all educational levels face worse health outcomes than white Americans with similar educational backgrounds, which many believe reflects not only unequal access to various life goods but also the physiological impact of racism (Figure 8.2).[58]

Numerous studies have shown that increased educational attainment does not translate into the same health benefits for all groups. Indeed, the health gap between blacks and whites is largest for those with college degrees.[59] One study by the CDC found disparate rates of preterm and low-birthweight babies even among college-educated black women:

More startling, the data showed that the rates of low birthweight and preterm delivery for college-educated African American women were more closely aligned with outcomes for non-college educated, unemployed, uninsured white women than they were with college-educated, employed, and insured white women.[60]

## Racism in Health Care

Though racial discrimination in health care is not as explicit as it once was, bias and stereotyping against black patients does persist and impacts quality of care, health outcomes, and individuals' relationships with the medical establishment. A seminal 2002 report from the Institute of Medicine (IOM) illustrated significant racial variations in the rates of medical procedures, even when controlling for income, age, health conditions, and insurance status.[61] The IOM report found that people of color receive a lower quality of care and are less likely to receive routine and also life-saving medical procedures, while they are more likely to receive less-desirable procedures.

A number of other studies have replicated similar findings.[62] A 2014 study of black women in Massachusetts found links between the implicit biases in doctor–patient interactions and racial disparities in cervical cancer screenings. The women in the study cited unconscious bias as one of the causes for the disparities, and two of the cervical cancer survivors surveyed reported feeling that "their doctors did not want to touch them."[63] Numerous other studies have connected implicit bias to "subtle nuances in physician–patient interactions, trust, and patient cooperativeness."[64]

Black women have reported receiving inadequate prenatal care and being treated by physicians who don't offer a full range of reproductive health options, making it difficult for women to make informed health decisions.[65] These circumstances contribute a mistrust of the medical community, making black Americans less likely to seek needed services. Bias and stereotyping compounds the structural factors that make it more difficult for blacks to receive timely, quality, and affordable care, and it serves as an additional source of stress that harms their overall well-being.

For black transgender Americans, the multiple and intersecting biases make accessing care especially difficult. Twenty-one percent of black trans people report being denied other kinds of medical treatment due to bias, and 34 percent of black trans people report delaying medical care due to fear of discrimination.[66]

## Toxic Stress

Throughout this section, we have described a number of underlying drivers and mediating factors that help explain persistent – and in some cases, growing – health disparities between black and white Americans. As we attempt to fully understand and address the impact of the racial rules, and economic inequality more broadly, we must acknowledge not only how individual stressors – the criminalization of black bodies, a lack of health coverage, neighborhood segregation, and inadequate education, and so on – lead to negative health outcomes. We must also acknowledge the growing body of research that illustrates how racism and the collective sum of those experiences create trauma inside the body and alter life outcomes. We now know that exposure to toxic stressors – racism, poverty, family crises, social unrest, and such – can create a chemical reaction that disrupts brain circuits essential for behavior, learning, memory, and problem solving. Essentially, toxic stress makes it harder for individuals to cope with general stress as well as the adverse situations they are more likely to encounter because of their race and class status, which increases the overall burden of stress for racial minorities.[67] These toxic stressors then serve as underlying risk factors for disease and other health complications later in life while also reducing individuals' capacity to manage with future stress.[68] They can also cause individuals to adopt coping mechanisms that potentially lead to negative health outcomes.[69] As with unequal economic outcomes, too often black Americans are blamed for making poor individual choices – such as having unhealthy diets or not seeking out medical care – when in fact behavioral choices are simply responses to systemic constraints driven by the racial rules.

Toxic stress has a particularly detrimental impact on black women. Amani Nuru-Jeter's work has shown that black women are more likely than men to think deeply about experiences with racism and are also more vigilant about future experiences, two important hallmarks of post-traumatic stress disorder.[70] A 2006 study by Arline Geronimus showed that black women have a higher probability of allostatic load (the overexposure to stress hormones that can cause wear and tear on important body systems) compared to white men and women, and also compared to black men; these patterns persist after adjusting for socioeconomic factors.[71] In another study focused on the length of telomeres – the stabilizing caps on chromosomes – Geronimus showed that black Americans may be biologically older than whites of the same chronological age as a result of cumulative and cellular impact of "repeated exposure to and high-effort coping with stressors."[72] Those stressors may actually shorten telomere length. She estimated that black women ages forty-nine to fifty-five are 7.5 years biologically older than white women, and that indicators of perceived stress and poverty account for 27 percent of this difference. This does not begin to account for the ways in which gender norms around caretaking intersect, such that black women not only personally experience the toxic stress of racism but then also take on the stress of community members who have experienced racism.[73]

Arline Geronimus argues that the effects of toxic stress may be felt more acutely by black women because of the "double jeopardy" of gender *and* racial discrimination, what Fleda Jackson calls "gendered racism."[74] Geronimus also calls attention to the ways in which changing socioeconomic dynamics impact the stress load on black women. "Gendered aspects of public sentiment on race may have limited Black men's role in providing social and economic security for their families, while raising expectations of Black women." As less-educated black men experienced a long secular decline in employment rates in recent decades, black women have shouldered an increasing amount of responsibility for the social and economic survival of black families, kinship networks, and communities. As black women work to fulfill those responsibilities, they may be more likely to be exposed to stressors "that require sustained and high-effort coping, along with the wear and tear on biological systems such repeated adaptation implies." She writes:

The findings suggest that progress in understanding and eliminating racial health inequality may require paying attention to the ways that American public sentiment on race, including its gendered aspects, exacts a physical price across multiple biological systems from Blacks who engage in and cope with the stressful life conditions presented to them.[75]

Toxic stress is particularly concerning given its impact on future generations. Numerous studies have shown that exposure to early life adversity – including during the prenatal phase – creates biological stress reactivity and lays the foundation for adult diseases.[76] Others have shown that prenatal stress can increase the risk of coronary heart disease and type-2 diabetes.[77] We now know that when mothers experience chronic stress during pregnancy, that stress reactivity can be transmitted to the fetus via cord blood and the fetus can be born more reactive to stress.[78] And research has shown that the more adverse experiences children have (such as emotional stress, household instability, or having an ill or incarcerated family member), the worse their health outcomes are later in life.[79] A recent study from researchers at Mt. Sinai in New York, which found that trauma suffered by Holocaust survivors was passed on to the genes of their offspring, forces us to ask how the trauma of slavery and the injustices that have followed from that long arc of history impact the health of black Americans today.[80]

### Roll Back in Reproductive Rights Disproportionately Impacts Black Women

Women's access to contraception – and therefore their ability to plan the timing and size of their families – has historically been shaped by their race, ethnicity, and economic status.[81] Today, access to reproductive health care is no different, and black women live at the precarious intersection of these categories. In the years following 2010, conservative lawmakers attempted to implement – many times successfully – countless legal barriers to reproductive health care that have a disproportionate impact on low-income women and women of color.[82] In states across the country, conservative lawmakers have passed medically unnecessary laws meant to eliminate abortion. These laws – Targeted Regulations of Abortion Providers, or TRAP laws – require clinics that provide abortions to make upgrades such as increasing the width of their hallways, adding janitor closets, and expanding operating rooms. These restrictions, along with efforts to defund Planned Parenthood and similar clinics and also to eliminate Title X (the federal family program), have shuttered publicly funded clinics across the country and left women without access to abortion services as well as basic reproductive health services.[83] The states that have been most aggressive in passing reproductive health restrictions are those with some of the largest uninsured populations of black women and high levels of teen and unintended pregnancy, sexually transmitted infections, and infant and maternal mortality.[84] Research from Texas – the state that has been most aggressive in curtailing reproductive health access – has shown the direct impact of these measures: a striking loss of health providers, an increase in unintended pregnancies and maternal mortality rates, and a rise in the number of self-induced abortions and later-term abortions.[85]

Reproductive health inequities levy a significant toll not only on women's physical and emotional well-being but also on their economic security. The recent Turnaway Study tracked women who sought out and either received or were "turned away" from abortion services. Two-thirds of participants had incomes below the poverty line, and for more than half the women who had an abortion, related travel and out-of-pocket costs totaled more than 30 percent of their monthly income. Forty percent of participants sought out abortion services because they believed they couldn't afford to have children, and over half of the women who had an abortion reported that needing to raise money for the procedure prolonged them in obtaining care, which led to a costlier and more complex procedure. The study showed that women denied an abortion had three times greater odds of ending up in poverty than women who had the procedure (when adjusting for previous differences in income).[86]

While access to family planning and abortion are critical elements of reproductive health care – and are central to the health and economic well-being of women and their families – they are inextricably linked to a much broader slate of health issues that concern black women: maternal mortality and morbidity, breast cancer, a lack of health coverage, and toxic stress, not to mention the countless other social and economic issues we have described in this book. As Loretta Ross wrote:

Abortion isolated from other social justice/human rights issues neglects issues of economic justice, the environment, criminal justice, immigrants' rights, militarism, discrimination based on race and sexual identity, and a host of other concerns directly affecting an individual woman's decision-making process.[87]

We must work to see abortion – and family planning – as part of a broader context of "empowering women, creating healthier families, and promoting sustainable communities."[88] Achieving those goals will require not only ensuring equitable access to reproductive health care but also addressing the full breadth of racial rules we describe in this report.

## Economic Status and Economic Inequality

We have illustrated the extent to which the racial rules shape the economic security – or lack thereof – of black Americans, and must also acknowledge how those rules extend well beyond the economics. Indeed, the link between income and negative health outcomes has been long established. Data have shown that individuals in the highest income bracket (400 percent FPL) live six years longer than those in the lowest bracket (100 percent FPL).[89] Poor adults are more than three times as likely as adults with family incomes at or above 400 percent FPL to have activity limitations as a result of chronic illness and are five times as likely to report being in poor or fair health.[90] Income is a particularly strong predictor for health outcomes that begin early in life. Infants born to low-income mothers experience the highest rates of low birthweight, which has been linked to child development and chronic conditions throughout the lifecycle.[91] The Robert Wood Johnson Foundation (RWJF) has shown that children in low-income families are "about seven times as likely to be in poor or fair health" as children in families with incomes at or above 400 percent FPL. Low-income children also have higher rates of heart conditions, hearing problems, digestive disorders, asthma, and elevated blood lead levels.[92]

There has been less research on the links between wealth (or a lack thereof) and health, but studies have shown that there is indeed a strong correlation. It is not surprising, of course, that one's ability to pay for preventive care, seek medical attention when needed, and weather a health crisis – particularly if uninsured – depends on one's ability to access funds that are not needed for other life necessities. A study by Hajat and colleagues showed that people with a negative net worth had a 62 percent increased risk of mortality compared with those with a net worth of more than $500,000.[93] That study also showed that the least wealthy had a 62 percent increased risk of poor or fair health and four excess deaths per one thousand persons. Women with less wealth had between a 24 and 90 percent greater risk of death, and the least wealthy men had six excess deaths compared with the wealthiest quintile.[94] According to RWJF, individuals with less income and wealth are also more likely to report experiencing "traumatic life events and the health-damaging psychosocial effects of neighborhood violence or disorder, residential crowding, and struggles to meet daily challenges with inadequate resources."[95]

There is a growing body of research that argues not only poverty and economic status, but also economic inequality itself, drive of negative health outcomes. In other words, being poor is bad for your health, and living in a society with large chasms between the rich and everyone else is makes it even worse. Work by epidemiologists Kate Pickett and Richard Wilkinson illustrates that countries with greater inequality also have higher rates of homicide, infant and maternal mortality, and mental illness and worse overall child well-being than countries that are more equal.[96] A recent University of Wisconsin study showed that even when average incomes were the same, individuals living in U.S. communities with higher levels of income inequality were more likely to die before the age of seventy-five than those in more equal communities. The researchers found that for each "one-point increase in the ratio between high and low earners in a county, there were about five years lost for every 1,000 people." This is approximately the same impact they observed when community rates of obesity and smoking increased by 3 and 4 percent, respectively.[97] The impacts of inequality are particularly harmful to communities of color. A study conducted by Nuru-Jeter showed that each unit increase in income inequality results in an additional twenty-seven to thirty-seven deaths among African Americans.[98]

## THE COST OF HEALTH DISPARITIES

We have illustrated how the racial rules shape health outcomes for black Americans, both directly through personally mediated racism and also indirectly through economic and social pathways. But we also know that those negative health outcomes carry significant costs for both families and the economy more broadly. One study conducted by researchers at Johns Hopkins found that over a four-year period, the indirect costs of lower worker productivity due to illness and premature death among black men was $317.6 billion. In that same period, the indirect costs for Hispanic men totaled $115 billion and for Asian men $3.6 billion.[99] A 2009 study by LaVeist and colleagues showed that between 2003 and 2006, eliminating health disparities for minorities would have reduced direct medical care expenditures by $229.4 billion, and that the combined costs of U.S. premature deaths and health inequalities were $1.24 trillion.[100]

This is to say nothing of the economic costs to individuals, families, and black communities more broadly. There is still much research needed to better understand the toll of high rates of maternal mortality and morbidity among black women, to quantify the economic impact of health expansions or rollbacks on black Americans, and to understand how racial health disparities among children impact their economic well-being later in life.

## CONCLUSION

While tackling the inequities we have outlined in this chapter may require complex solutions, the goal is clear: we need an equitable health system that is affordable, accessible, reliable, and able to provide culturally competent care to all individuals. As we have presented in this chapter and throughout this book, there is ample evidence that tinkering around the edges of inequality and modifying individual policies is not sufficient, and a comprehensive policy overhaul is needed.

We have tried to show how the one-size-fits-all model has failed black communities; health care is no exception. As Monica Peek writes:

"We can no longer exclusively have a conversation about individuals ... but must begin to broaden the dialogue to include community infrastructure (e.g. safe housing, primary care facilities), resources (e.g. grocery stores, fitness centers), and the built environment (e.g. bike paths, local parks)" in order to "address community health and health disparities.[101]

So too must the rule makers understand that health – the very foundation of our ability to care for our families, participate in our communities, engage in the labor market, and carry on our lives – is both a result and a cause of social and economic inequities. These inequities, in turn, are driven by the rules – rules that we can and must rewrite.

# 9

# The Racial Rules of Democratic Participation

The right to vote is one of the central and most basic components of a democracy, and the expansion of the franchise has been one of the most consistent themes in U.S. political history. In fact, more than half of the constitutional amendments ratified after the Bill of Rights have dealt with voting rights.[1] The suffrage struggle has been central to demands of African Americans and women to be recognized as full citizens and to have comprehensive access to the rights associated with citizenship. Even after the Fifteenth Amendment extended the franchise to black Americans, it took the Civil Rights Movement and the subsequent Voting Rights Act of 1965 (VRA) for African Americans to even come close to realizing the promise of citizenship. As in other areas of life affecting black Americans, racial progress around the right to vote has been an "unsteady march" – two steps forward and one step back.[2] As with education, wealth, and all the other topics this book has covered, the rules around voting and political inclusion both create and reinforce racially unequal outcomes in the economy and society writ large.

For more than two-thirds of U.S. history, the majority of the domestic adult population was ineligible for full citizenship because of race, country of origin, or gender.[3] While we have made progress in rolling back explicit pre–Civil War exclusions, the rules of the electoral system continue to be racialized.

The history of electoral rules maps cleanly onto the history of other racial rules we have outlined throughout this book. Since the abolition of slavery, social movements and political actors have sought to expand the electorate, and with each iteration of progress there has been a corresponding backlash to fuller inclusion, including new mechanisms to suppress the vote through both explicit and implicit rules. For instance, in response to the post–Civil War Reconstruction-era Fifteenth Amendment, which extended the franchise to black men, exclusionary Jim Crow laws emerged all across the South in the late nineteenth and twentieth centuries.[4] The racial rules of elections embedded in "Black Codes" and Jim Crow laws had the clear intention of excluding African American voters.

In this chapter, we first outline the rules that blocked access to voting for black Americans between the Reconstruction and Civil Rights eras. We then demonstrate how the explicitly inclusionary racial rules of the Civil Rights era opened up unprecedented access to the franchise for black Americans. Finally, we argue that under the current electoral rules, black Americans continue to have unequal access to voting due to a set of policies at both the state and federal levels that, while on their face are race-neutral, are implicitly racially exclusive.

Black voting participation in the modern era is circumscribed by three sets of racialized rules: the increased disenfranchisement of those with a criminal record, the 2013 Supreme Court decision that effectively gutted the Voting Rights Act, and the passage of implicitly exclusionary "voter suppression" laws. These contemporary voter suppression laws, enacted with increasing frequency since 2010, are a response to the expansion of the electorate after the "Second Reconstruction": the 1965 Voting Rights Act; the Twenty-Fourth Amendment, which ended the poll tax; and the Twenty-Sixth Amendment, which expanded the franchise to eighteen-year-olds. While in some cases they are less obvious, these twenty-first century racial rules of political exclusion are no less insidious than the exclusionary rules of the previous three centuries.

## PRE-CIVIL RIGHTS EXCLUSIONARY RULES

### Racial Electoral Exclusion and Jim Crow (1877–1954)

Following passage of the Fifteenth Amendment in 1870, black Americans experienced a brief period of sharply increased political participation and representation during the Reconstruction era. During that time, only black *men* enjoyed the right to vote, as the Fifteenth Amendment only guaranteed that prohibitions against black *men* from voting were unconstitutional, as black women wouldn't obtain that right until well into the twentieth century.[5] During the Reconstruction years, black Americans experienced political representation at the local as well as the national level for the first time, electing sixteen black Americans to Congress between 1870 and 1877.[6] These victories, however, were short lived. With whites in the South calling for "Southern Redemption" and "Restoration," essentially the preservation of white supremacy and the revocation of black Southerners' rights, massive disenfranchisement and political exclusion soon followed.[7] From 1890 to 1910, most southern states, in order to circumvent the Fifteenth Amendment, "creatively" enacted racially exclusionary laws that were race-neutral on their face but had the impact of disenfranchising the vast majority of southern blacks, who comprised the majority of all black Americans at that time.

These so-called race-neutral laws were implicitly exclusionary. Poll taxes limited voting access to those who could afford it, and many former slaves could not. Literacy tests targeted black Americans who had been forbidden from learning to read under slavery. Grandfather clauses specifically allowed white citizens to evade these restrictions.[8] And criminal disenfranchisement provisions disproportionately impacted blacks, whose every move was increasingly criminalized in the post-Reconstruction era. In 1890, Mississippi replaced a provision of its constitution that originally disenfranchised all citizens convicted of any crime with one that disenfranchised only those convicted of crimes that blacks were supposedly more likely than whites to commit, such as burglary, theft, and arson.[9] Southerners in the Democratic Party held "white primaries" in which southern blacks were excluded from voting – which effectively excluded them from voting at all, as the "Solid South" was dominated by a single party. These rules follow the trend we have identified throughout each of these chapters: in response to strides toward greater inclusion, implicitly exclusive racial rules replace the previously explicitly exclusive rules to covertly – and in some cases legally – perpetuate the same effects.

The effects of the southern Redemption disenfranchisement campaign on newly freed blacks were devastating. By the turn of the twentieth century, virtually all black Americans in southern states had lost the right to vote. The cumulative effect of all of these disenfranchisement methods was to exclude almost all blacks and a significant number of poor whites from full citizenship. But the economic and social effects of disenfranchisement were equally as significant. According to economist Suresh Naidu, as disenfranchisement policies became more common, the amount of public goods the government distributed decreased, especially spending on education for schools in black communities. This would have decades-long effects on generations of southern black children.[10]

## THE CIVIL RIGHTS ERA: EXPLICIT INCLUSION

### Enforcing Racial Inclusion in Voting Rights (1955–1980)

As we have described in earlier chapters, the beginning of a Second Reconstruction around racial justice and full political inclusion began

ten years before the historic *Brown v. Board of Education* Supreme Court
decision effectively reversed *Plessy v. Ferguson*. The 1944 Supreme Court
case *Smith v. Allwright*, which overturned the use of white primaries that
arose during the First Reconstruction, was the first blow to exclusionary
primaries. Subsequent blows came from the Civil Rights Movement, especially Fannie Lou Hamer and the Mississippi Freedom Democratic Party's
challenge to the Democratic Party at the 1964 convention. The party was
created to challenge the all-white and anti–civil rights delegation that
the Mississippi Democratic Party planned on sending to the Democratic
National Convention. Hamer, who was elected vice chair of the Mississippi
Freedom Democratic Party, brought national light on the issues facing black
Americans. This began the story of electoral realignment, where southern
whites and conservative southern Democrats fled the Democratic Party for
what until that point had been the "party of Lincoln."[11]

The 1965 Voting Rights Act (VRA), heralded by some as the most significant single piece of legislation of the Civil Rights Movement, successfully eliminated most of the structural barriers to full citizenship for
African Americans erected during the Jim Crow era. The VRA increased
black political empowerment for the next thirty years, and throughout
the post–Civil Rights era, thousands of black elected officials took office
at all levels.[12] Black communities in large metropolitan areas were even
able to elect black mayors, but the black working class and black poor
populations benefited little from this triumph of black electoral power.[13]
Despite its limitations, the strength and heart of the VRA was in its explicitly race-conscious approach: by requiring states and jurisdictions who
had a history of disenfranchising black voters to seek permission from
the Justice department before making changes to their voting laws, the
law placed the onus on those jurisdictions to prove they *weren't* discrim-
inating, which proved effective in increasing black voter turnout at the
polls.[14] The law prevented more than one thousand attempts to change
local voter laws that would have had a disproportionately negative affect
on black voters.[15]

Racial inclusion as a result of the Second Reconstruction and black political empowerment at the local, state, and national levels during the Civil
Rights movement actively created a new and expanded black middle class
that still occupies an "ethnic niche" in public employment today, though a
precarious one.[16] Yet black political empowerment occurred simultaneously
with deindustrialization, globalization, and increased class divisions within
black communities. The result has been that economic and social distress in
the post–Civil Rights era has been a "countervailing force" against political

empowerment, weakening the black civic capacity that the landmark pieces of legislation from the Civil Rights era had expanded.[17]

## THE CURRENT RULES

### The Rise of Race-Neutral Exclusion (1980–Present)

Much like the massive disenfranchisement of blacks following Reconstruction, the voting rights of black Americans continue to be targeted, and the events in the 2000s and 2010s have demonstrated the vulnerabilities of Civil Rights era progress. Three sets of racial rules that continue to create structural barriers to civic participation have emerged despite brief extensions of the Voting Rights Act and voter access provisions. These are the growth of the prison industry and mass incarceration, leading to increased disenfranchisement of those with a criminal record; the Supreme Court's 2013 curtailment of the key provisions of the Voting Rights Act; and, since 2010, the passage of ostensibly race-neutral but in fact racially exclusionary voter suppression laws.

#### Disenfranchisement and Incarceration Interact

One of the major consequences of the punitive criminal justice and mass incarceration policies enacted over the past four decades is the disenfranchisement of people who have been convicted of felonies.[18] From the late 1990s to the early 2000s, police dramatically increased arrests for felony charges, especially for nonviolent, drug-related crimes. Up from just 1.17 million in 1976, as of 2010 5.8 million Americans, including 2.2 million black Americans, are ineligible to vote due to a felony conviction.[19] In other words, more than one-third of all of those disenfranchised are black even though blacks constitute only 14 percent of the population. As of 2010, one in thirteen black Americans nationwide are unable to vote because of felony convictions, and one in five are disenfranchised in Virginia (20 percent), Kentucky (22 percent), and Florida (23 percent).[20] According to Chris Uggen and Jeff Manza, the effects of felony disenfranchisement on potential black voters have significant political consequences, including being a decisive factor in the presidential election of 2000 and in at least seven Senate races since 1978.[21]

There is no national or constitutional right to vote in America; the Fifteenth Amendment merely "prohibits" efforts to prevent protected groups from voting. Thus, states' rights reign supreme when it comes to voting. And because state laws determine voting rights for all elections, there is great variation in voting eligibility. For instance, in forty-six states, convicted felons lose the right to vote while incarcerated; thirty-two states prohibit felons on probation or parole the right to vote; and in eleven states, anyone convicted of a felony is disenfranchised for life.[22] Thus, an eighteen-year-old convicted of a felony in Florida for writing a bad check is permanently disenfranchised even if she completes a two-year sentence.

The processes that are available in some states to regain the right to vote are just as varied and cumbersome as the disenfranchisement laws themselves. In Mississippi, ex-felons must either have a legislator introduce a bill on their behalf, which must be passed by a two-thirds vote, or secure an executive order from the governor. In at least sixteen states, ex-felons convicted of federal offenses are ineligible to seek state procedures for restoring their voting rights and instead must obtain a presidential pardon, which are very rare for nonviolent drug offenders (whose sentences are typically commuted rather than pardoned if granted clemency by the president).[23]

These rules, which we also described in the chapter on criminal justice, have second-order effects that contribute to limiting black Americans' right to vote. First, the laws that currently disenfranchise black citizens are vestiges of Jim Crow and other previous efforts to disenfranchise – these laws were never completely repealed. Second, the rising incarceration of black Americans has interacted with these rules to further exclude millions of ex-felons, and this population is comprised disproportionately of black men. These racialized rules not only have severe consequences for civic engagement and electoral results, but also negative implications for civic participation. According to Vesla Weaver, Americans with no criminal justice contact turn out to vote at a rate of 60 percent, while turnout drops for those who have been stopped by the police (52 percent), been arrested (44 percent), been convicted (42 percent), or served a prison sentence (38 percent).[24] Put simply, the harsher an individual's contact with the state, the less likely they are to either want to or be able to participate in it (Figure 9.1).

### The Curtailing of the Voting Rights Act

Civil rights and racial justice organizations made tremendous efforts to pass the 1982 extension of the VRA. This extension renewed the VRA for an additional twenty-five years and made permanent Section 2, which made all race-based voter discrimination illegal, regardless of whether or not the rules had been adopted with the intent to discriminate. The VRA extension faced strong resistance from President Reagan, but he eventually

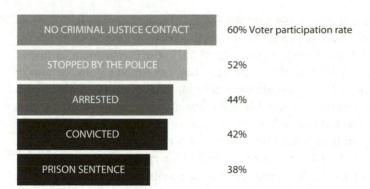

| NO CRIMINAL JUSTICE CONTACT | 60% Voter participation rate |
| STOPPED BY THE POLICE | 52% |
| ARRESTED | 44% |
| CONVICTED | 42% |
| PRISON SENTENCE | 38% |

Figure 9.1.  Voter participation rates decrease with severity of criminal police contact. *Source*: Data courtesy of National Longitudinal Study of Adolescent Health, Black Youth Culture Survey, and Fragile Families and Child Wellbeing Survey. Based on a chart published in *Boston Review* by Weaver, Vesla (2014).

signed the bill.[25] Since the 1980s, civil rights organizations have mobilized nationally in support of legislation extending and protecting the right to vote for black Americans and other politically excluded groups. This legislation has included the 1982 and 1992 extensions of the VRA, the 1991 Civil Rights Act, and the 1993 Motor Voter Act (which allowed the Department of Justice to bring civil actions in federal court to enforce its requirements and developed a national mail registration form),[26] in addition to numerous court challenges and advocacy on the local and state levels.

Despite the success of the VRA in ensuring full political inclusion for blacks long denied the right to vote and enabling thousands of black Americans to get elected to local, state, and national offices, the conservative majority on the Supreme Court has defanged some of the most important provisions of the act. In the 2013 *Shelby County v. Holder* case, the Court invalidated a key provision (Section 4) that covered voting rules in states and localities with a history of racial discrimination in voting. The Court majority argued that a new formula is necessary for assessing which voting jurisdictions require "preclearance" from the Justice Department to approve new voting rules; this essentially invalidated Section 5 of the VRA, which was one of the most important in ending racial exclusion of blacks in voting. Chief Justice Roberts wrote in the majority opinion that "[t]he conditions that originally justified these measures no longer characterize voting in the covered jurisdictions" and that the law "punish[es] the past,"[27] meaning that discrimination against black voters in historically exclusionary jurisdictions was no longer an issue.

The argument that racism and the racial rules are over ignored the role that the VRA itself played and continued to play in that progress at the time of the Court's ruling. As recently as 2012, the Department of Justice blocked requested electoral rule changes that they found would have had a discriminatory effect on hundreds of thousands of minority voters.[28] As a result of the Court's decision, black American voters in many states, particularly southern states, will have restricted voting access, and many states have subsequently enacted a range of new laws to restrict the right to vote. A mere twenty-four hours after the *Shelby County v. Holder* decision, five of the nine states that had been required to acquire preclearance from the Department of Justice before changing electoral rules introduced new voter suppression laws, some of which had already been found discriminatory by the federal government before the Court's decision.[29] The gutted VRA may have been one of many factors that affected the outcome of the 2016 presidential election. According to Sherrilyn Ifill, president of the NAACP Legal Defense and Education Fund, "In jurisdictions formerly covered by the Voting Rights Act, voters saw 868 polling places closed, forcing too many people to travel as far as 25 miles just to be able to vote."[30] Though it is impossible to measure the direct causal effects of the VRA's stripped powers on the election, it is certainly clear that the change to the law will have long-term effects on black Americans' access to the ballot box, and therefore on the very issues that impact their lives.

### Nonracial Electoral Rules with Racial Consequences

There are also nonracial electoral rules with significant racial consequences that structure how our democracy operates. From Congress to state and city legislatures, most citizens must vote for their elected representatives in a geography-based "winner-take-all" system. In this system, the winner only needs 51 percent of the electorate in a given district to be elected as legislative representative, which means that up to 49 percent of voters are not represented based on their vote choice.[31] Gerrymandering – the manipulation of electoral boundaries – is another "nonracial rule" that has significant racial consequences. By selecting the boundaries around an electoral constituency, politicians functionally choose their voters, not the other way around. "Racial gerrymandering" refers to drawing legislative districts in a race-conscious way to either advance black or Latino representation in legislatures, or to strategically "pack" black voters into a few concentrated districts to expand the representation of white voters in surrounding districts, a practice that became more common after the Voting Rights Act of 1965. This combination of electoral rules – winner-take-all geographic districts and political and racial gerrymandering – has undercut the political voice of blacks and other racially marginalized groups.[32]

Between 2010 and 2014, twenty-two states planned to enact new voting restrictions. In all but four, the rules passed entirely through GOP-controlled bodies.[33] Seventeen of these states enacted new restrictions after the 2012 presidential election.[34] In 2016, fourteen states put in place voting restrictions ranging from photo ID requirements to curtailing early voting.[35] The majority of these voter restriction efforts are voter ID laws, which make it more difficult to register and vote because of the limited types of identification allowed, and research has demonstrated that voter ID laws have the direct effect of suppressing minority votes.[36] Proponents argue that these laws are necessary to combat fraud,[37] but there is no evidence of significant electoral fraud, and many of the conservative elected officials advancing these efforts have stated the real intention behind them: advancing their own partisan interests. In 2012, for example, Pennsylvania House Majority Leader Mike Turzai was quoted as saying, "We are focused on making sure that we meet our obligations that we've talked about for years. Voter ID, which is gonna allow Governor Romney to win the state of Pennsylvania, done."[38] As several voting rights advocates have noted, in 2016 it was easier to register and obtain a gun than it was to vote in many states. Other voter restrictions include cutbacks or elimination of early and weekend voting and same-day registration. Fewer options for voting early or on weekends make it harder for black voters to get to the polls, where research from the Brennan Center shows they face lines that are twice as long as those in majority-white areas due to underresourced poll workers and fewer voting machines (Figure 9.2).[39]

While the letter of these laws is racially neutral, the effect of these efforts is to restrict the rights and participation of black Americans, other voters of color, students, and constituencies that traditionally lean Democratic.[40] Recent empirical studies show the disproportionate effect of these laws on black voters and other voters of color. Zoltan Hajnal and coauthors find that "strict voter ID laws double or triple the gap in turnout between whites and nonwhites."[41] Similarly, a report from the Government Accountability Office shows that voter ID laws have a disproportionate impact on black Americans, who are less likely to have the required identification.[42] In Texas, which has one of the nation's strictest voter ID laws, it is estimated that six hundred thousand voters – disproportionately black and Latino – lack the required ID.[43] Another study illustrated that voter turnout rates among Latino and black voters were lower in states that had voter ID laws.[44]

Figure 9.2. States with new voting restrictions since 2010 elections.
*Source*: Map based on data and maps originally published by the Brennan Center for Justice by Weiser, Wendy R. and Erik Opsal (2014).

## IMPLICATIONS FOR RACIAL INEQUALITY

The clear implication of structural biases against black Americans is that political and economic elites – those who make the rules – fear expansive and inclusive electoral democracy. This fear is directly related to the overall distribution of income and wealth. One theory, the "redistribution thesis," suggests that if the majority of "eligible voters" in an electorate are poor, working class, or middle class, and everyone has an equal vote, then that majority will use the vote to demand downward redistribution by the state.[45] Elites in the status quo have clear incentives to discourage this kind of redistributive politics. As political theorist Ian Shapiro argues, "Democracy offers the possibility of downwardly redistributive politics, but there are no guarantees that it will happen, and many cards are stacked against it, particularly in the American system."[46] T. H. Marshall's thesis – that the continual expansion of civil, political, and social rights was an inevitable trend among advanced democracies and would empower citizens to make successful demands on nation-states to address inequality – has also been particularly influential.[47]

Scholars and political actors alike have long believed that increased inclusion in, and democratization of, American institutions would challenge racial, economic, and gender inequalities. In other words, fairer rules for the political game would lead to fairer economic rules and more equitable outcomes. In practice, inclusive democratic participation (whether peaceful or disruptive) has led to enduring structural and institutional changes. In many counties in the Deep South, for instance, blacks saw increased redistribution through social welfare benefits as a direct result of enfranchisement by the 1965 VRA.[48] However, the overall empirical reality of the post–Civil Rights era poses serious problems for this assumption, particularly as increased black inclusion in American society has coincided with increased economic inequality.

## CONCLUSION

This chapter has explored the racialized rules that prevent black Americans from exercising their constitutional right to vote. Of course, voter participation is also linked to the range of socioeconomic factors described in previous chapters: wealth, income, education, health, and criminal justice. The unequal outcomes for black Americans in each of these areas compound with implicit exclusions to further curtail civic participation. This creates a vicious cycle in which limited political power and limited economic power feed upon each other. However, as our next chapter will illustrate, we can take concrete steps to rewrite the rules that implicitly exclude black Americans from full participation. In doing so, we can eliminate the legal strictures that serve as modern-day poll taxes preventing electoral outcomes that lead toward equity.

# 10

## What Will It Take to Rewrite the Hidden Rules of Race?

Throughout this book, we have illustrated how the racial rules – from the explicitly racist and exclusionary rules of slavery and Jim Crow to the implicitly racist and exclusionary rules of our current economic, education, health, criminal justice, and electoral systems – have disadvantaged black Americans over the course of our nation's history. We have also identified examples of inclusionary rules that have effectively reduced unequal opportunities and outcomes throughout our history. For example, we noted the success of school desegregation in reducing the education gap between whites and blacks and the success of inclusive public employment in reducing the employment gap.

We now argue that it is time again to write inclusionary rules that will redress the past and present rules and inequities that shape the lives of black Americans. Policy makers would be wise to remember what President Lyndon Johnson said in his 1965 Howard University Commencement Address about the historical legacy of racism:

> You do not take a person who, for years, has been hobbled by chains and liberate him, bring him up to the starting line of a race and then say, "you are free to compete with all the others," and still justly believe that you have been completely fair. Thus it is not enough just to open the gates of opportunity. All our citizens must have the ability to walk through those gates.[1]

We agree. As we have demonstrated throughout this book, we believe that we must both reopen the gates of opportunity and ensure that everyone, particularly black Americans, is equipped to walk through those gates.

Critics of the agenda we propose will likely push two lines of argument: first, that in our "colorblind" society implementing such racially targeted policies is unnecessary; and second, that doing so is too expensive. We believe that the preceding pages have sufficiently addressed the first line of criticism. We will now address the second strain of argument.

First and foremost, the status quo deprives black Americans of their fundamental rights. It denies them not only justice but also the public goods that white Americans – particularly those who are economically secure – often take for granted. As Franklin Roosevelt recognized, economic rights are human rights, and human rights should be universal. It is not possible for black Americans to have the full measure of their rights as participating citizens of the United States given the abject levels of inequity and injustice we see today. This is unacceptable, and we argue that it is our moral duty to change the system. However, in this section we will also address the material costs associated with a true reform agenda.

First, we reiterate our earlier point: contrary to traditional economic arguments, recent research, from case studies to cross-country analyses, shows no negative relationship between redistribution and economic performance.[2] This is to say that if the chief argument against enacting the kind of policy agenda identified in this chapter is a concern about long-term economic growth, the preponderance of evidence suggests there is no validity to that concern. Even Arthur Okun, who believed deeply in the trade-off between equality and efficiency, argued that the relationship did not hold when it came to addressing discrimination because of the great inefficiencies of underutilizing human capital.

It may even be possible that rewriting policies to be more racially inclusive could have a positive influence on economic growth and our country's prosperity. Intuitively, removing the barriers that people of color face – for example, higher interest rates on business loans or higher incarceration rates – would unleash economic potential that would be important not only for them and their families but for society and the broader economy as well.

While we do not yet fully understand how rewriting the racial rules might positively impact economic growth, some interesting preliminary evidence does exist. For example, in 1962 the Council of Economic Advisors (CEA) compiled the very first calculations of the economic drag of racial discrimination, and John F. Kennedy presented these data in his economic report to Congress.[3] According to the late economist Andrew F. Brimmer, the CEA estimated the economic cost of racial discrimination at about $17.8 billion or 3.2 percent of the gross national product. More recently, economists Chris Benner and Manuel Pastor looked at what could explain "growth spells" for a number of regions in the United States in the past two decades and found that the duration of these growth spells is strongly connected to income and race equality. As Brenner and Pastor state in their paper, "the punchline of this work is that regions that are more equal and more integrated – across income, race, and place – are better able to sustain growth over time."[4] We believe, based on both existing research evidence and common sense, that as the United States moves toward a majority-minority population, continued barriers to building or utilizing human capital will impoverish not only black families and communities but our nation as a whole.

Finally, despite the overall economic gain that could come from true inclusion of people of color, we acknowledge that we cannot claim the following proposals will be an economic win for every American. As under any set of rules that shapes our economic system, some may benefit more than others. Just as the current corporate governance rules prioritize the claims of wealth holders over the claims of workers; just as current trade policies favor exporters over local producers; just as current bankruptcy laws protect financial institutions ahead of graduates with student debt, so too will rewriting the racial rules reward some people more than others.

## GUIDING PRINCIPLES

We believe that there are a series of principles that are required to successfully rewrite the racial rules:

1. **We must reckon with our history.** Our nation has not fully reckoned with its fraught racial history, whether by acknowledging the truth of our often horrific and undemocratic history of racial apartheid or by recognizing and celebrating the times that we have made progress. In all policy-making processes and political discourse, an acknowledgment of the complex reasons for our unequal starting places is important.

2. **We need to acknowledge that race-neutral policies are rarely race-neutral.** As we have shown in each section of this report, prima facie "race-neutral" policies are rarely race-neutral. In fact, race-neutral rules have both racial origins and racial consequences. From New Deal policies to mandatory minimum sentencing, race-neutral or color-blind policies have most often led to racially unequal outcomes. Some policies, such as the Affordable Care Act or minimum-wage increases, have helped to reduce racial disparities. But even so, it is rare that such policies address the root causes of racial disparities. Moreover, we cannot look at rules in isolation. It is important to acknowledge that rules manifest themselves in the context of longer-term economic trends.

3. **Trickle-down policies have disproportionately hurt people of color, but also the white middle and working classes.** The rise of

trickle-down ideology has led to a rollback of policies designed to pro-mote inclusive growth and rein in rent seeking. Disinvestment from public goods and the safety net, permissiveness among regulators, and the erosion of worker power have increased economic insecurity and life outcomes for people of color, but also for low- and middle-income white Americans. Recent reports about rising mortality rates among low-income white Americans are a stark example of how these individuals and communities have been affected by the intersection of racial rules and economic inequality. In short, the consequences of racism are literally killing low-income white Americans. As Ira Katznelson notes, the era in which government programs and invest-ments built the white middle class was ended just as black Americans achieved equal access to these public goods. Neoliberal policies have destabilized the middle class.

4. **We must move away from universal policies and toward *targeted universal policies*.** In this book, we have shown that universal pol-icies have, as john powell argues, not only failed to address the needs of marginalized communities but disproportionately benefited whites and exacerbated the racial gaps.[5] But these policies have not benefited whites uniformly, and in fact over the past thirty years neoliberalism has also hurt the white middle class. As Ian Haney-López argues, dog-whistle politics kept most working- and middle-class whites from see-ing the true culprit of their economic pains.[6] Now is the time to adopt a strategy of targeted universalism – one that benefits all but is crafted to favor the most disadvantaged and therefore provides race-specific results.[7]

5. **Explicitly inclusive rules work.** Explicitly inclusive racial rules are still needed to reverse the long legacy of explicitly exclusive racial rules. In the past, we have seen race-focused policies help to close the gap in outcomes between black and white. Further, we have seen the promotion of race-neutral policies stall and even roll back some of the progress furthered by racially explicit programs. A twenty-first-century plan for inclusion must accept the reality of unequal starting points and opportunities.

6. **Who writes the rules matters.** People make rules, and it is critical that people in power are in every way diverse: diverse in terms of economic, racial, and ethnic backgrounds, and diverse with respect to gender and age. We have shown in this book how black disenfranchisement and political exclusion throughout the majority of American history have resulted in a power imbalance in who gets to write the rules. In

periods of greater racial political inclusion, representation, and power, we rewrote the racial rules to become more inclusive. Therefore, we should rewrite our electoral rules to ensure full political inclusion of marginalized communities – people of color and poor and working-class Americans of all races – who have been on the losing end of economic and racial rules written by a small, powerful elite over the last forty years. Moreover, it is important that we build institutions – labor organizations, political parties, movement groups – that prioritize diversity and build countervailing power for those who historically have been shut out.

## NEW RACIAL RULES: EXAMPLES

Just as it is beyond our scope to catalogue *every* racial rule, we are not able here to enumerate every rule that must be written or rewritten in order to create the conditions and opportunities that correct our past and present injustices. A true agenda to tackle racial inequality in America must go beyond superficial fixes to tackle the structures beneath the surface that shape unequal outcomes. The sample of policies we provide later in this chapter is meant to identify pathways toward deeper structural change; however, we do not argue that these proposals are sufficient to achieve true equality. Indeed, volumes could be – and have been – written about the need for more inclusive transportation policy, a revolution in housing policy, a concentrated effort to desegregate neighborhoods, and the many other issues the following proposals leave out or only reference in passing.

Many have called for reparations – which some describe as investments (and reinvestments) in black communities to correct for historical exclusions and current wrongs, and others define more broadly as the "full acceptance of our collective biography and its consequences."[8] In many ways, our analysis and recommendations are consistent with those conceptualizations.

The key policy point is that we have a choice. It is possible to rewrite the rules that shape unequal opportunities and produce unequal outcomes. The policies outlined in the following begin to answer the question of how.

These policies span a range of issue areas and goals. We begin with a call for a kind of "truth and reconciliation," focusing on the importance of the United States officially acknowledging the cost of past wrongs in order to begin to set the stage for more trust and a different kind of politics. We then address access to opportunity in education and the labor market, as well as health and safety – very immediate concerns that are related to, but go beyond, the economic. And finally, we propose ways to advance both income and wealth equity very directly, and to restructure parts of the economy so they work better for people of color and for all Americans more broadly.

## Politics and the Political System

**Acknowledge the cost of federally backed discriminatory policies:** Congress should pass H.R. 40, which calls for a commission to study proposals for reparations, and which, since introduced by Representative John Conyers in 1989, has never even received a vote. The bill's aim is simple:

> To acknowledge the fundamental injustice, cruelty, brutality, and inhumanity of slavery in the United States and the 13 American colonies between 1619 and 1865 and to establish a commission to examine the institution of slavery, subsequently de jure and de facto racial and economic discrimination against African-Americans, and the impact of these forces on living African-Americans, to make recommendations to the Congress on appropriate remedies, and for other purposes.[9]

The failure of the U.S. government to even debate the merits of such a commission, much less actually support its findings, speaks to the lengths we have yet to travel as a nation before achieving true reconciliation. While it would not change the concrete structures shaping unequal outcomes in America, the passage of H.R. 40 would be both an acknowledgment of and a first step toward a serious debate about the continued influence of racialized rules on the country.

**Guarantee democratic inclusion and expand political power:** Today our democracy consists of fifty different and unequal sets of voting rules for American citizens, which has pernicious effects on black Americans. The current rules of our democracy result in the lowest rates of participation among wealthy democracies; this must end. Our Constitution must once and for all positively guarantee the right to vote for all Americans. We have expanded the franchise by amending our Constitution half a dozen times throughout our history, and now is the time to do so again. This would include a constitutional amendment guaranteeing the right to vote for all and implementing a fully national system of universal voter registration, which should no longer be left up to states. Such an amendment would also prohibit policies that place an undue burden on exercising the right to vote, including the racially insidious permanent disenfranchisement of those with a criminal record.

Congress should also pass the Voting Rights Advancement Act, introduced in the House of Representatives in June 2015, which updates the Voting Rights Act of 1965.[10] The bill has a number of provisions that would expand access to voting, including ensuring that last-minute voting changes won't negatively impact voters; preventing voting changes that are most likely to disproportionately impact people of color and "language minorities"; and expanding the Federal Observer Program, which enables the attorney general to dispatch federal observers to any location where there is deemed to be a substantial risk of racial discrimination.[11]

Mandatory or universal voting is another democratic rule the United States should advance. Americans are required to pay taxes, and registered voters are required to participate in jury duty. We should extend this logic to voting, like other democracies have done. In most mandatory voting systems, the penalty for not showing up to vote is equivalent to a fine, much like a ticket for a driving violation. Requiring all citizens to vote on a national election day holiday would ensure greater participation in our democracy and promote fuller inclusion.

Another important rule of democracy is how we apportion representation in our state and national legislatures. As Lani Guinier has long argued, our current system of winner-take-all geographic representation not only disadvantages black Americans but also silences the political voices of almost half the country. A system of proportional representation in our legislatures would guarantee fuller representation of minorities of all types, particularly racial, ethnic, and ideological minorities. Proportional representation systems eliminate partisan gerrymandering, which disempowers too many citizens; enable more robust political ideas and interests to have a voice in our democracy; and result in better gender representation in elected offices in democracies around the world. Several states in the United States also have had versions of proportional representation electoral systems for legislative seats. Until 1980, Illinois used a "cumulative voting" system of proportional representation that enabled more women and people of color to get elected compared to geography-based, winner-take-all systems.

## Opportunity and Justice

**Divestment from the Criminal Justice System and Reinvestment in Communities:** Policy makers must divest from the tangle of supposedly race-neutral policies and institutions that have disproportionately affected black Americans and guaranteed that no level of income or wealth can purchase their safety and justice. A key lever for reform is removing the money that fuels a corrupt justice system. Policies from the War on Drugs coupled with the recent militarization of police forces after 9/11 have perpetuated and sustained massive investments in policing.

Noncustodial forms of policing – such as fines, fees, and other economic penalties – affect more individuals and their families than physical confinement and are often used as revenue generators for cities and counties. Measures such as the No Money Bail Act, which was before Congress in 2016, would help do away with cash bail, which has largely resulted in the incarceration of individuals simply because of their low-income status.[12] As funds are divested from the penal system, it is important that a portion be reinvested in repairing the damage wrought by the rules we have described throughout this book.

The profit of policing extends even further through its privatization, which incentivizes states and localities to incarcerate people for longer periods of time under such things as "bed guarantee provisions." These provisions, often embedded in contractual agreements between a private entity and a municipality, typically express the need to satisfy a quota whereby 80 to 100 percent of prison beds are to remain filled. Private profits from this scheme are fueled by the roughly $80 billion the United States spends annually to lock up more than 2.4 million individuals. These are expenses that could, instead, be invested in communities – particularly in communities of color that are disproportionately affected by criminal justice practices and policies.

Police budgets should be reduced and for-profit prison systems must be done away with. As Black Youth Project 100 (BYP100) notes, "The profit motive in the penal system is a corrupting force that motivates police and judges to unnecessarily incarcerate and criminalize in order to maintain profitability of powerful monied interests."[13] States and localities should replace fines for minor crimes and misdemeanors as well as administrative fees for probationers and parolees with debt collection practices that account for one's ability to pay.[14] Furthermore, the government should divest from for-profit prison systems and invest in such things as public education, higher education, and community policing. "Establishing participatory municipal and state budgets," says BYP100 in a recent report, "is an avenue that would allow the public to democratically decide how to allocate funds toward services and institutions critical to our survival and success."[15]

Finally, we must make a concentrated effort to reduce our prison population, at least in part by decriminalizing drugs and also by bringing U.S. sentencing practices more in line with those of other nations. We must also recognize the critical role that prosecutors play in driving mass incarceration. The choices they make in how aggressively they file felony charges are the link between arrests and sentences.[16]

As this report has illustrated, more prisons and more police have not made our communities safer. Research has shown that the other investments we, and many others, are calling for would significantly improve the safety of our communities.[17]

**Massive Public Investment in Asset-Poor Communities:** In this book, we have outlined the range of rules that have led to continued unequal access to public goods in black communities, from infrastructure and education to green space and safe streets. The reasons include historic appropriation of black wealth and de jure segregation, continued underinvestment in black communities due to "trickle-down" cuts in public spending and the devastating employment effects of deindustrialization, and continued implicit discrimination on both the institutional and individual levels. In response, we echo the Center for Community Change's (CCC) proposal for a domestic Marshall Plan in which the federal government would invest at least $200 billion a year over ten years in areas with the highest levels of concentrated poverty.[18] It is critically important that this plan focus on building infrastructure for long-term economic growth as well as direct job creation. Infrastructure that provides greater transportation access to low-income people, who tend to live far from job centers, would increase access to the labor market. Investment in affordable municipal broadband is not only a critical way to increase access to jobs and income but also important in addressing the deep digital divide that cuts through our country.[19]

CCC's proposal builds on a long history of demands for public investment in black communities. In 1966, civil rights leader A. Philip Randolph advocated for a "Freedom Budget" that would invest $10 billion a year for ten years in urban "ghettos." He argued that a federal policy of employing workers for a good wage in activities beneficial to the community would end, once and for all, the debate around individual deficits.[20] Our proposed community investment program would adhere to the principles of targeted universalism and bring much-needed resources to large portions of America.[21] Fully 11.2 percent of U.S. counties are persistently poor, meaning that for the past thirty years at least 20 percent of the population has been living in poverty. By 2013, 13.8 million Americans were living in high-poverty neighborhoods in which 40 percent or more of residents live below the poverty line, according to the most recent data.[22] In fact, the fastest-growing population living in concentrated poverty is white Americans.

Nonetheless, the proposed public investment would disproportionately benefit black Americans, more than 25 percent of whom live in high-poverty neighborhoods.[23] These investments should be targeted to sectors that will continue to produce jobs of the future, including the "care infrastructure" (child care, day care, home care, and elder care jobs), green jobs, jobs to rebuild our crumbling physical infrastructure, and public service jobs that promote the common good.[24] According to CCC's analysis, a proposed $200 billion annual investment in infrastructure and a jobs program that addresses high unemployment in high poverty communities would create 2 million jobs directly and stimulate growth.[25]

**Labor Standards and Bargaining Rights:** As described in previous chapters, black workers have tended to make strides in closing the income gap when backed by the power of the government or a labor union. Among other factors, when hiring and promotions are more rules-based, as in unionized and public sectors, rather than subject to personal discretion, legal protections can blunt the role of institutional or individual racial and gender bias. Unsurprisingly, the neoliberal attack on collective bargaining, public employment, and labor standards has been particularly destabilizing for the black middle class. Of course, the destruction of middle-class work and the associated ladders to opportunity have decimated the white middle class as well, resulting in rising white mortality, white out-of-wedlock births, and white drug addiction, all outcomes that might have once been written off as stereotypical "black pathology." As described in *Rewriting the Rules*, this decline in labor standards and bargaining rights has not been an inevitable outcome of globalization and technology, but rather a choice. The 10 percent unionization rate in the United States is well below the Organization for Economic Cooperation and Development (OECD) average of 17 percent and significantly lower than comparable economies such as Canada (26.4 percent) and the United Kingdom (25.4 percent).[26]

Clearly there is no silver bullet for building middle-class jobs in the new economy, but a strong start would include protecting existing bargaining rights and promoting new rules that support work power in the fissured workplace.[27] Elected officials can move toward these goals by moving beyond the traditional National Labor Relations Act (NLRA) definitions of "bargaining unit," "employer," and "secondary action" to increase scope for bargaining in the new economy. Elected officials can set the standard for fair pay and benefits for fair labor practices through government employment and government contracts. Further, leaders should increase funding for enforcement and penalties for violation of existing labor law.

**Health Care Expansion:** Access to affordable and universal health care is critically important. A number of efforts will be required to achieve racial health equity, including increased investments in community health centers, particularly in underresourced and underserved areas, along with strengthening the current capacity of providers to guarantee culturally competent care and services. To ensure the health of women and families before, during, and after pregnancy, we must guarantee high-quality preconception, prenatal, and postpartum care. Congress should strengthen the family planning safety net – including Title X – and also pass federal reproductive health protections, such as the EACH Woman Act, which would overturn the Hyde Amendment and ensure abortion access regardless of a woman's income.[28]

Additionally, lawmakers at the state and federal level should make every effort to overturn – or prevent the passage of – Targeted Regulation of Abortion Provider laws, which make it more difficult for low-income women to access reproductive health services.[29] In addition to these measures, we must also consider the health impacts of disparities in wealth, income, and education, as we have discussed throughout this book, and acknowledge that striving for equity in each of those areas is necessary to achieve both social and economic well-being and actual physical health.

## Assets and Wealth

**Child Trust Accounts or "Baby Bonds":**[30] Just as history, geography, and policy perpetuate unequal community wealth between black and white Americans, so too do these factors perpetuate the massive race gap in individual and community wealth. As described in this book, the unequal distribution of income pales in comparison to the unequal distribution of wealth. Overall, individual actions – in terms of education, jobs, or savings – have little power to close this gap. Further, individual wealth serves as a key driver in education, health, income, and other outcomes.

The kind of universal (yet targeted) "baby bond" proposed by William Darity and Darrick Hamilton would provide every American at birth with a wealth grant to be accessed at age eighteen. The size of the grant would vary depending on the wealth of the child's family, and such a program would have a pronounced benefit for the 77 percent of black American families with less than the national median household wealth.[\*, 31] Darity and Hamilton propose a graduated wealth grant of up to $60,000 for children born to families with less than the median wealth. The numbers average out to approximately $20,000 per child, for an annual cost of about $60 billion

---

\*   In 2013, median family wealth stood at $81,456, with 41 percent of white families, 49 percent of Asian, 75 percent of Hispanic, and 77 percent of black families below the median (Federal Reserve Bank of St. Louis. 2015).

annually, not accounting for potential increased births or reduced government spending on other safety net programs. In comparison, individual tax expenditures total approximately $335 billion a year, with at least a third benefiting households earning more than $1 million annually.[32]

**Financial and Corporate Reform:** In tandem with the undermining of worker rights and standards, trickle-down policies have promoted the ascendancy of corporate and financial power to the detriment of middle- and low-income Americans disproportionately represented by people of color. As detailed in the Roosevelt Institute's *Rewriting the Rules* and in *Untamed: How to Check Corporate, Financial, and Monopoly Power*, the deregulation agenda of the last thirty-five years has really been an effort to "re-regulate" the economy in favor of the powerful and privileged. The policies associated with increasing the wealth of the richest Americans at the expense of average Americans have been refracted through the web of racialized rules to particularly disadvantage people of color. A quick survey of examples makes the clear point that privatization of public resources – such as the water infrastructure in Flint, Michigan, the free rein of financial institutions to target communities of color with predatory loans, and a shift in monetary policy away from full-employment to protect wealth holders from inflation – has disproportionately impacted black Americans.[33]

It will not be easy to reform the structures that have contributed to the current high-inequality, low-growth economy, which prioritizes the claims of wealth holders over the claims of workers. However, we must take key steps toward those goals. Specifically, we can promote policies aimed at fostering full employment. Beyond monetary policy, this includes boosting public investment by ensuring corporations pay their fair share of taxes and boosting private investment by reining in short-termism on Wall Street.

Further, we can strive for policies that promote financial services that benefit, rather than prey upon, communities of color. A public option for banking run through the postal service can reach communities, both urban and rural, from which banks have withdrawn. It can also use its scale to provide baseline services to the 33.3 percent of Americans who are unbanked or underbanked.[34]

## Neighborhoods and Schools: Reducing Racial Isolation

**Racially Explicit Rules:** Many of the policies recommended here aim to address problems of racial exclusion by using economic status as a proxy for race. Wealth-building programs and public investments targeted to the least wealthy Americans will overwhelmingly benefit black Americans. These are important. But while economic and class-based policies will provide significant support for black and other minority communities, overcoming structural racial inequities will necessarily require policies that explicitly target black individuals and black communities as beneficiaries – particularly in contexts such as school desegregation, a renewed effort at affirmative action, and a broader focus on promoting not just de jure but de facto racial equality.

The evidence shows that reducing racial isolation is very important educationally and economically, and as a driver of overall well-being. We argue strongly for a renewed look at affirmative action, or directly targeted efforts to build the pool of qualified educational and job applicants, in order to continue to ensure the reality of equal opportunity. We argue strongly for policies that incentivize and allow school districts to achieve better racial balance among and within schools, with the goal of ending the extreme race- and class-based isolation of black and also Latino children we see today. These include everything from more support for "voluntary transfers" and stronger district school assignment policies to more equitable housing policy.[35]

**A Shift in Constitutional Doctrine:** To make racially explicit rules a possibility, we need a significant shift in the current state of constitutional jurisprudence on issues of racial inequality, discrimination, and affirmative action. Racially explicit rules, even when geared toward remedying past structural discrimination, are, under current Supreme Court precedent, subject to a standard of "strict scrutiny" in judicial review. This means that such policies will be upheld only if they meet a "compelling government interest" and are "narrowly tailored" to that end. This, in itself, is not fatal to such proposals: as suggested in this book, achieving racial equity and inclusion and overcoming the deep legacy of racial segregation and inequality should be understood as a compelling governmental interest that justifies targeted policies of the kind proposed here.

Even so, Supreme Court practice as of 2017 poses a problem, as it is focused predominantly on race neutrality.[†] This sort of constitutional

---

† In cases like *Parents Involved* (2007), the Supreme Court held that racially targeted policies such as school desegregation can be oriented toward goals of diversity, and remedying explicit, de jure, prior segregation of the sort in the Jim Crow South, but that racial balance alone is not considered a sufficiently compelling interest. In *Fisher I* (2013), the Court suggested that *Brown v. Board* and the Fourteenth Amendment's guarantee of Equal Protection require a "color-blind" reading of the Constitution, such that policies must be facially race-neutral – and more strongly, that if schools and other institutions have race-neutral alternatives present, those alternatives must be preferred.

doctrine makes impossible the kind of racially targeted policies that, as this book has suggested, are essential for undoing structural racial inequities. To rewrite the racial rules, we need to shift our constitutional understanding of the Equal Protection Clause and the governmental interest in remedying past discrimination using racially targeted policies. As some justices on the Court (including Stevens, Breyer, Sotomayor, and Ginsburg) have suggested, neither the Fourteenth Amendment nor *Brown v. Board* requires the kind of colorblind, race-neutral approach that excludes such remedial actions. Remedying racial inequality – including both the inequalities that arise from our history of de jure segregation and today's de facto racial disparities – should be understood as a compelling government interest under the Equal Protection Clause. This compelling interest should in turn be understood to justify the kinds of racially targeted policies described in this book.

**Racial Equity Impact Assessments:** To reduce the adverse consequences of "race-neutral" policies on communities of color, all policies and programs should be evaluated with racial impact assessments. Our research makes clear that policies are almost never race-neutral, even when their intent may be. Further, race-neutral policies do, at times, hide discriminatory intent, as in the case of mandatory minimums associated with different types of illicit drugs. Just as environmental impact studies assess whether proposed policies might cause environmental harm, racial impact assessments analyze proposed policies to better understand and clarify the consequences of policies, practices, programs, plans, and budgetary decisions.[36] Such assessments allow us to evaluate proposals not simply by their intent, veiled or otherwise, but also by their likely outcomes. As Race Forward explains, racial equity impact assessments "can be a vital tool for preventing institutional racism and for identifying new options to remedy long-standing inequities." Both Connecticut and Iowa now require minority impact statements in advance of passing new sentencing laws.[37] The city of Seattle requires such analysis on a range of policy and budgetary decisions, and the city of St. Paul is considering a similar proposal. We must consider ways to implement these assessments at all levels of government.

## Areas for Future Research

This book marks the Roosevelt Institute's first significant effort to identify, understand, and suggest corrections to the structures perpetuating unequal racial outcomes in the American economy. We know that our own work remains incomplete.

There are a number of areas for future research, including a deeper dive on gendered rules, a better understanding of how racial and economic inequity operates *within* race categories (for example, for black immigrants, LGBT black Americans, etc.), and more work on the economic effects of immigration rules. We look forward to advancing these efforts in the future.

Most importantly, the policy proposals outlined in this book would benefit from a more rigorous analysis of macroeconomic, and also social, effects. Note that some of our proposals – including voting rights, labor standards, and financial reform, as well as our support for H.R. 40 and our call for racial impact assessments – are not massive new public spending programs, and would therefore have modest costs and outsized market benefits. But we also propose some programs, including major job creation and infrastructure investment in low-income communities and community wealth grants (or "baby bonds"), that do require major expenditures.

Improving our understanding of these macroeconomic costs and benefits, including long-term growth effects, will help us further prioritize and also argue effectively for our comprehensive approach to rewriting the racial rules. Given the inefficiency in today's economy, we strongly believe that the multiplier effects of the spending we propose will bring outsized gains. But a better understanding of potential economic gains and distributional effects is an essential next step in this line of research.

While many of the policies proposed in this chapter are targeted toward federal policy, there is extensive work to be done at the state and local level. State and local rules, too, have both racialized origins and consequences. From restructuring the way in which public education is funded to changing redistricting rules, there are many policies that local and state governments can implement – even in the absence of friendly federal policy makers – to address race-based inequities.

While we acknowledge the need for future research and a sustained national conversation about our racial past and racial future, none of this will be possible without the hundreds and thousands of activists and ordinary people willing to mobilize and take collective action. As of 2017, we are living through a "movement moment." Sparked by the continued police and vigilante violence inflicted on black Americans, the Movement for Black Lives has forced a national conversation about racial injustice in America, much like an earlier generation in the 1960s. We applaud their efforts to raise these painful and unresolved issues, but more importantly, to lead campaigns around the country to change the racial rules of our economy and society and advance racial and economic justice.

# Conclusion

In recent years, economic inequality has moved to the fore of America's public debate. Middle- and working-class families are working harder and harder and enjoying less economic security while those at the top amass an ever-growing share of the nation's wealth.

Many progressive political leaders have responded to these rapidly widening gaps by arguing that addressing economic inequality would be a cure-all for the problems we face. Because white working-class voters abandoned the Democratic Party during the 2016 election, many argue that progressives should give up on "identity politics" – that is, a focus on race, gender, immigration status, and so on – and instead focus exclusively on class.[1] In some cases, the strategy of courting white working-class voters at the expense of a more nuanced and intersectional analysis may be a cynical political calculation. In other cases, it may be the result of leaders assuming that the potent discrimination that is cemented into our social and economic systems will fall away as a more just economy evolves. But focusing solely on class and economics presumes that progressive economic policies will trickle down and lead to equality in other domains. Throughout this book, we have resoundingly rejected that notion, arguing that race and class are inextricably linked.

We have illustrated how a vast web of racial rules perpetuates stark inequities and injustices, reaching into every domain of our society and economy. They drive racial gaps in wages and wealth. They enable the overreach and continued human rights violations of our criminal justice system. They perpetuate racial segregation in our schools and lead to unequal educational outcomes for black students. These rules lead to poor health access and negative health outcomes for black Americans, particularly black women. And they prevent black Americans from exercising their right to vote, thereby preventing them from shaping the rules that govern their lives.

171

Today, many blame these disparate opportunities and outcomes on a lack of personal ambition on the part of black Americans, or – as conservatives have long explained – a lack of personal responsibility. They argue that we have closed the book on the era of slavery and Jim Crow, and as such, all Americans today begin life with the same potential and tools for success, regardless of their race or ethnicity. And they argue that equal opportunity for all is considered by many to be part of the fabric of American life.

But as we have shown, the legacy of our darkest days continues to impede social and economic well-being for black Americans. We have demonstrated how economic progress is not shared evenly across racial groups in the United States, and that even when black Americans achieve economic gains, the role of racism is so pervasive that it prevents well-being in many other domains. As we have described, black Americans at higher income and education levels experience the same police violence and the unchecked discrimination of the criminal justice system as less wealthy black Americans. Even if we raised the minimum wage and enabled black workers to take home a paycheck that more accurately reflects the value of their labor, it would not prevent black Americans from being channeled into low-wage work in the first place. As the doors to education and high-paying jobs have been opened for black women, rates of maternal death have also risen across all education and income levels, signifying the pervasive nature of both racism and sexism.

In many ways, racial inequality is the most intractable problem for our politics and our society. The vast web of racial rules that shape unequal outcomes cannot be untangled easily, so perhaps it is somewhat brazen to end this book on a hopeful note. But racial inequality is – and has always been – a choice. That means we can rewrite our racial rules for better outcomes.

Despite a history of rules borne from a desire to maintain a stratified racial order, we have also made real – though incomplete – progress at times. Reconstruction-era rules brought newly freed slaves into the real economy and the labor market, expanded black social and political power, and opened educational opportunities to black Americans from which they had long been prohibited. Civil Rights–era rules led to the integration of schools, an increase in voting rights, expanded rights for women, and a rise in incomes and economic opportunities for many black Americans. But each time, a politics of resentment and retrenchment tapped into racial and economic anxieties and built support for recycled exclusionary policies that preserve white power and privilege at the great expense of people of color.

However brief and incomplete our periods of progress may have been, they prove that only when we account for race and gender do we begin to level the playing field for people of color and women. Conversely, gender- and race-neutral policies and programs have disproportionately benefited white Americans at the peril of everyone else. We must not accept inequality as inevitable. We believe we are at an inflection point, and thanks to the organizing, advocacy, bravery, and protest of those who will not accept the status quo, there is hope for a "third Reconstruction."

Persistent racial inequities and the reigniting of social and economic retrenchment demand that progressives reimagine, rebuild, and recommit to a politics of inclusion. The era demands an economic narrative and agenda that comprehensively addresses the obstacles and opportunities facing black Americans – and, for that matter, all people of color, women, immigrants, the LGBT community, and beyond – such as those put forth by gender and racial justice leaders in the policy platforms for the Women's March on Washington and the Movement for Black Lives.[2] This agenda must acknowledge the ways in which politicians have strategically used racism to ratchet up fear and resentment of these communities against white Americans in service of a neoliberal economic agenda that has a disproportionate impact on people of color but is also bad for the majority of Americans.

For too long, progressives have talked about the symptoms of the rules without naming the rules, the people who wrote them, or the process by which they were made. They have not connected the dots between a neoliberal economic agenda that funnels investments and financial promise away from hard-working Americans and into the pockets of the top 1 percent and an agenda that advocates for slashing the safety net, curbing health coverage and health access, expanding the criminal justice enterprise, and erecting barriers to voting. But these phenomena are two sides of the same coin. The challenge for progressives in the twenty-first century will be to hold onto the truth that the racial rules of the last 40 – indeed, 140 – years have not worked for any Americans, neither black nor white. Racial and economic justice is not a zero-sum gain. Achieving equity for black Americans would benefit all Americans, and to do so, we must tackle the hidden rules of race and racism head on.

# Notes

## INTRODUCTION

1 Pew Research Center. 2007. "Optimism About Black Progress Declines: Blacks See Growing Values Gap Between Poor and Middle Class." Retrieved May 4, 2016. www .pewsocialtrends.org/files/2010/10/Race-2007.pdf.

2 Austin, Algernon, Darrick Hamilton, and William Darity. 2011. "Whiter Jobs, Higher Wages: Occupational Segregation and the Lower Wages of Black Men." Retrieved November 5, 2015. www.epi.org/files/page/-/BriefingPaper288.pdf. See also Bucknor, Cherrie. 2015. "Young Black America Part Four: The Wrong Way to Close the Gender Wage Gap." Washington, DC: Center for Economic and Policy Research. Retrieved on February 17, 2016. cepr.net/publications/ reports/young-black-america-part-four-the-wrong-way-to-close-the-gender-wage-gap.

3 Stiglitz, Joseph E. 2015. *Rewriting the Rules of the American Economy: An Agenda for Growth and Shared Prosperity*. New York: W.W. Norton. Page 4.

4 Jones, Camara Phyllis. 2000. "Levels of Racism: A Theoretic Framework and a Gardener's Tale." *American Journal of Public Health* 90(8): 1212–1215. Page 1212. See also Lieberman, Robert C. 2008. "Legacies of Slavery? Race and Historical Causation in American Political Development." In Joseph E. Lowndes, Julie Novkov, and Dorian T. Warren, Eds. *Race and American Political Development*. New York: Routledge.

5 Bureau of Labor Statistics. 2015. "Median Weekly Earnings by Educational Attainment in 2014." Retrieved April 11, 2016. www.bls.gov/opub/ted/2015/median-weekly-earnings-by-education-gender-race-and-ethnicity-in-2014.htm.

6 Becker, Gary. 1957. *The Economics of Discrimination*. Chicago, IL: University of Chicago Press.

7 Pager Devah, Bruce Western, and Bart Bonikowski. 2009. "Discrimination in a Low-Wage Labor Market: A Field Experiment." *American Sociological Review* 74(5): 777–799.

8 Harvey, David. 2005. *A Brief History of Neoliberalism*. Oxford: Oxford University Press.

9  Ostry, Jonathan D., Andrew Berg, and Charalambos G. Tsangarides. 2014. "Redistribution, Inequality, and Growth." Washington, DC: International Monetary Fund. Retrieved May 8, 2015. www.imf.org/external/pubs/ft/sdn1402.pdf.

10 Heckman, James J. 1998. "Detecting Discrimination." *Journal of Economic Perspectives* 12(2): 101–116.

11 Hacker, Jacob S. 2011. "The Institutional Foundations of Middle-Class Democracy." Policy Network Publication: Priorities for a New Political Economy: Memos to the Left.

12 Krueger, Anne O. 1974. "The Political Economy of the Rent-Seeking Society." *American Economic Review* 64: 291–303.

13 Stiglitz, Joseph E. 2015. *Rewriting the Rules of the American Economy: An Agenda for Growth and Shared Prosperity*. New York: W. W. Norton.

14 Austin et al., "Whiter Jobs, Higher Wages."

15 Haney-López, Ian. 2014. *Dog Whistle Politics: How Coded Racial Appeals Have Reinvented Racism and Wrecked the Middle Class*. Oxford: Oxford University Press.

16 Jones, "Levels of Racism."

17 Ibid.

18 Bonilla-Silva, Eduardo. 2009. *Racism Without Racists: Color-Blind Racism and the Persistence of Racial Inequality in America*. New York: Rowman & Littlefield.

19 powell, john a. 2015. *Racing to Justice: Transforming Our Conceptions of Self and Other to Build an Inclusive Society*. Bloomington: Indiana University Press. Page 23.

20 powell, john a., Stephen Menendian & Jason Reece. 2009. "The Importance of Targeted Universalism." *Poverty & Race* (March/April). Retrieved February 23, 2017. www.prrac.org/full_text.php?text_id=1223&item_id=11577&newsletter_id=104&header=Miscellaneous&kc=1.

21 Cohen, Cathy J. 1999. *The Boundaries of Blackness: AIDS and the Breakdown of Black Politics*. Chicago, IL: University of Chicago Press. See also Reed, Adolph, Jr. 1999. *Stirrings in the Jug: Black Politics in the Post-Segregation Era*. Minneapolis: University of Minnesota Press. See also Brown, Michael K., Martin Carnoy, Elliott Currie, Troy Duster, David B. Oppenheimer, Marjorie M. Schultz, and David Wellman. 2005. *Whitewashing Race: The Myth of a Color-Blind Society*. Berkeley: University of California Press. See also Thompson, J. Phillip. 2005. *Double Trouble: Black Mayors, Black Communities, and the Call for a Deep Democracy*. New York: Oxford University Press. See also Shapiro, Thomas M. 2005. *The Hidden Cost of Being African American: How Wealth Perpetuates Inequality*. New York: Oxford University Press.

22 Darity, William. 2005. "Stratification Economics: The Role of Intergroup Inequality." *Journal of Economics and Finance* 29(2): 144–153. Page 144.

23 Marable, Manning. 1983. *How Capitalism Underdeveloped Black America*. Brooklyn, NY: South End Press. See also Sharkey, Patrick. 2013. *Stuck in Place: Urban Neighborhoods and the End of Progress Toward Racial Equality*. Chicago, IL: University of Chicago Press.

24 Wilson, William Julius. 1978. *The Declining Significance of Race*; Chicago, IL. University of Chicago Press. See also Wilson, William Julius. 1987. *The Truly Disadvantaged*. Chicago, IL: University of Chicago Press. See also Wilson, William Julius. 2010. *More than Just Race: Being Black and Poor in the Inner City*. W. W. Norton.

25 Waquant, Loic. 2000. "The New 'Peculiar Institution.': On the Prison as Surrogate Ghetto." *Theoretical Criminology* 4(3): 377–389.

26 Harris Fredrick C., Valeria Sinclair-Chapman, and Brian D. McKenzie. 2005. *Countervailing Forces in African-American Civic Activism, 1973–1994*. New York: Cambridge University Press.

27 Massey, Douglas S. and Nancy A. Denton. 1990. *American Apartheid: Segregation and the Making of the Underclass*. Cambridge, MA: Harvard University Press. See also Sampson, Robert J. 2013. *Great American City: Chicago and the Enduring Neighborhood Effect*. Chicago, IL: University of Chicago Press.

28 Sharkey, *Stuck in Place*.

29 Guinier, Lani and Gerald Torres. 2003. *The Miner's Canary: Enlisting Race, Resisting Power, Transforming Democracy*. New York: Harvard University Press.

# 1 AMERICAN POLITICS AND ECONOMIC OUTCOMES FOR AFRICAN AMERICANS

1 PBS. N.d. "Bacon's Rebellion: 1675–1676." Retrieved February 14, 2017 (www.pbs.org/wgbh/aia/part1/1p274.html).

2 Lawrence, Keith and Terry Keleher. 2004. "Structural Racism." *Race and Public Policy Conference Proceedings*. Retrieved February 13, 2017 (www.intergroupresources.com/rc/Definitions%20of%20Racism.pdf).

3 Coates, Ta-Nehisi. 2014. "The Case for Reparations." *The Atlantic*, June. Retrieved April 11, 2016. (www.theatlantic.com/magazine/archive/2014/06/the-case-for-reparations/361631/).

4 Stiglitz, Joseph et al. 2015. *Rewriting the Rules of the American Economy: An Agenda for Growth and Shared Prosperity*. New York: W. W. Norton.

5 Polanyi, Karl. 1944. *The Great Transformation: The Political and Economic Origins of Our Time*. Boston, MA: Beacon Press.

6 Thompson J. Phillip III. 1998. "Universalism and Deconcentration: Why Race Still Matters in Poverty and Economic Development." *Politics and Society* (26)2, 188.

7 Library of Congress. N.d. "The African American Odyssey: A Question for Full Citizenship. Slavery – The Peculiar Institution." Washington, DC: Library of Congress.

8 Ibid.

9 Foner, Eric. 1988. *Reconstruction: America's Unfinished Revolution, 1863–1877*. New York: Harper Collins.

10 National Archives. N.d. "African American Records: Freemen's Bureau." Washington, DC: National Archives and Records Administration. Retrieved February 13, 2017 (www.archives.gov/research/african-americans/freedmens-bureau).

11 Foner, Eric. 2015. "Why Reconstruction Matters."*New York Times*, March 28. Campbell, James T. 1995. *Songs of Zion: The African Methodist Church in the United States and South Africa*, p. 54.

12 History, Art & Archives, U.S. House of Representatives. N.d. "Black Americans in Congress." Retrieved January 10, 2017 (history.house.gov/Exhibitions-and-Publications/BAIC/Black-Americans-in-Congress/).

13 Foner, Eric. 1990. *A Short History of Reconstruction*. New York: Harper Perennial, p. 46.

14  U.S. House of Representatives. N.d. "The Civil Rights Bill of 1866." Washington, DC: U.S. House of Representatives – History, Art & Archives. Retrieved February 14, 2017 (history.house.gov/Historical-Highlights/1851–1900/The-Civil-Rights-Bill-of-1866/). Halbrook, Stephen P. 1998. *Freedmen, the Fourteenth Amendment, and the Right to Bear Arms, 1866–1876.* Westport, CT: Praeger Publishers.

15  Smith, Rogers M. 1997. *Civic Ideals: Conflicting Versions of Citizenship in U.S. History.* New Haven: Yale University Press.

16  Foner, "Why Reconstruction Matters.".

17  Foner, *A Short History of Reconstruction*, p. 53.

18  McBride, Alex. N.d. "Landmark Cases: Slaughterhouse Cases (1873)." PBS. Retrieved February 14, 2017 (www.pbs.org/wnet/supremecourt/antebellum/landmark_slaughterhouse.html).

19  Tucker, Ronnie Bernard. 2000. *Affirmative Action, The Supreme Court, and Political Power in the Old Confederacy.* New York: Rowman & Littlefield.

20  Pope, James Gray. 2016. "Why Is There No Socialism in the United States?" *Texas Law Review* 94: 1555–1590.

21  Blackmon, Douglas A. 2008. *Slavery by Another Name: The Re-enslavement of Black People in America from the Civil War to World War II.* New York: Doubleday.

22  Foner, "Why Reconstruction Matters."

23  Jaynes, Gerald D. 2005. *Encyclopedia of African American Society*, Volume 1. Thousand Oaks, CA: SAGE Publishing.

24  Valelly, Richard M. 2004. *The Two Reconstructions: The Struggle for Black Enfranchisement.* Chicago, IL: University of Chicago Press Books, p. 1.

25  Salvatore, Susan Cianci, Neil Foley, Peter Iverson, and Steven F. Lawson. 2007. "Civil Rights in America: Racial Voting Rights. A National Historic Landmarks Theme Study." Washington, DC: National Historic Landmarks Program, Cultural Resources, National Park Service, U.S. Department of the Interior. Retrieved February 14, 2017 (www.nps.gov/nhl/learn/themes/CivilRights_VotingRights.pdf).

26  Wilkerson, Isabel. 2011. *The Warmth of Other Suns.* New York: Vintage Books.

27  Ibid.

28  Warren, Dorian T. 2013. "Racial Inequality in Employment in Postracial America." In Frederick C. Harris and Robert C. Lieberman, Eds. *Beyond Discrimination: Racial Inequality in a Post-Racist Era, Page 141.* New York: Russell Sage. Farhang, S., & I. Katznelson, 2005. "The Southern Imposition: Congress and Labor in the New Deal and Fair Deal." *Studies in American Political Development, 19*(01), 1–30. Frymer, P. 2008. *Black and Blue: African Americans, the Labor Movement, and the Decline of the Democratic Party.* Princeton, NJ: Princeton University Press.

29  Katznelson, Ira. 2006. *When Affirmative Action Was White.* New York: W. W. Norton & Company. See also Katznelson, Ira. 2014. *Fear Itself: The New Deal and the Origins of Our Time.* New York: W. W. Norton & Company.

30  Goluboff, Risa L. 2009. *The Lost Promise of Civil Rights.* Cambridge, MA: Harvard University Press.

31  Bobo, Lawrence D., Camille Z. Charles, Maria Krysan, and Alicia D. Simmons. 2012. "The Real Record on Racial Attitudes." In Peter V. Marsden, Ed. *Social Trends in American Life: Findings from the General Social Survey Since 1972.* Princeton, NJ: Princeton University Press, pp. 38–83.

32  López, Ian Haney. 2015. *Dog Whistle Politics: How Coded Racial Appeals Have Reinvented Racism and Wrecked the Middle Class*. New York: Oxford University Press.

33  Bobo et al., "Real Record."

34  Dobbin, Frank. 2011. *Inventing Equal Opportunity*. Princeton, NJ: Princeton University Press.

35  Rustin, Bayard. 1965. "From Protest to Politics: The Future of the Civil Rights Movement." *Commentary* 2(39).

36  Flippen, Alan. 2014. "Black Turnout in 1964 and Beyond." *New York Times*, October 17. Retrieved January 12, 2017. www.nytimes.com/2014/10/17/upshot/black-turnout-in-1964-and-beyond.html.

37  Colburn, David R. and Jeffrey S. Alder. 2001. *African-American Mayors: Race, Politics, and the American City*. Urbana, IL: University of Illinois Press. Page 1.

38  Goluboff, *Lost Promise*.

39  Warren, "Racial Inequality in Employment." Page 142.

40  Austin, Algernon. 2013. "The Unfinished March: An Overview." Washington, DC: Economic Policy Institute. Retrieved January 12, 2017 www.epi.org/publication/unfinished-march-overview/.

41  Foderaro, Lisa W. 2016. "Dispute as Westchester Housing Pact Nears End: Did the County Honor It?" *New York Times*, July 7. Retrieved January 12, 2017 www.nytimes.com/2016/07/08/nyregion/dispute-as-westchester-housing-pact-nears-end-did-the-county-honor-it.html. On Shelby, see Fuller, Jaime. 2014. "How Has Voting Changed Since Shelby County v. Holder?" *Washington Post*, July 7. Retrieved January 12, 2017. www.washingtonpost.com/news/the-fix/wp/2014/07/07/how-has-voting-changed-since-shelby-county-v-holder/?utm_term=.0b6186897969.

42  Kruse, Kevin M. 2005. *White Flight: Atlanta and the Making of Modern Conservatism*. Princeton, NJ: Princeton University Press.

43  Williams, Lucy A. 1997. *Decades of Distortion: The Right's 30-year Assault on Welfare*. Somerville, MA: Political Research Associates; Abramowitz, Mimi. 1996. *Regulating the Lives of Women: Social Welfare Policy from Colonial Times to the Present*. Boston: South End Press.

44  Rowthorn, Robert and Ramana Ramaswamy. 1997. "Deindustrialization– Its Causes and Implications." International Monetary Fund. Retrieved February 14, 2017. www.imf.org/EXTERNAL/PUBS/FT/ISSUES10/issue10.pdf. See also U.S. Bureau of Labor Statistics. "Percent of Employment in Manufacturing in the United States (DISCONTINUED) [USAPEFANA]." St. Louis, MO: Federal Reserve Bank of St. Louis. Retrieved February 14, 2017. fred.stlouisfed.org/series/USAPEFANA.

45  Wilson, William Julius. 1998. *When Work Disappears: The World of the New Urban Poor*. New York: Vintage.Page iv.

46  Snyder, Thomas D. 1993. "120 Years of American Education: A Statistical Portrait." Washington, DC: National Center for Education Statistics. Retrieved February 6. nces.ed.gov/pubs93/93442.pdf.

47  American Sociological Association. 2005. "Race, Ethnicity, and the American Labor Market: What's at Work?" Retrieved January 12, 2017. www.asanet.org/sites/default/files/savvy/images/research/docs/pdf/RaceEthnicity_LaborMarket.pdf.

48  Warren, "Racial Inequality in Employment." Page 144.

49  American Sociological Association, "Race, Ethnicity, and the American Labor Market," Page 5.

50  See Reskin, Barbara F. and Patricia Roos. 1990. *Job Queues, Gender Queues.* Philadelphia, PA: Temple University Press.

51  Looney, Adam and Michael Greenstone. 2012. "A Record Decline in Government Jobs: Implications for the Economy and America's Workforce." Washington, DC: Brookings Institution. Retrieved February 6, 2017. www.brookings.edu/blog/jobs/2012/08/03/a-record-decline-in-government-jobs-implications-for-the-economy-and-americas-workforce/.

52  Cowie, Jefferson. 1999. *Capital Moves: RCA's Seventy-Year Quest for Cheap Labor.* Ithaca, NY: Cornell University Press. See also Gordon, David M. 1977. "Class Struggle and the Stages of American Urban Development." In *The Rise of the Sunbelt Cities,* D. C. Perry and A. J. Watkins, Eds. Beverly Hills, CA: Sage. 74–75; Kain, John. 1968, "The Distribution and Movement of Jobs and Industry." In James Q. Wilson, Ed. *The Metropolitan Enigma.* Cambridge, MA: Harvard University Press.

53  Gobillon, Laurent, Harris Selod, and Yves Zenou. 2007. "The Mechanisms of Spatial Mismatch." *Urban Studies* 44(12): 2401–2427. Retrieved February 6, 2017 www.parisschoolofeconomics.eu/IMG/pdf/ArticleZenou1.pdf.

54  Kruse, *White Flight.* Page 8.

55  Ibid.

56  Wilson, *When Work Disappears*; Kruse *White Flight.*

57  Wilson, *When Work Disappears.*

58  Teaford, Jon C. 1993. *The Twentieth Century American City: Problem, Promise, and Reality.* Baltimore, MD: Johns Hopkins University Press. Page 150.

59  Gottschalk, Marie. 2015. *Caught: The Prison State and the Lockdown of American Politics.* Princeton, NJ: Princeton University Press.

60  Rustin, Bayard. 1965. "The Meaning of the March on Washington." *Liberation* (October).

61  Ibid.

## 2 STRATIFICATION ECONOMICS

1  For example, Easterlin, Richard A. 1973. "Does Money Buy Happiness?" *Public Interest* 30 (Winter): 3–8; Easterlin, Richard A. 1995. "Will Raising the Incomes of All Increase the Happiness of All?" *Journal of Economic Behavior and Organization* 27(1, June): 35–47; Clark, Andrew E. and Andrew J. Oswald. 1996. "Satisfaction and Comparison Income." *Journal of Public Economics* 61 (3, September): 359–381; Solnick, Sara and David Hemenway. 1998. "Is More Always Better: A Survey on Positional Concerns." *Journal of Economic Behavior and Organization* 37(3, November): 373–383.

2  Veblen, Thorstein. 1899. *The Theory of the Leisure Class: An Economic Study of Institutions.* moglen.law.columbia.edu/LCS/theoryleisureclass.pdf, p. 14.

3  Kuziemko, Ilyana, Ryan W. Buell, Taly Reich, and Michael I. Norton. 2012. "'Last Place Aversion': Evidence and Redistributive Implications." NBER Working Paper No. 17234, July.

4  Tajfel, Henri and John Turner. 1979. "An Integrative Theory of Intergroup Conflict." In W. G. Austin and S. Worchel, Eds. *The Social Psychology of Intergroup Relations.* Monterey, CA: Brooks-Cole. 33–47, at 40.

5 For example, Goldsmith, Arthur H., Darrick Hamilton, and William Darity, Jr. 2007. "From Dark to Light: Skin Color and Wages Among African Americans." *Journal of Human Resources* 42 (4, Fall): 701–738; Goldsmith, Arthur H., Darrick Hamilton, and William Darity, Jr. 2006. "Shades of Discrimination: Skin Tone and Wages." *American Economic Review* 96(2, May): 242–245; Mason, Patrick L. 2007. "Intergenerational Mobility and Interracial Inequality: The Return to Family Values." *Industrial Relations* 46(1, January): 51–80; Senik, Claudia and Thierry Verdier. 2011. "Segregation, Entrepreneurship and Work Values: The Case of France." *Journal of Population Economics* 24(4, October): 1207–1234.

6 Stewart, James B. 1995. "Toward Broader Involvement of Black Economists in Discussions of Race and Public Policy: A Plea for a Reconceptualization of Race and Power in Economic Theory, NEA Presidential Address, 1994," *Review of Black Political Economy* 23(3): 13–36.

7 For example, Steele, Claude M., Steven J. Spencer, and Joshua Aronson. 2002. "Contending with Group Image: The Psychology of Stereotype and Social Identity Threat." *Advances in Experimental Psychology* 34: 379–440; Armenta, Brian E. 2010. "Stereotype Boost and Stereotype Threat Effects: The Moderating Role of Ethnic Identification." *Cultural Diversity and Ethnic Minority Psychology* 16(1, January): 94–98; Walton, Gregory and Geoffrey L. Cohen. 2003. "Stereotype Lift." *Journal of Experimental Psychology* 39(5, September): 455–467.

8 Steele et al., "Contending with Group Image"; Hoff, Karla and Priyanka Pandey. 2006. "Discrimination, Social Identity, and Durable Inequalities." *American Economic Review* 96(2 May): 206–211; Croizet, Jean-Claude and Theresa Claire. 1998. "Extending the Concept of Stereotype Threat to Social Class: The Intellectual Underperformance of Students from Low Socioeconomic Backgrounds." *Personality and Social Psychology Bulletin* 24(6, June): 588–594.

9 Steele et al., "Contending with Group Image."

10 Armenta, "Stereotype Boost."

11 Shih, Margaret, Todd L. Pittinsky, and Nalini Ambady. 1999. "Stereotype Susceptibility: Identity, Salience and Shift in Quantitative Performance." *Psychological Science* 10(1, January): 80–83.

12 Smith, Jessi L. and Camille Johnson. 2006. "A Stereotype Boost or Choking Under Pressure: Positive Gender Stereotypes and Men Who Are Low in Domain Identification." *Basic and Applied Psychology* 28(1): 51–63.

13 Walton and Cohen, "Stereotype Lift."

14 Darity, William, Jr. 2005. "Stratification Economics: The Role of Intergroup Inequality." *Journal of Economics and Finance* 29(2): 144–153.

15 Darity, William, Jr., Patrick L. Mason, and James B. Stewart. 2006. "The Economics of Identity: The Origin and Persistence of Racial Identity." *Journal of Economic Behavior and Organization* 60(3, July): 283–306.

16 Stewart, James B. 2009. "Be All That You Can Be? Racial Identity Production in the U.S. Military." *Review of Black Political Economy* 36(1, March): 51–78.

17 Sherif, Muzafer. 1966. *In Common Predicament*. Boston: Houghton Mifflin.

18 Tajfel and Turner, "An Integrative Theory," p. 33.

19 Tajfel and Turner, "An Integrative Theory," p. 34.

20 Goette, Lorenz, David Huffman, Stephen Meier. 2012. "The Impact of Social Ties on Group Identification: Evidence from Minimal Groups and Randomly Assigned Real Groups." *American Economic Journal* 4(1 February): 101–116.

21   Allport, Gordon. 1954. *The Nature of Prejudice*. Reading: Addison-Wesley, MA.

22   Blumer, Herbert. 1958. "Race Prejudice as a Sense of Group Position." *Pacific Sociological Review* 1(1, Spring): 3–7

23   Allport, *The Nature of Prejudice*.

24   Cook, Stuart W. 1978. "Interpersonal and Attitudinal Outcomes in Cooperating Interracial Groups" *Journal of Research and Development in Education* 12(1): 97–113.

25   Pettigrew, Thomas F. and Linda R. Tropp. 2006. "A Meta-Analytic Test of Intergroup Contact Theory." *Journal of Personality and Social Psychology* 90(5, May): 751–783; Forbes, H. D. 1997. *Ethnic Conflict: Commerce, Culture and the Contact Hypothesis.* New Haven, CT: Yale University Press.

26   Ridgeway, Cecilia and Lynn Smith Lovin. 1999. "The Gender System and Interaction." *Annual Review of Sociology* 25: 199–216.

27   Forbes, *Ethnic Conflict*.

28   Tropp, Linda and Thomas Pettigrew. 2005. "Differential Relationships Between Intergroup Contact and Affective and Cognitive Dimensions of Prejudice." *Personality and Social Psychology Bulletin* 31(8, August): 1145–1157.

29   Blumer, ""Race Prejudice as a Sense of Group Position," p. 4.

30   Blumer, ""Race Prejudice as a Sense of Group Position," p. 4.

31   Bobo, Lawrence and Vincent L. Hutchings. 1996. "Perceptions of Racial Group Competition: Extending Blumer's Theory of Group Position to a Multiracial Context." *American Sociological Review* 61(6, December): 951–972; Perry, Pamela. 2007. "White Universal Identity as a 'Sense of Group Position.'" *Symbolic Interaction* 30(3, Summer): 375–393.

32   Hechter, Michael. 1984. *Principles of Group Solidarity*. Berkeley: University of California Press.

33   Du Bois, W. E. B. 1992 (1935). *Black Reconstruction in America 1860–1880*. New York: Free Press, p. 700.

34   Du Bois, *Black Reconstruction*, p. 700.

35   Roithmayr, Daria. 2014. *Reproducing Racism: How Everyday Choices Lock in White Advantage*. New York: New York University Press.

36   Perry, "White Universal Identity."

37   Sue, D. W. 2010. *Microaggressions in Everyday Life: Race, Gender, and Sexual Orientation*. Hoboken, NJ: John Wiley and Sons.

38   Calhoun, John C. 2012. "Speech on the Oregon Bill." In Hillsdale College Politics Department, Eds. *The U.S. Constitution: A Reader*. Hillsdale, MI: Hillsdel College, 419-426, at 420.

39   Goldsmith et al., "From Dark to Light."

40   Hamilton, Darrick, Arthur H. Goldsmith, and William Darity, Jr. 2009. "Shedding 'Light' on Marriage: The Influence of Skin Shade on Marriage for Black Females." *Journal of Economic Behavior and Organization* 72(1, October): 30–56.

41   Eberhardt, Jennifer L., Paul G. Davies, Valerie T. Purdie-Vaughns, and Sherilyn Johnson. 2006. "Looking Deathworthy: Perceived Stereotypicality of Black Defendants Predicts Capital Sentencing." *Psychological Science* 17(5, May): 383–386; Gyimah-Brempong, Kwabena and Gregory Price. 2006. "Crime and Punishment and Skin Hue Too?" *American Economic Review* 96(2, May): 246–250.

42   Stewart, James B. "Economics, Stratification." 2008. In William Darity, Jr. Ed., *International Encyclopedia of the Social Sciences*, 2nd Edition, Volume 2. Detroit: Thomson Gale. 530–531.

43 Stewart, "Economics, Stratification."

44 Alesina, Alberto., Reza Baqir, and William Easterly. 1999. "Public Goods and Ethnic Divisions." *Quarterly Journal of Economics* 114: 1243–1284; Hopkins, Daniel J. 2009. "The Diversity Discount: When Increasing Ethnic and Racial Diversity Prevents Tax Increases." *Journal of Politics* 71: 160–177; Luttmer, Erzo F. P. 2001. "Group Loyalty and the Taste for Redistribution." *Journal of Political Economy* 109: 500–528.

45 Cutler, David M., Douglas W. Elmendorf, and Richard J. Zeckhauser. 1993. "Demographic Characteristics and the Public Bundle." *Public Finance* 48: 178–198; Halcoussis, Dennis and Anton D. Lowenberg. 1998. "Local Public Goods and Jim Crow." *Journal of Institutional and Theoretical Economics* 154: 599–621.

46 Alesina, Alberto, Edward Glaeser, and Bruce Sacerdote. 2001. "Why Doesn't the United States Have a European-Style Welfare State?" *Brookings Papers on Economic Activity* 2: 1–70.

47 Alesina, Glaeser and Sacerdote, "Why Doesn't the United States Have a European-Style Welfare State?"

48 Fogel, Robert W. 2004. "Health, Nutrition, and Economic Growth." *Economic Development and Cultural Change* 52: 643–658; Fogel, Robert W. and Dora Costa. 1997. "A Theory of Technophysio Evolution, with Some Implications for Forecasting Population, Health Care Costs, and Pension Costs." *Demography* 34: 49–66.

49 Alesina, Glaeser and Sacerdote, "Why Doesn't the United States Have a European-Style Welfare State?"

50 Andrews, Marcellus. 2008. "Risk, Inequality and the Economics of Disaster." *Real-World Economics Review* 45: 2–9.

51 Price, Gregory N. 2008. "Hurricane Katrina: Was There a Political Economy of Death?" *Review of Black Political Economy* 35(4, December): 163–180.

52 Lowe, Jeffrey S. and Todd C. Shaw. 2009. "After Katrina: Racial Regimes and Human Development Barriers in the Gulf Coast Region." *American Quarterly* 61: 803–827.

53 Banerjee, Lopamudra. 2010. "Creative Destruction: Analysing Flood and Flood Control in Bangladesh." *Environmental Hazards* 9(1): 102–117.

54 Tilly, Charles. 1998. *Durable Inequality*. Berkeley and Los Angeles: University of California Press. 147–169.

55 Darity, "Stratification Economics," 146–147.

56 Moore, Solomon and Robin Fields. 2002. "The Great 'White' Influx." *Los Angeles Times*, July 31. articles.latimes.com/2002/jul/31/local/me-white31.

57 Duncan, Brian and Stephen J. Trejo. 2011. "Tracking Intergenerational Progress for Immigrant Groups: The Problem of Ethnic Attrition." *American Economic Review* 101(3, May): 603–608.

58 Darity et al., "Economics of Identity."

59 Mason, Patrick L. and Andrew Matella. 2014. "Stigmatization and Racial Selection after September 11, 2001: Self-Identity Among Arab and Islamic Americans." *IZA Journal of Migration* 3(20, December): 1–21.

60 Antman, Francisca and Brian Duncan. 2015. "Incentives to Identify: Racial Identity in the Age of Affirmative Action." *Review of Economics and Statistics* 97(3, July): 710–713.

61 Telles, Edward E. and Edward Murguia. 1990. "Phenotypic Discrimination and Income Differences Among Mexican Americans. *Social Science Quarterly* 71: 682–696; Bohara, Alok K. and Alberto Dávila. 1992. "A Reassessment of Phenotypic Discrimination and Income Differences Among Mexican Americans." *Social*

*Science Quarterly* 73(1): 114–119; Mason, Patrick L. 2004. "Annual Income, Hourly Wages, and Identity Among Mexican-Americans and Other Latinos?" *Industrial Relations: A Journal of Economy and Society* 43(4): 817–834; Golash-Boza, Tanya and William Darity, Jr. 2008. "Latino Racial Choices: The Effects of Skin Colour and Discrimination on Latinos' and Latinas' Racial Self-Identifications." *Ethnic & Racial Studies* 31(5): 899–934; Hersch, Joni. 2008. "Profiling the New Immigrant Worker: The Effects of Skin Color and Height." *Journal of Labor Economics* 26(2): 345–386.

62  Dávila, Alberto, Marie T. Mora, and Sue Stockly. 2011. "Does Mestizaje Matter in the US? Economic Stratification of Mexican Immigrants." *American Economic Review* 101(3, May): 593–597.

63  Metcalf, Hilary and Heather Rolfe. December 2010. *Caste Discrimination and Harassment in Great Britain*. London: NIESR. www.homeoffice.gov.uk/publications/ equalities/research/caste-discrimination/caste-discrimination?view=Binary.

64  Telles, Edward E. 2004. *Race in Another America: The Significance of Skin Color in Brazil*. Princeton, NJ: Princeton Unive rsity Press; Villarreal, Andres. 2010. "Stratification by Skin Color in Contemporary Mexico." *American Sociological Review* 75(5, October): 652–678.

65  Frank, Reanne, Ilana Redstone Akresh, and Bo Lu. 2010. "Latino Immigrants and the US Racial Order: How and Where Do They Fit In?" *American Sociological Review* 75(3, June): 378–401; Dávila et al., "Does Mestizaje Matter?"

66  Darity, William A., Jr. 1989. "What's Left of the Economic Theory of Discrimination?" In Seve Shulman and William Darity, Jr., *The Question of Discrimination*. Middletown, CT: Wesleyan University Press. 335–374.

67  For example, Dávila et al., "Does Mestizaje Matter?"

68  Nopper, Tamara. 2011. "Colorblind Racism and Institutional Actors: Explanations of Korean Immigrant Entrepreneurship." *Critical Sociology* 37(5 September): 651–671.

69  Becker, Gary S. 1971 (1957). *The Economics of Discrimination*. Chicago: University of Chicago Press.

70  Lang, Kevin and Michael Manove. 2011. "Education and Labor Market Discrimination." *American Economic Review* 101(4): 1467–1496.

71  Darity, William, Jr. and Patrick L. Mason. 1998. "Evidence on Discrimination in Employment: Codes of Color, Codes of Gender." *Journal of Economic Perspectives* 12(2, Spring): 63–90.

72  Agesa, Jacqueline and Darrick Hamilton. 2004. "Competition and Wage Discrimination: The Effects of Interindustry Concentration and Import Penetration." *Social Science Quarterly* 85(1, March): 121–135.

73  O'Connell, Geoffrey F. X. 2001. "The Mysterious 364th." *Philadelphia City Paper*, May 17–24. archives.citypaper.net/articles/051701/cs.coverstory1.shtml?CFTOKE N=29468257&CFID=7817445.

74  Hamilton, Darrick, Algernon Austin, and William Darity, Jr. 2011. *White Jobs, Higher Wages: Occupational Segregation and the Lower Wages of Black Men* Economic Policy Institute Briefing Paper.

75  Devah Pager. 2003. "The Mark of a Criminal Record." *American Journal of Sociology* 108: 937–75.

76  Bertrand, Marianne and Sendhil Mullainathan. (2004). "Are Emily and Greg More Employable than Lakisha and Jamal? A Field Experiment on Labor Market

Discriminaton." *American Economic Review* 94(4): 991–1013.Bertrand and Mullainathan (2004)

77 For example, see Darity and Mason, "Evidence on Discrimination in Employment," 81–86; and Basu, Kaushik. 2011 *Beyond the Invisible Hand: Groundwork for a New Economics*. Princeton, NJ: Princeton University Press. 77–129.

78 Basu, *Beyond the Invisible Hand.*

79 Krueger, Anne. 1963. "The Economics of Discrimination." *Journal of Political Economy* 71(5, October): 481–486.

## 3 CREATING STRUCTURAL CHANGES

1 Crenshaw, Kimberle. 1989. "Demarginalizing the Intersection of Race and Sex: A Black Feminist Critique of Antidiscrimination Doctrine, Feminist Theory and Antiracist Politics." *University of Chicago Legal Forum* 1989 (1): Article 8.

2 For information on the "All Lives Matter" phrase, see Victor, Daniel. 2016. "Why 'All Lives Matter' Is Such a Perilous Phrase." *New York Times*, July 15. Accessed March 1, 2017. www.nytimes.com/2016/07/16/us/all-lives-matter-black-lives-matter.html.

3 Movement for Black Lives. N.d. "Platform." Accessed March 1, 2017. policy.m4bl.org/platform.

4 Cohn, D'Vera. 2015. "Future Immigration Will Change the Face of America by 2065." *Pew Research Center*, October 5. Accessed March 1, 2017. www.pewresearch.org/fact-tank/2015/10/05/future-immigration-will-change-the-face-of-america-by-2065/.

5 Pastor, Manuel, Juan De Lara, and Justin Scoggins. 2011. *All Together Now? African Americans, Immigrants and the Future of California*, report. Los Angeles: University of Southern California.

6 McNamee, Stephen J. and Robert K. Miller. 2014. *The Meritocracy Myth*, 3rd ed. Lanham, MD: Rowman & Littlefield.

## 4 THE RACIAL RULES OF WEALTH

1 Nam, Yunju, Darrick Hamilton, William A. Darity, and Anne E. Price. 2015. "Bootstraps Are for Black Kids: Race, Wealth, and the Impact of Intergenerational Transfers on Adult Outcomes." Retrieved February 3, 2016. www.insightcced.org/wp-content/uploads/2015/07/Bootstraps-are-for-Black-Kids-Sept.pdf.

2 McCulloch, Heather. 2017. "Closing the Women's Wealth Gap: What Is It, Why It Matters, and What Can Be Done About It." Retrieved January 25, 2017. assetbuild-ingstrategies.com/wp-content/uploads/2017/01/Closing-the-Womens-Wealth-Gap-Jan2017.pdf.

3 Shapiro, Thomas, Tatjana Meschede, and Sam Osoro. 2013. "The Roots of the Widening Racial Wealth Gap: Explaining the Black–White Economic Divide." Waltham, MA: Institute on Assets & Social Policy. Retrieved February 2, 2016. iasp.brandeis.edu/pdfs/Author/shapiro-thomas-m/racialwealthgapbrief.pdf.

4 Tippett, Rebecca, Avis Jones-DeWeever, Maya Rockeymoore, Darrick Hamilton, and William Darity. 2011. "Beyond Broke: Why Closing the Racial Wealth Gap Is a Priority for National Economic Security." Washington, DC: Center on Global Policy

Solutions. Retrieved February 3, 2016. globalpolicysolutions.org/wp-content/uploads/2014/04/Beyond_Broke_FINAL.pdf.

5　Hamilton, Darrick. 2000. "Issues Concerning Discrimination and Measurements of Discrimination in U.S. Labor Markets." *African American Research Perspectives*, 6(3):116–20. Kochhar, Rakesh, and Richard Fry. 2014. "Wealth Inequality Has Widened Along Racial, Ethnic Lines Since End of Great Recession." Retrieved February 3, 2016. www.pewresearch.org/fact-tank/2014/12/12/racial-wealth-gaps-great-recession/.

6　Chang, Mariko. 2015. "Women and Wealth: Insights for Grantmakers." *Asset Funders Network*. Retrieved February 28, 2017. www.mariko-chang.com/AFN_Women_and_Wealth_Brief_2015.pdf.

7　McCulloch, "Closing the Women's Wealth Gap."

8　Chang, Mariko Lin. 2010. *Shortchanged: Why Women Have Less Wealth and What Can Be Done About It*. New York: Oxford University Press.

9　Kids Count Data Center. N.d. "Children in Single-Parent Families By Race." Retrieved May 5, 2016. datacenter.kidscount.org/data/tables/107-children-in-single-parent-families-by#detailed/1/any/false/869,36,868,867,133/10,11,9,12,1,185,13/432,431)

10　Richard, Katherine. 2014. "The Wealth Gap for Women of Color." Center for Global Policy Solutions. Retrieved April 11, 2016. globalpolicysolutions.org/wp-content/uploads/2014/10/Wealth-Gap-for-Women-of-Color.pdf.

11　McCulloch, "Closing the Women's Wealth Gap."

12　Richard, "The Wealth Gap for Women of Color."

13　Bhaskaran, Suparna. 2016. "Pinklining: How Wall Street's Predatory Products Pillage Women's Wealth, Opportunities & Futures." June. Retrieved January 25, 2017. d3n8a8pro7vhmx.cloudfront.net/acceinstitute/pages/100/attachments/original/1466121052/acce_pinklining_VIEW.pdf?1466121052.

14　Richard, "The Wealth Gap for Women of Color."

15　Institute for Women's Policy Research. 2017. "Wealth Inequality and Asset Depletion Among Single Early Baby Boomers: Differences by Gender, Race/Ethnicity and Home Ownership in Retirement Readiness." January. Retrieved January 25, 2017. iwpr.org/publications/pubs/weath-inequality-asset-depletion-single-boomers/.

16　Kochhar and Fry, "Wealth Inequality Has Widened."

17　Hamilton, Darrick, William Darity, Jr., Anne E. Price, Vishnu Sridharan, and Rebecca Tippett. 2015. "Umbrellas Don't Make it Rain: Why Studying and Working Hard Isn't Enough for Black Americans." New School. Duke Center for Social Equity. Insight. Retrieved February 2, 2016. www.insightcced.org/wp-content/uploads/2015/08/Umbrellas_Dont_Make_It_Rain_Final.pdf.

18　Henry J. Kaiser Family Foundation. 2014. "Poverty Rate by Race/Ethnicity." Retrieved May 5, 2016. kff.org/other/state-indicator/poverty-rate-by-raceethnicity/; National Partnership for Women & Families. 2015. "African American Women and the Wage Gap." Retrieved May 5, 2016. www.nationalpartnership.org/research-library/workplace-fairness/fair-pay/african-american-women-wage-gap.pdf.

19　Kids Count Data Center. N.d. "Children Living in Areas of Concentrated Poverty by Race and Ethnicity." Retrieved May 5, 2016. datacenter.kidscount.org/data/Tables/7753-children-living-in-areas-of-concentrated-poverty-by-race-and-ethnicity?loc=1&loct=1#detailed/1/any/false/1485,1376,1201,1074,880/10,11,9,12,1,185,13/14943,14942.

20  Shapiro et al., "Roots of the Widening Racial Wealth Gap."

21  Hamilton et al., "Umbrellas Don't Make It Rain."

22  Cuffee, Jocelyn. 2008. "Slave Codes." In Orville Vernon Burton, Ed. *Gale Library of Daily Life: Slavery in America*. Farmington Hills, MI: Gale.

23  Vinik, Danny. 2014. "The Economics of Reparations: Why Congress Should Meet Ta-Nehisi Coates's Modest Demand." *New Republic*, May 21. Retrieved May 5, 2016. newrepublic.com/article/117856/academic-evidence-reparations-costs-are-limited.

24  Greene, Lorenzo Johnston. 1942. *The Negro in Colonial New England*. New York: Columbia University Press; Beckert, Sven. 2014. *Empire of Cotton: A Global History*. New York: Vintage.

25  Bailey, Ronald. 1990. "The Slave(ry) Trade and the Development of Capitalism in the United States: The Textile Industry in New England." *Social Science History* 14(3): 373–414.

26  Beckert, Sven. 2014. "Slavery and Capitalism." *Chronicle Review*, December 12. Retrieved February 3, 2016. chronicle.com/article/SlaveryCapitalism/150787/.

27  Beckert, *Empire of Cotton*; Bailey, "Slave(ry) Trade."

28  Ibid.

29  Beckert, Sven and Seth Rockman. 2012. "How Slavery Led to Modern Capitalism: Echoes." *Bloomberg View*, May 14. Retrieved February 3, 2016. www .bloombergview.com/articles/2012-01-24/how-slavery-led-to-modern-capitalism-echoes.

30  Blackmon, Douglas A. 2008. *Slavery by Another Name: The Re-Enslavement of Black Americans from the Civil War to World War II*. New York: Doubleday.

31  Frymer, Paul. 2008. *Black and Blue: African Americans, the Labor Movement, and the Decline of the Democratic Party*. Princeton, NJ: Princeton University Press; Katznelson, Ira. 2014. *Fear Itself: The New Deal and the Origins of Our Time*. New York: Liveright; King, Desmond S. and Rogers M. Smith. 2005. "Racial Orders in American Political Development." *American Political Science Review* 99: 75–92. Leiberman, Robert C. 2003. "Race and the Limits of Solidarity: American Welfare State Development in Comparative Perspective." In S. Schram, J. Soss, and R. C. Fording, Eds. *Race and the Politics of Welfare Reform* (Ann Arbor: University of Michigan Press), 23–46.

32  Franklin D. Roosevelt Presidential Library and Museum. N.d. "FDR and Housing Legislation, 75th Anniversary of the Wagner-Steagall Housing Act of 1937." Retrieved September 18, 2015. www.fdrlibrary.marist.edu/aboutfdr/housing.html.

33  The Fair Housing Center of Greater Boston. N.d. "1934: Federal Housing Administration Created." Retrieved September 18, 2015. www.bostonfairhousing .org/timeline/1934-FHA.html. See, more generally, Denton, Nancy and Douglass Massey. 1990. *American Apartheid: Segregation and the Making of the Underclass*. Cambridge, MA: Harvard University Press; Hirsch, Arnold R. 1998. *Making the Second Ghetto: Race & Housing in Chicago 1940–1960*. Chicago: University of Chicago Press; Oliver, Melvin and Thomas Shapiro. 2006. *Black Wealth/White Wealth: A New Perspective on Racial Inequality*. New York: Routledge; Conley, Dalton. 2009. *Being Black, Living in the Red: Race, Wealth and Social Policy in America*. Oakland: University of California Press.

34  Katznelson, Ira. 2005. *When Affirmative Action Was White: An Untold History of Racial Inequality in Twentieth-Century America*. New York: W. W. Norton. Page 140.

35   Sharkey, Patrick. 2014. "Spatial Segmentation and the Black Middle Class." *American Journal of Sociology* 119(4): 903–954; Sharkey, Patrick. 2013. *Stuck in Place: Urban Neighborhoods and the End of Progress Toward Racial Equality.* Chicago: University of Chicago Press.

36   Cashin, Sheryll. 2004. *The Failures Of Integration: How Race and Class Are Undermining the American Dream.* New York: Public Affairs; Pattillo, Mary. 2005. "Black Middle-Class Neighborhoods." *Annual Review of Sociology* 31: 305–329.

37   Chetty, Ray, Nathaniel Hendren, Patrick Kline, and Emmanuel Saez. 2014. "Where Is the Land of Opportunity? The Geography of Intergenerational Mobility." *Quarterly Journal of Economics* 129(4): 1553–1623.

38   Austin Turner, Margery and Felicity Skidmore, Eds. 1999. "Mortgage Lending Discrimination: A Review of Existing Evidence." Washington, DC: Urban Institute. Retrieved February 4, 2016. www.urban.org/sites/default/files/alfresco/publication-pdfs/309090-Mortgage-Lending-Discrimination.PDF.

39   Federal Financial Institutions Examination Council. 1998. "Press Release, August 6." Retrieved May 6, 2016. www.ffiec.gov/hmcrpr/hm080698.htm. See also Ross, Stephen and John Yinger. 1999. "Does Discrimination in Mortgage Lending Exist? The Boston Fed Study and Its Critics." In Margery Austin Turner and Felicity Skidmore, Eds. *Mortgage Lending Discrimination: A Review of Existing Evidence.* Washington, DC: Urban Institute, 43–75.

40   Dymski, Gary. 1999. *The Bank Merger Wave: The Economic Causes and Social Consequences of Financial Consolidation.* Armonk, NY: M. E. Sharp. See also Ezeala-Harrison, Fidel and Glenda B. Glover. 2008. "Determinants of Housing Loan Patterns Toward Minority Borrowers in Mississippi." *Journal of Economic Issues* 42 (1): 75–96.

41   Rugh, Jacob S. and Douglas S. Massey. 2010. "Racial Segregation and the American Foreclosure Crisis." *American Sociological Review* 75(5): 629–651.

42   Konzcal, Mike and Nell Abernathy. 2015. "Defining Financialization." Retrieved February 15, 2017. rooseveltinstitute.org/wp-content/uploads/2015/10/Defining_Financialization_Web.pdf.

43   Heintz, James and Radhika Balakrishnan. 2012. "Debt, Power, and Crisis: Social Stratification and the Inequitable Governance of Financial Markets." *American Quarterly* 64(3): 387–409. See also Williams, Richard, Reynold Nesiba, and Eileen Diaz McConnell. 2005. "The Changing Face of Inequality in Home Mortgage Lending." *Social Problems* 52(2): 181–208.

44   U.S. Department of Housing and Urban Development. 2000. "Unequal Burden: Income and Racial Disparities in Subprime Lending in America." Retrieved September 30, 2015. www.huduser.org/publications/fairhsg/unequal.html; Gramlich, Edward M. 2007. "Booms and Busts: The Case of Subprime Mortgages." Kansas City, MO: Federal Reserve Bank of Kansas City. Retrieved September 30, 2015. www.kansascityfed.org/publicat/econrev/PDF/4q07Gramlich.pdf.

45   Ibid.

46   Campen, Jim. 2008. "Changing Patterns XIV: Mortgage Lending to Traditionally Underserved Borrowers & Neighborhoods in Boston, Greater Boston and Massachusetts, 2006." Boston, MA: ScholarWorks at UMass Boston. Retrieved April 11, 2016. scholarworks.umb.edu/cgi/viewcontent.cgi?article=1107&context=gaston_pubs.

47  National Council of Negro Women. 2009. "Assessing the Double Burden: Examining Racial and Gender Disparities in Mortgage Lending." Retrieved April 11, 2016. ncnw.org/images/double_burden.pdf.

48  Jones-DeWeever, Avis. 2008. "Losing Ground: Women and the Foreclosure Crisis." *National Council of Jewish Women*. Retrieved January 25, 2017. www.ncjw.org/content_1441.cfm.

49  Hill, Anita. 2012. *Reimagining Equality: Stories of Gender, Race, and Finding Home.* Boston, MA: Beacon Press. Page 110.

50  Ibid.

51  Williams, Nesiba, and McConnell, "Changing Face."

52  Wolff, Sarah D. 2015. "The State of Lending in America & Its Impact on U.S. Households." Washington, DC: Center for Responsible Lending. Retrieved April 1, 2016. www.responsiblelending.org/state-of-lending/reports/13-Cumulative-Impact.pdf.

53  Tippett, Rebecca, Avis Jones-DeWeever, Maya Rockeymoore, Darrick Hamilton, and William Darity. 2014. "Beyond Broke: Why Closing the Racial Wealth Gap Is a Priority for National Economic Security." Washington, DC: Center for Global Policy Solutions. Retrieved February 3, 2016. globalpolicysolutions.org/wp-content/uploads/2014/04/Beyond_Broke_FINAL.pdf.

54  Ibid.

55  Oliver and Shapiro, *Black Wealth/White Wealth.*

56  Steuerle, C. Eugene, Benjamin H. Harris, Signe-Mary McKernan, Caleb Quakenbush, and Caroline Ratcliffe. 2014. "Who Benefits from Asset Building Tax Subsidies?" Washington, DC: Urban Institute. Retrieved May 5, 2016. www.urban.org/sites/default/files/alfresco/publication-pdfs/413241-Who-Benefits-from-Asset-Building-Tax-Subsidies-.PDF.

57  Saunders, Laura. 2014. "The New Rules of Estate Planning." *Wall Street Journal*, October 28. Retrieved May 5, 2016. www.wsj.com/articles/the-new-rules-of-estate-planning-1414167302.

58  Kochhar and Fry, "Wealth Inequality Has Widened."

59  Corporation for Enterprise Development (CFED). 2013. "Why Assets Matter: An Overview of Research on Assets and Their Effect on Financial Stability and Economic Opportunity." Retrieved February 4, 2016. cfed.org/assets/pdfs/WhyAssetsMatter_2013updates.pdf.

60  Ibid.

61  Kiel, Paul and Annie Waldman. 2015. "The Color of Debt: How Collection Suits Squeeze Black Neighborhoods." New York: ProPublica. Retrieved February 4, 2016. www.propublica.org/article/debt-collection-lawsuits-squeeze-black-neighborhoods.

62  Chiteji, Ngina and Darrick Hamilton. 2002. "Family Connections and the Black-White Wealth Gap Among the Middle Class." *Review of Black Political Economy* 30(1): 9–27; Nam et al., "Bootstraps Are for Black Kids."

63  Kiel and Waldman, "Color of Debt."

64  Conley, Dalton. 2001. "Capital for College: Parental Assets and Postsecondary Schooling." *Sociology of Education* 74(1): 59–72.

65  Elliott, William. 2011. "When Effort and Ability Are Not Enough to Reduce the College Enrollment Gap, Does College Savings Help? Center for Social

Development Working Papers No. 11–31. Retrieved February 4, 2016. csd.wustl.edu/publications/documents/wp11-31.pdf.

## 5 THE RACIAL RULES OF INCOME

1 Weil, David. 2014. *The Fissured Workplace: Why Work Became So Bad for So Many and What Can Be Done to Improve It*. Cambridge, MA: Harvard University Press.

2 Thomas-Breitfeld, Sean, Linda Turnham, Steven Pitts, Marc Bayard, and Algernon Austin. 2015. "#BlackWorkersMatter." Brooklyn, NY: Discount Foundation. Retrieved May 5, 2016. www.discountfoundation.org/sites/all/files/black_workers_matter.pdf.

3 Wilson, Valerie. 2015. "Black Unemployment Is Significantly Higher Than White Unemployment Regardless of Educational Attainment." Washington, DC: Economic Policy Institute. Retrieved May 5, 2016. www.epi.org/publication/black-unemployment-educational-attainment/; Desilver, Drew. "5 Facts About Economic Inequality." Washington, DC: Pew Research Center. Retrieved May 5, 2016. www.pewresearch.org/fact-tank/2014/01/07/5-facts-about-economic-inequality/.

4 DeNavas-Walt, Carmen and Bernadette D. Proctor. 2015. "Income and Poverty in the United States: 2014." Washington, DC: U.S. Census Bureau. Retrieved May 5, 2016. www.census.gov/content/dam/Census/library/publications/2015/demo/p60-252.pdf; Pew Research Center. 2013. "King's Dream Remains an Elusive Goal; Many Americans See Racial Disparities." Retrieved May 5, 2016. www.pewsocialtrends.org/2013/08/22/kings-dream-remains-an-elusive-goal-many-americans-see-racial-disparities/.

5 Desilver, Drew. 2013. "U.S. Income Inequality, on Rise for Decades, Is Now Highest Since 1928." Washington, DC: Pew Research Center. Retrieved January 27, 2017. www.pewresearch.org/fact-tank/2013/12/05/u-s-income-inequality-on-rise-for-decades-is-now-highest-since-1928/.

6 Austin, Algernon, Darrick Hamilton, and William Darity. 2011. "Whiter Jobs, Higher Wages: Occupational Segregation and the Lower Wages of Black Men." Washington, DC: Economic Policy Institute. Retrieved on November 5, 2015. www.epi.org/files/page/-/BriefingPaper288.pdf.

7 Bucknor, Cherrie. 2015. "Young Black America Part Four: The Wrong Way to Close the Gender Wage Gap." Washington, DC: Center for Economic and Policy Research. Retrieved on February 17, 2016. cepr.net/publications/reports/young-black-america-part-four-the-wrong-way-to-close-the-gender-wage-gap.

8 Ibid.

9 Ibid. See also Holzer, H. J. 2000. "Career Advancement Prospects and Strategies for Low-Wage Minority Workers." Working Paper. Washington, DC: Urban Institute. Retrieved May 5, 2016. www.urban.org/sites/default/files/alfresco/publication-pdfs/410403-Career-Advancement-Prospects-and-Strategies-for-Low-Wage-Minority-Workers.pdf. See also O'Connor, Rachel, Jeff Hayes, and Barbara Gault. 2014. "Paid Sick Days Access Varies by Race/Ethnicity, Sexual Orientation, and Job Characteristics." WPR#B337. Washington, DC: Institute for Women's Policy Research. Retrieved on February 17, 2016. www.iwpr.org/publications/pubs/paid-sick-days-access-varies-by-race-ethnicity-sexual-orientation-and-job-characteristics. See

also Glied, Sherry A., Allyson G. Hall, and Karen Scott Collins. 1999. "Employer-Sponsored Health Insurance: Implications for Minority Workers." New York: Commonwealth Fund. Retrieved on February 17, 2016. www.commonwealthfund.org/publications/fund-reports/1999/feb/employer-sponsored-health-insurance--implications-for-minority-workers.

10  U.S. Bureau of Labor Statistics. 2015. "Characteristics of Minimum Wage Workers, 2014." Retrieved on February 17, 2016. www.bls.gov/opub/reports/cps/characteristics-of-minimum-wage-workers-2014.pdf.

11  Card, David and Krueger, Alan. 1992. "School Quality and Black–White Relative Earnings: A Direct Assessment." *Quarterly Journal of Economics* 107(1): 151–200.

12  Wilson, "Black Unemployment Is Significantly Higher"; Bureau of Labor Statistics, U.S. Department of Labor. "Median Weekly Earnings by Educational Attainment in 2014." Economics Daily, January 23. Retrieved December 17, 2016. www.bls.gov/opub/ted/2015/median-weekly-earnings-by-education-gender-race-and-ethnicity-in-2014.htm.

13  Annie E. Casey Foundation. 2016. "Children in Single-Parent Families by Race." Retrieved December 17, 2016. datacenter.kidscount.org/data/tables/107-children-in-single-parent-families-by#detailed/1/any/false/869,36,868,867,133/10,11,9,12,1,185,13/432,431.

14  Harris, Linda Harris. 2013. "Feel the Heat: The Unrelenting Challenge of Young Black Male Unemployment." Washington, DC: CLASP. Accessed April 1, 2016. www.clasp.org/resources-and-publications/files/Feel-the-Heat_Web.pdf.

15  Pew Research Center. 2015. "Parenting in America." December 17. Accessed December 17, 2016. www.pewsocialtrends.org/2015/12/17/1-the-american-family-today/; Darity, Jr., William A. and Samuel L. Myers, Jr. 1998. *Persistent Disparity: Race and Economic Inequality in the United States Since 1945.* Cheltenham, UK: Edward Elgar.

16  Fields, Barbara J. 1982. "Ideology and Race in American History." Pp.143–177 In J. M. Kousser and J.M. McPherson, Eds. *Region, Race, and Reconstruction: Essays in Honor of C. Vann Woodward.* New York: Oxford University Press. See also Fields, Barbara. 1990. "Slavery, Race and Ideology in the United States of America." *New Left Review* 1(181): 95–118.

17  Roberts, Neil. 2015. *Freedom as Marronage.* Chicago, IL: University of Chicago Press; Holt, Thomas C. 2010. *Children of Fire: A History of African Americans.* New York: Hill and Wang.

18  Blackmon, Douglas A. *Slavery by Another Name: The Re-Enslavement of Black Americans from the Civil War to World War II.* New York: Anchor.

19  Amenta, Edwin. 2000. *Bold Relief: Institutional Politics and the Origins of Modern American Social Policy.* Princeton, NJ: Princeton University Press; Hacker, Jacob S. and Paul Pierson. 2002. "Business Power and Social Policy: Employers and the Formation of the American Welfare State." *Politics & Society* 30(2): 277–325. See also Lieberman, Robert C. 1998. *Shifting the Color Line: Race and the American Welfare State.* Cambridge, MA: Harvard University Press; Skocpol, Theda. 1995. *Social Policy in the United States: Future Possibilities in Historical Perspective.* Princeton, NJ: Princeton University Press.

20  Smith, Roger M. 1997. *Civic Ideals: Conflicting Visions of Citizenship in U.S. History.* New Haven, CT: Yale University Press. See also Lichtenstein, Nelson. 2002. *State*

*of the Union: A Century of American Labor*. Princeton, NJ: Princeton University Press; Mettler, Suzanne. 1998. *Dividing Citizens: Gender and Federalism in New Deal Public Policy*. Ithaca, NY: Cornell University Press. See also Skocpol, Theda. 1992. *Protecting Soldiers and Mothers: The Political Origins of Social Policy in the United States*. Cambridge, MA: Harvard University Press.

21 Farhang, Sean and Ira Katznelson. 2005. "The Southern Imposition: Congress and Labor in the New Deal and Fair Deal." *Studies in American Political Development* 19(1): 1–30; Frymer, *Black and Blue*.

22 United States Census Bureau. 1930. "Color and Nativity of Gainful Workers."

23 Ibid.; National Domestic Workers Alliance. N.d. "Employment Protections for Domestic Workers: An Overview of Federal Law." Retrieved on February 17, 2016. www.domesticworkers.org/sites/default/files/Domestic_Worker_Employment_Protections_Federal.pdf.

24 Frymer, *Black and Blue*; McCall, Leslie. 2001. *Complex Inequality: Gender, Class and Race in the New Economy*. New York: Routledge. See also Stein, Judith. 1998. *Running Steel, Running America: Race, Economic Policy and the Decline of Liberalism*. Chapel Hill: University of North Carolina Press. See also Sides, Josh. 2003. *L.A. City Limits: African American Los Angeles from the Great Depression to the Present*. Berkeley: University of California Press.

25 Card and Krueger, "School Quality and Black–White Relative Earnings."

26 Collins, Sharon M. 1983. "The Making of the Black Middle Class." *Social Problems* 30(4): 369–382.

27 Brimmer, Andrew. 1976. "The Economic Position of Black Americans: 1976." In *A Special Report to the National Commission for Manpower Policy, Special Report No. 9*. Washington, DC: Commission for Manpower, 25–30; Freeman, Richard. 1973. "Changes in the Labor Market for Black Americans, 1948–72." *Brookings Papers on Economic Activity* 1973(1): 67–120; Purcell, Theodore V. 1977. "Management and Affirmative Action in the Late Seventies." In Leonard J. Hausman and Orley Ashenfelter, Eds. *Equal Rights and Industrial Relations*. Madison: Industrial Relations Research Association, University of Wisconsin, 71–103.

28 Sides, *L.A. City Limits*; Lehman, Nicholas. 1992. *The Promised Land: The Great Black Migration and How It Changed America*. New York: Vintage. See also Wilkerson, Isabel. 2010. *The Warmth of Other Suns: The Epic Story of America's Great Migration*. New York: Vintage; Wilson, William Julius. 1978. *The Declining Significance of Race*. Chicago, IL: University of Chicago Press. See also Wilson, William Julius. 1996. *When Work Disappears: The World of the New Urban Poor*. New York: W. W. Norton. See also Wilson, William Julius. 2009. *More Than Just Race: Being Black and Poor in the Inner City*. New York: W. W. Norton.

29 Tye, Larry. 2005. *Rising from the Rails: Pullman Porters and the Making of the Black Middle Class*. New York: Henry Holt; Zeitlin, Maurice and Frank L. Weyher. 2001. "Black and White, Unite and Fight: Interracial Working-Class Solidarity and Racial Employment Equality." *American Journal of Sociology* 107(2):430–467. See also Rosenfeld, Jack. 2014. *What Unions No Longer Do*. Cambridge, MA: Harvard University Press.

30 Gottschalk, Marie. 2015. *Caught: The Prison State and the Lockdown of American Politics*. Princeton, NJ: Princeton University Press.

31  Sides, *L.A. City Limits*, 183.

32  Stein, *Running Steel*. See also McCall, *Complex Inequality*.

33  Stiglitz, Joseph E. 2015. *Rewriting the Rules of the American Economy: An Agenda for Growth and Shared Prosperity*. New York: W. W. Norton. See also Wright, Eric Olin and Rachel E. Dwyer. 2003. "The Patterns of Job Expansions in the USA: A Comparison of the 1960s and 1990s." *Socio-Economic Review* 1: 289–325. See also Stone, Katherine V.W. 2004. *From Widgets to Digits: Employment Regulation for the Changing Workplace*. New York: Cambridge University Press. See also Weil, David. 2014. *The Fissured Workplace: Why Work Became So Bad for So Many and What Can Be Done to Improve It*. New York: Harvard University Press.

34  Johnston, Paul. 1994. *Success While Others Fail: Social Movement Unionism and the Public Workplace*. Ithaca, NY: Cornell University Press. See also Parks, Virginia. 2010. "Revisiting Shibboleths of Race and Urban Economy: Black Employments in Manufacturing and the Public Sector Compared, Chicago 1950–2000." *International Journal of Urban and Regional Research* 35(1): 110–129.

35  Donohue, John J. and James Heckman. 1991. "Continuous Versus Episodic Change: The Impact of Civil Rights Policy on the Economic Status of Blacks." National Bureau of Economic Research Working Paper No. 3894. Retrieved May 6, 2016. www.nber.org/papers/w3894.pdf.

36  Collins, "Making of the Black Middle Class," 371.

37  Parks, "Revisiting Shibboleths."

38  Wilson, *Declining Significance of Race*; Wilson, *When Work Disappears*; Wilson, *More Than Just Race*.

39  Reed, Adolph, Jr. 1999. *Stirrings in the Jug: Black Politics in the Post-Segregation Era*. Minneapolis: University of Minnesota Press. See also Thompson, J. Phillip III. 2006. *Double Trouble: Black Mayors, Black Communities and the Call for a Deep Democracy*. New York: Oxford University Press.

40  Sides, *L.A. City Limits*, 179.

41  Stainback, Kevin and Donald Tomaskovic-Devey. 2012. *Documenting Desegregation: Racial and Gender Segregation in Private-Sector Employment Since the Civil Rights Act*. New York: Russell Sage Foundation.

42  Ibid.

43  Hegewisch, Ariane and Heidi Hartmann. 2014. "Occupational Segregation and the Gender Wage Gap: A Job Half Done." Washington, DC: Institute for Women's Policy Research. Retrieved May 6, 2016. www.iwpr.org/publications/pubs/occupational-segregation-and-the-gender-wage-gap-a-job-half-done.

44  Austin et al., "Whiter Jobs, Higher Wages."

45  Tilly, Chris and Philip Moss. 2001. *Stories Employers Tell: Race, Skill, and Hiring in America*. New York: Russell Sage Foundation. See also Beirnat, Monica and Diane Kobrynowicz. 1997. "Gender- and Race-Based Standards of Competence: Lower Minimum Standards but Higher Ability Standards for Devalued Groups." *Journal of Personality and Social Psychology* 72(3): 544–557.

46  Pager et al., "Discrimination in a Low-Wage Labor Market."

47  Bertrand, Marianne and Sendhil Mullainathan. 2004. "Are Emily and Greg More Employable than Lakisha and Jamal? A Field Experiment on Labor Market Discrimination." *American Economic Review* 94(4): 991–1013; Mincy, Ronald B. 1993. "The Urban Institute Audit Studies: Their Research and Policy

Context." In Michael Fix and Raymond J. Struyk, Eds. *Clear and Convincing Evidence: Measurement of Discrimination in America.* Washington, DC: Urban Institute. 165–186. See also Bendick, Marc, Jr., Charles W. Jackson, and Victor A. Reinoso. 1997. "Measuring Employment Discrimination Through Controlled Experiments." In James B. Stewart, Ed. *African Americans and Post Industrial Labor Market.* New Brunswick, NJ: Transaction. 77–100.

48 Mincy, "Urban Institute Audit Studies."

49 Pager, Devah, Bruce Western, and Bart Bonikowski. 2009. "Discrimination in a Low-Wage Labor Market: A Field Experiment." *American Sociological Review* 74(5):777-799. www.ncbi.nlm.nih.gov/pmc/articles/PMC1497358/.

50 Pager, Devah. 2003 "The Mark of a Criminal Record." *American Journal of Sociology* 108(5): 937–975.

51 Ibid.; Stiglitz, *Rewriting the Rules.* See also Wilson, *When Work Disappears*; *Op. Cit.* Holt, *Children of Fire*; Holt, Thomas C. 2000. *The Problem of Race in the 21st Century.* New York: Harvard University Press.

52 Schmitt, John and Ben Zipperer. 2008. "The Decline in African American Representation in Unions and Manufacturing, 1979–2007." Washington, DC: Center for Economic Policy Research. Retrieved May 6, 2016. cepr.net/documents/publications/unions_aa_2008_02.pdf.

53 Ibid.

54 Jones, Janelle and John Schmitt. 2014. "Union Advantage for Black Workers," Center for Economic Policy Research, February. Accessed December 17, 2016. cepr.net/documents/black-union-2014-02.pdf.

55 Zipperer, Ben. 2016. "African American Workers Are Hurt More by the Decline in Union and Manufacturing Jobs." Washington, DC: Washington Center for Equitable Growth, March 31. Accessed December 17, 2016. equitablegrowth.org/equitablog/african-american-workers-are-hurt-more-by-the-decline-in-union-and-manufacturing-jobs/.

56 Pierce, Justin R. and Peter K. Schott. 2012. "The Surprisingly Swift Decline of U.S. Manufacturing Employment." Cambridge, MA: National Bureau of Economic Research. December. Retrieved January 20, 2017. www.nber.org/papers/w18655; McCormack, Richard. 2013. *ReMaking America.* Washington, DC: Alliance for American Manufacturing.

57 DeSilver, Drew. 2015. "5 Facts About the Minimum Wage." Washington, DC: Pew Research Center. Retrieved May 5, 2016. www.pewresearch.org/fact-tank/2015/07/23/5-facts-about-the-minimum-wage.

58 Economist. 2015. "Pay Dirt." May. Retrieved February 17, 2016. www.economist.com/blogs/graphicdetail/2015/05/minimum-wages.

59 colorofchange.org. "Hold Walmart Accountable to Black Workers." Retrieved May 5, 2016. colorofchange.org/campaign/tell-walmart-meet-workers/original_email/; Retail Justice Alliance. 2016. "Basic Facts About Walmart." Retrieved May 5, 2016. retailjusticealliance.org/basic-facts-about-walmart/.

60 McCarty, Nolan, Keith T. Poole, and Howard Rosenthal. 2008. *Polarized America: The Dance of Ideology and Unequal Riches.* Cambridge, MA: MIT Press. See also Pierson, Paul and Theda Skocpol. 2007. *The Transformation of American Politics: Activist Government and the Rise of Conservatism.* Princeton, NJ: Princeton University Press. See also Hacker, Jacob S. and Paul Pierson. 2006. *Off Center: The Republican Revolution and the Erosion of American Democracy.*

New Haven, CT: Yale University Press. See also Bartels, Larry M. 2008. *Unequal Democracy: The Political Economy of the New Gilded Age.* New York: Russell Sage Foundation.

61 Levi, Margaret. 2003. "Organizing Labor: the Prospects for an American Labor Movement." *Perspectives on Politics* 1(1): 45–68. See also Hacker, Jacob S. and Paul Pierson. 2010. *Winner-Take-All Politics: How Washington Made the Rich Richer – and Turned Its Back on the Middle Class.* New York: Simon & Schuster.

62 Stiglitz, *Rewriting the Rules.*

63 Ibid.

64 Ibid.; Center for Popular Democracy. "Building a National Campaign for a Strong Economy: Fed Up." Retrieved May 5, 2016. populardemocracy.org/campaign/building-national-campaign-strong-economy-fed.

65 Pitts, Steven. 2011. "Black Workers and the Public Sector." Berkeley: University of California Berkeley Center for Labor Research and Education. Retrieved May 6, 2016. laborcenter.berkeley.edu/pdf/2011/blacks_public_sector11.pdf.

66 Ibid.

67 Greenstone, Michael and Adam Looney. 2012. "A Record Decline in Government Jobs: Implications for the Economy and America's Workforce." Washington, DC: Brookings Institution. Retrieved May 5, 2016. www.brookings.edu/blogs/jobs/posts/2012/08/03-jobs-greenstone-looney.

68 Laird, Jennifer. 2016. "Public Sector Employment Inequality and the Great Recession." Seattle: University of Washington. Retrieved May 5, 2016. students.washington.edu/jdlaird/laird_public_sector_inequality_042716.pdf.

69 Cooper, David, Mary Gable and Algernon Austin. 2012. "The Public-Sector Jobs Crisis: Women and African Americans Hit Hardest by Job Losses in State and Local Governments." Washington, DC: Economic Policy Institute. Accessed April 5, 2016. www.epi.org/files/2012/bp339-public-sector-jobs-crisis.pdf.

70 Laird, "Public Sector Employment Inequality."

71 Ibid.

## 6 THE RACIAL RULES OF EDUCATION

1 Hanushek, Eric A. and Steven G. Rivkin. 2008. "Harming the Best: How Schools Affect the Black–White Achievement Gap." National Bureau of Economic Research Working Paper No 14211. Retrieved May 10, 2016. www.nber.org/papers/w8741.pdf; Johnson, Rucker C. 2011. "Long-Run Impacts of School Desegregation & School Quality on Adult Attainments." National Bureau of Economic Research Working Paper No. 16664, January 2011. Retrieved May 6, 2016. www.nber.org/papers/w16664.pdf. See also Ashenfelter, Orley, William J. Collins, and Albert Yoon. 2005. "Evaluating the Role of *Brown v. Board of Education* in School Equalization, Desegregation, and the Income of African Americans." National Bureau of Economic Research Working Paper Working Paper No. 11394. Retrieved May 6, 2016. www.nber.org/papers/w11394.pdf.

2 Coleman, James S., et al. 1966. "Equality of Educational Opportunity." Washington, DC: National Center for Education Statistics. Retrieved January 4, 2017. files.eric.ed.gov/fulltext/ED012275.pdf.

3 For an extensive contemporary overview of non-school-based drivers, including family environment, see Research on the Factors for School Success. Sandra

L. Christenson, Ph.D, Professor, College of Education and Human Development and Cathryn Peterson, Teacher, Armstrong High School, Robbinsdale, MN. Revised June 2013 by Kathleen A. Olson, Program Director, Partnering for School Success.

4  Hanushek, Eric A., John F. Kain and Steven G. Rivkin. 2002. "New Evidence About *Brown v. Board of Education*: The Complex Effects of School Racial Composition on Achievement." National Bureau of Economic Research Working Paper No 8741. Retrieved May 10, 2016. www.nber.org/papers/w8741.pdf.

5  Farkas, George. 2008. "How Educational Inequality Develops." In A. C. Lin and D. R. Harris, Eds. *The Colors of Poverty: Why Racial and Ethnic Disparities Persist.* New York: Russell Sage Foundation. 105–134.

6  Ibid.

7  Ahmad, Farah Z. and Katie Hamm. 2013. "The School-Readiness Gap and Preschool Benefits for Children of Color." Washington, DC: Center for American Progress. Retrieved February 2, 2016. cdn.americanprogress.org/wp-content/uploads/2013/11/PreschoolBenefits-brief-2.pdf.

8  Heckman, James. 2006. "Skills Formation and the Economics of Investing in Disadvantaged Children," *Science* (June): 1900–1902.

9  Cascio, Elizabeth U. and Diane Schanzenbach. 2013. "The Impacts of Expanding Access to High Quality Preschool Education." *Brookings Papers on Economic Activity* (Fall): 127–192.

10  National Center for Education Statistics. "Public High School Graduation Rates." Retrieved May 6, 2016. nces.ed.gov/programs/coe/indicator_coi.asp.

11  National Center for Education Statistics. "The Condition of Education 2015." Retrieved May 6, 2016. nces.ed.gov/programs/coe/pdf/coe_caa.pdf.

12  Orfield, Gary and Erika Frankenberg. 2014. "Brown at 60: Great Progress, a Long Retreat, and an Uncertain Future." Los Angeles, CA: Civil Rights Project/Proyecto Derechos Civiles at UCLA. Retrieved May 6, 2016. civilrightsproject.ucla.edu/research/k-12-education/integration-and-diversity/brown-at-60-great-progress-a-long-retreat-and-an-uncertain-future/Brown-at-60-051814.pdf.

13  National Equity Atlas. "Percentage of Students by Poverty Level." Retrieved March 26, 2015. nationalequityatlas.org/indicators/School_poverty/By_race~ethnicity:35576/United_States/false/Year(s):2014/School_type:All_public_schools/.

14  Irons, Peter. 2004. "Jim Crow's Schools." Washington, DC: American Federation of Teachers. Retrieved May 6, 2016. www.aft.org/periodical/american-educator/summer-2004.

15  See Johnson, "Long-Run Impacts."

16  McGuinn, Patrick and Frederick Hess. 2005. "Freedom from Ignorance? The Great Society and the Evolution of the Elementary and Secondary Education Act of 1965." In S. M. Milkis and J. Mileur, Eds. *The Great Society and the High Tide of Liberalism.* Amherst: University of Massachusetts Press. 289–320.

17  Hannah-Jones, Nikole. 2014. "Segregation Now." *ProPublica.* propublica.org/article/segregation-now-the-resegregation-of-americas-schools/#intro. See also Guryan, Jonathan. 2004. "Desegregation and Black Dropout Rates." *American Economic Review* 94 (4): 919–943.

18  Orfield, Gary. 2009. "Reviving the Goal of an Integrated Society: A 21st Century Challenge." Los Angeles, CA: Civil Rights Project/Proyecto Derechos Civiles at UCLA. Retrieved February 2, 2016. civilrightsproject.ucla.edu/research/k-12-education/integration-and-diversity/reviving-the-goal-of-an-integrated-society-a-21st-century-challenge.

19 Barton, Paul and Richard Coley. 2010. "The Black–White Achievement Gap: When Progress Stopped." Educational Testing Service Policy Information Report. Retrieved February 3, 2016. www.ets.org/Media/Research/pdf/PICBWGAP.pdf.

20 Guryan, Jonathan. 2004. "Desegregation and Black Dropout Rates." *American Economic Review* 94 (4): 919–943.

21 Grissmer, D. Flanagan, A., & Williamson, S. 1998. "Why Did the Black–White Score Gap Narrow in the 1970s and 1980s?" In C. Jencks & M. Phillips, Eds. *The Black–White Test Score Gap*. Washington, DC: Brookings Institution Press. Pages 182-226.

22 Johnson, "Long-Run Impacts."

23 Reardon, Sean F. 2011. "The Widening Academic Achievement Gap Between the Rich and the Poor: New Evidence and Possible Explanations." In G. J. Duncan and R. J. Murnane, Eds. *Whither Opportunity? Rising Inequality, Schools, and Children's Life Chances*. New York: Russell Sage Foundation. 91–116.

24 Johnson, "Long-Run Impacts."

25 Reardon, Sean F. 2016. "School Segregation and Racial Academic Achievement Gaps." Stanford Center for Education Policy Analysis Working Paper No 15–21. Retrieved April 30, 2016. cepa.stanford.edu/sites/default/files/wp15-12v201601.pdf.

26 For a summary of this debate, see Biddle, Bruce J. and David C. Berliner. 2002. "A Research Synthesis/Unequal School Funding in the United States," *Educational Leadership* 59(8): 48–59.

27 Jackson, C. Kirabo, Rucker Johnson, and Claudia Persico. 2014. "The Effect of School Finance Reforms on the Distribution of Spending, Academic Achievement, and Adult Outcomes." National Bureau of Economic Research Working Paper No. 20118. Retrieved May 6, 2016. www.nber.org/papers/w20118.

28 Orfield, Gary and Erica Frankenberg. 2014. "Brown at 60: Great Progress, a Long Retreat, and an Uncertain Future." Los Angeles, CA: The Civil Rights Project/Proyecto Derechos Civiles at UCLA. Retrieved May 6, 2016. civilrightsproject.ucla.edu/research/k-12-education/integration-and-diversity/brown-at-60-great-progress-a-long-retreat-and-an-uncertain-future; Orfield, Gary, John Kucsera, and Genevieve Siegel-Hawley. 2012. "E Pluribus...Separation: Deepening Double Segregation for More Students," The Civil Rights Project. Accessed May 5, 2016. civilrightsproject.ucla.edu/research/k-12-education/integration-and-diversity/mlk-national/epluribus...separation-deepening-double-segregation-for-more-students/orfield_epluribus_revised_omplete_2012.pdf.

29 Ibid.

30 Lukas, J. Anthony. *Common Ground: A Turbulent Decade in the Lives of Three American Families*. New York: Vintage.

31 Kozol, Jonathan. 2005. *The Shame of the Nation: The Restoration of Apartheid Schooling in America*. New York: Random House.

32 Reardon, Sean F., Elena Grewal, Demetra Kalogrides and Erica Greenberg. 2012. "Brown Fades: The End of Court-Ordered School Desegregation and the Resegregation of American Public Schools." *Journal of Policy Analysis and Management*. 31(4): 876–904.

33 Kucsera, John and Gary Orfield. 2014. "New York State's Extreme School Segregation Inequality, Inaction and a Damaged Future," March. Los Angeles, CA: Civil Rights Project/Proyecto Derechos Civiles at UCLA. Retrieved April 11, 2016. files.eric.ed.gov/fulltext/ED558739.pdf.

34 Rothstein, Richard. 2014. "The Racial Achievement Gap, Segregated Schools, and Segregated Neighborhoods – a Constitutional Insult." Washington, DC: Economic Policy Institute. Retrieved May 6, 2016. www.epi.org/publication/the-racial-achievement-gap-segregated-schools-and-segregated-neighborhoods-a-constitutional-insult/.

35 Borjas, George. 1994. "Ethnicity, Neighborhoods, and Human Capital Externalities." National Bureau of Economic Research Working Paper No. 4912. Retrieved May 6, 2016. www.nber.org/papers/w4912.pdf.

36 Sampson, Robert J. and Patrick Sharkey. 2008. "Neighborhood Selection and the Social Reproduction of Concentrated Racial Inequality." *Demography* 45: 1–29; Orfield, Gary and Chungmei Lee. 2007. "Historic Reversals, Accelerating Resegregation, and the Need for New Integration Strategies." Los Angeles, CA: Civil Rights Project/Proyecto Derechos Civiles at UCLA. Retrieved May 6, 2016. civilrightsproject.ucla.edu/research/k-12-education/integration-and-diversity/historic-reversals-accelerating-resegregation-and-the-need-for-new-integration-strategies-1/orfield-historic-reversals-accelerating.pdf.

37 Hawkins, Carey Ash and Chaneé D. Anderson. 2013. "The Same but Different: 'Post-Racial' Inequality in American Public Education." In J. K. Donnor and A. Dixson, Eds. *Resegregation of Schools: Education and Race in the Twenty-First Century.* New York: Routledge. 1–26. Page 1.

38 See Spatig-Amerikaner, Ary. 2012. "Unequal Education: Federal Loophole Enables Lower Spending on Students of Color." Washington, DC: Center for American Progress. Retrieved May 6, 2016. www.americanprogress.org/wp-content/uploads/2012/08/UnequalEduation.pdf.

39 Bush. George W. "NAACP 91st Annual Convention." Retrieved April 11, 2016. www.washingtonpost.com/wp-srv/onpolitics/electronics/bushtext071000.htm.

40 Orfield and Frankenberg, "Brown at 60." Page 4.

41 See Reardon, Sean F., Erica H. Greenberg, Demetra Kalogrides, Kenneth A. Shores, and Rachel A. Valentino. 2013. "Left Behind? The Effect of No Child Left Behind on Academic Achievement Gaps." Stanford, CA: Stanford Center for Education Policy Analysis. Retrieved May 6, 2016. cepa.stanford.edu/content/left-behind-effect-no-child-left-behind-academic-achievement-gaps.

42 McKinsey and Company. "The Economic Impact of the Achievement Gap in America's Schools." Retrieved May 6, 2016. mckinseyonsociety.com/downloads/reports/Education/achievement_gap_report.pdf.

43 Darling-Hammond, Linda. 2000. "Teacher Quality and Student Achievement: A Review of State Policy Evidence." *Education Policy Analysis Archives* 8(1): 1–44.

44 Darling-Hammond, "Teacher Quality."

45 Johnson, "Long-Run Impacts."

46 Belway, Shakti. 2010. "Access Denied: New Orleans Students and Parents Identify Barriers to Public Education." New Orleans, LA: Southern Poverty Law Center. Retrieved April 11, 2016. www.splcenter.org/sites/default/files/d6_legacy_files/downloads/publication/SPLC_report_Access_Denied.pdf; Welner, Kevin. G. 2013. "The Dirty Dozen: How Charter Schools Influence Student Enrollment." Teachers College Record. Retrieved May 6, 2016. nepc.colorado.edu/publication/TCR-Dirty-Dozen.

47 Kim, J. & Sunderman, G. L. 2004. "Does NCLB Provide Good Choices for Students in Low Performing Schools?" Cambridge, MA: Civil Rights Project at

Harvard University. Retrieved May 6, 2016. civilrightsproject.ucla.edu/research/ k-12-education/integration-and-diversity/does-nclb-provide-good-choices-for-students-in-low-performing-schools/kim-sunderman-does-nclb-provide-choices-2004.pdf; "Data Snapshot: School Discipline." *Department of Education*, Issue Brief No. 1, March 2014. ocrdata.ed.gov/Downloads/CRDC-School-Discipline-Snapshot.pdf.

48  Losen, Daniel J., Michael A. Keith II, Cheri L. Hodson, and Tia E. Martinez. 2016. "Charter Schools, Civil Rights and School Discipline: A Comprehensive Review." Civil Rights Project, March 15. Retrieved December 21, 2016. www.civilrightsproject.ucla.edu/ resources/projects/center-for-civil-rights-remedies/school-to-prison-folder/federal-reports/charter-schools-civil-rights-and-school-discipline-a-comprehensive-review.

49  Bruenig, Matt. "Why White High School Drop Outs Have More Wealth Than Black College Graduates." New York: Demos. Retrieved February 2, 2016. www.demos.org/blog/10/ 24/14/why-white-high-school-drop-outs-have-more-wealth-black-college-graduates.

50  Sullivan, Laura, Tatjana Meschede, Lars Dietrich, and Thomas Shapiro. 2015. "The Racial Wealth Gap." New York: Demos. Retrieved May 6, 2016. www.demos.org/ sites/default/files/publications/RacialWealthGap_1.pdf.

51  Hamilton et al., "Umbrellas Don't Make it Rain."

52  Rothstein, Richard. 2004. *Class and Schools: Using Social, Economic, and Educational Reform to Close the Black–White Achievement Gap*. Washington, DC, and New York: Economic Policy Institute and Teachers College Press; Ravitch, Diane. 2013. *Reign of Error: The Hoax of the Privatization Movement and the Danger to America's Public Schools*. New York: Vintage.

53  Persson, Jonas. 2015. "Vouchers on the Move: Return to School Segregation?" *PRWatch*, April 28. Retrieved December 20, 2016. www.prwatch.org/news/2015/ 02/12730/segregation-school-vouchers.

54  Ibid.

55  Brunner, Eric J., Jennifer Imazeki, and Stephen L. Ross. 2006. "Universal Vouchers and White Flight." *Economics Working Papers*, January. Retrieved December 20, 2016. digitalcommons.uconn.edu/cgi/viewcontent.cgi?article=1038&context=econ_ wpapers.

56  Ravitch, Diane. 2013. *Reign of Error: The Hoax of the Privatization Movement and the Danger to America's Public Schools*. Alfred A. Knopf: New York. Page 206.

57  Kucsera, John and Gary Orfield. 2014. "New York State's Extreme School Segregation: Inequality, Inaction and a Damaged Future." Los Angeles, CA: The Civil Rights Project. civilrightsproject.ucla.edu/research/k-12-education/ integration-and-diversity/ny-norflet-report-placeholder/Kucsera-New-York-Extreme-Segregation-2014.pdf. Page iv.

58  McKinsey, "Economic Impact."

## 7 THE RACIAL RULES OF CRIMINAL JUSTICE

1  Dolovich, Sharon. 2012. "Creating the Permanent Prisoner." *UCLA School of Law Public law & Legal Research Paper Series*. Retrieved April 10, 2016. papers.ssrn.com/ sol3/papers.cfm?abstract_id=1845904.

2  Clear, Todd. 2007. *Imprisoning Communities: How Mass Incarceration Makes Disadvantaged Neighborhoods Worse*. New York: Oxford University Press, p. 3.

3  Waquant, Loïc. 2000. "The New 'Peculiar Institution': On the Prison as Surrogate Ghetto." *Theoretical Criminology* 4(3): 377–389. Retrieved May 5, 2016. www.soc .umn.edu/~uggen/Wacquant_TC_00.pdf.

4  Alexander, Michelle. 2012. *"The New Jim Crow: Mass Incarceration in the Age of Colorblindness."* New York: New Press.

5  American Civil Liberties Union. 2014. "Racial Disparities in Sentencing Hearing on Reports of Racism in the Justice System of the United States." New York: American Civil Liberties Union. Retrieved May 5, 2016. www.aclu.org/sites/default/files/ assets/141027_iachr_racial_disparities_aclu_submission_0.pdf.

6  United States Department of Justice Civil Rights Division. 2015. *Investigation of the Ferguson Police Department.* Washington, DC: United States Department of Justice. Retrieved May 5, 2016. www.justice.gov/sites/default/files/opa/press-releases/ attachments/2015/03/04/ferguson_police_department_report.pdf.

7  Pelaez, Vicky. 2014 "The Prison Industry in the United States: Big Business or a New Form of Slavery?" New York: El Diario-La Prensa. Retrieved May 5, 2016. www.globalresearch.ca/the-prison-industry-in-the-united-states-big-business-or- a-new-form-of-slavery/8289.

8  The Sentencing Project. Nd. "Americans with Criminal Records." Washington, DC: Sentencing Project. Retrieved May 5, 2016. www.sentencingproject.org/doc/ publications/cc_HiT_CriminalRecords_profile_1.pdf.

9  Wagner, Peter and Bernadette Rabuy. 2016. "Mass Incarceration: The Whole Pie 2016." Northhampton, MA: Prison Policy Initiative. Retrieved May 5, 2016. www .prisonpolicy.org/reports/pie2016.html.

10  Quigley, Bill. 2015. "40 Reasons Our Jails and Prisons Are Full of Black and Poor People." *Common Dreams.* Retrieved May 5, 2016. www.commondreams .org/views/2015/06/02/40-reasons-our-jails-and-prisons-are-full-black-and- poor-people.

11  Sentencing Project. Nd. "Racial Disparity." Washington, DC: Sentencing Project. Retrieved May 5, 2016. www.sentencingproject.org/template/page.cfm?id=122.

12  Ibid.

13  Hogg, R. S., E. F. Druyts, S. Burris, E. Drucker, and S. A. Strathdee. 2008. "Years of Life Lost to Prison: Racial and Gender Gradients in the United States of America." *Harm Reduction Journal* 5(4). Retrieved May 4, 2016. www.ncbi.nlm.nih.gov/ pubmed/18221538.

14  Ibid.

15  Sentencing Project. 2015. "Incarcerated Women and Girls." Washington, DC: Sentencing Project. Retrieved May 5, 2016. www.sentencingproject.org/doc/ publications/cc_Incarcerated_Women_Factsheet_Sep24sp.pdf.

16  Carson, Ann E. 2014. *Prisoners in 2013.* Washington, DC: U.S. Department of Justice. Retrieved May 5, 2016. www.bjs.gov/content/pub/pdf/p13.pdf.

17  ACLU, "Hearing on Reports."

18  Mitchell, Michael. 2014. "The Causes and Costs of High Incarceration Rates." Washington, DC: Center on Budget and Policy Priorities. Retrieved April 1, 2016. www.cbpp.org/blog/the-causes-and-costs-of-high-incarceration-rates.

19  United States Department of Justice Civil Rights Division, *Invesigation of the Ferguson Police Department.*

20  Chesney-Lind, Meda. 2002. ""Imprisoning Women: The Unintended Victims of Mass Imprisonment." In Mauer, Marc and Meda Chesney-Lind, Eds. *Invisible*

*Punishment: The Collateral Consequences of Mass Imprisonment.* New York: New Press.

21 Ibid.

22 Ibid., 79–94.

23 Ibid.

24 Ibid.

25 Haviland, M., V. Frye, V. Rajah, J. Thukral, and M. Trinity. 2001. "The Family Protection and Domestic Violence Intervention Act of 1995: Examining the Effects of Mandatory Arrest in New York City." New York: Family Violence Project, Urban Justice Center.

26 Sentencing Project. 2015. "Incarcerated Women and Girls." Washington, DC: Sentencing Project. Retrieved May 5, 2016. www.sentencingproject.org/doc/ publications/cc_Incarcerated_Women_Factsheet_Sep24sp.pdf; James, Doris J. and Lauren E. Glaze. 2006. *Mental Health Problems of Prison and Jail Inmates* (Bureau of Justice Statistics Special Report). Washington, DC: Department of Justice. Retrieved May 2, 2016. www.bjs.gov/content/pub/pdf/mhppji.pdf.

27 Correctional Association of New York. 2015. "Reproductive Injustice: The State of Reproductive Health Care for Women in New York State Prisons." Retrieved May 3, 2016. www.correctionalassociation.org/press-release/correctional-association-releases-5-year-study-of-reproductive-healthcare-for-women-in-new-york-prisons.

28 Clear, Todd R. 2007. *Imprisoning Communities: How Mass Incarceration Makes Disadvantaged Neighborhoods Worse.* New York: Oxford University Press, p. 10.

29 National Center for Transgender Equality. 2012. "Prison and Detention Reform." Washington, DC: National Center for Transgender Equality. Retrieved January 6, 2017. www.transequality.org/sites/default/files/docs/resources/NCTE_Blueprint_ for_Equality2012_Prison_Reform.pdf.

30 Shames, Alison, Jessa Wilcox, and Ram Subramanian. 2015. "Solitary Confinement: Common Misconceptions and Emerging Safe Alternatives." New York: Vera Institute of Justice Center on Sentencing and Corrections. Retrieved January 6, 2017. archive.vera.org/sites/default/files/resources/downloads/solitary-confinement-misconceptions-safe-alternatives-report_1.pdf.

31 Weir, Kirsten. 2012. "Alone, in 'the Hole.'" *American Psychological Association* 43(5): 54. Retrieved January 7, 2017. www.apa.org/monitor/2012/05/solitary.aspx.

32 Sears, Clare, Ed. 2010. "Introduction: Sexuality, Criminalization, and Sexual Control." *Social Justice* 31(1): 1–6.

33 Beck, Allen J. 2014. "Sexual Victimization in Prisons and Jails Reported by Inmates, 2011–2012." Washington, DC: Bureau of Justice Statistics, U.S. Department of Justice Office of Justice Programs. Retrieved January 6, 2017. www.bjs.gov/content/ pub/pdf/svpjri1112_st.pdf.

34 Beck, Allen J. 2015. "PREA Data Collection Activities, 2015." Washington, DC: Bureau of Justice Statistics. Retrieved August 19, 2016 (www.bjs.gov/index .cfm?ty=pbdetail&iid=5320).

35 Blackmon, *Slavery by Another Name.*

36 Ibid, Page 7.

37 Ibid.

38 Ibid.; Browne, Jaron. 2007. "Rooted in Slavery: Prison Labor Exploitation." *Race, Poverty & the Environment* (Spring). Accessed May 5, 2016. www.reimaginerpe.org/ files/RPE14-1_Browne-s.pdf.

39 Blackmon, *Slavery by Another Name*, Page 96.
40 Travis, Jeremy. 2002. "Invisible Punishment: An Instrument of Social Exclusion." In Mauer and Chesney-Lind, Eds. *Invisible Punishment*. 20–21.
41 Ibid.
42 Ibid, Page 21.
43 Ibid, Page 21.
44 Dolovich, "Creating the Permanent Prisoner," Page 102.
45 Western, Bruce. 2006. *Punishment and Inequality in America*. New York: Russell Sage Foundation. 4.
46 Gottschalk, Marie. 2014. *Caught: The Prison State and the Lockdown of American Politics*. Princeton, NJ: Princeton University Press.
47 Khalil Gibran Muhammad. 2011. *The Condemnation of Blackness: Race, Crime and the Making of Modern Urban America*. Cambridge, MA: Harvard University Press.
48 Clear, *Imprisoning Communities*, Page 50.
49 Harris, Andrew M. 2016. "Mandatory Minimum Sentencing: Second Thoughts about Preset Prison Terms." *Bloomberg View*, January 12. Retrieved May 2, 2016. www.bloombergview.com/quicktake/mandatory-minimum-sentencing.
50 Rovner, Joshua. 2016. "Juvenile Life Without Parole: An Overview." Washington, DC: Sentencing Project. Retrieved January 5, 2017. www.sentencingproject.org/publications/juvenile-life-without-parole/.
51 ACLU, "Hearing on Reports."
52 Clear, *Imprisoning Communities*, Page 51.
53 Kelling, George L. and James Q. Wilson. 1982. "Broken Windows: The Police and Neighborhood Safety," March, *The Atlantic*. theatlantic.com/magazine/archive/1982/03/broken-windows/304465/.
54 Childress, Sarah. 2016. "The Problem with 'Broken Windows' Policing." *PBS Frontline*, June 28. Retrieved January 6, 2017. www.pbs.org/wgbh/frontline/article/the-problem-with-broken-windows-policing/.
55 Eure, Philip K., Inspector General, Office of the Inspector General for the NYPD. 2016. "The New York City Department of Investigation's Office of the Inspector General for the New York City Police Department Releases a Report and Analyses on the NYPD's Quality-of-Life Enforcement." City of New York Department of Investigation. Retrieved January 6, 2017. www1.nyc.gov/assets/oignypd/downloads/pdf/OIGNYPD-Quality-of-Life-2010-2015-PR.pdf.
56 Haney-Lopez, Ian. 2014. *Dog Whistle Politics*. New York: Oxford University Press.
57 Schwartzapfel, Beth and Bill Keller. 2015. "Willie Horton Revisited." Marshall Project. Retrieved January 5, 2017. www.themarshallproject.org/2015/05/13/willie-horton-revisited#.1I0JfGW4h.
58 Hinton, Elizabeth, Julilly Kohler-Hausman, and Vesla Weaver. 2016. "Did Blacks Really Endorse the 1994 Crime Bill?" *New York Times*, April 13. Retrieved April 28, 2016. www.nytimes.com/2016/04/13/opinion/did-blacks-really-endorse-the-1994-crime-bill.html?_r=0.
59 Ibid.
60 ACLU, "Hearing on Reports," 5.
61 Ibid.
62 Vagins, Deborah J. and Jesselyn McCurdy. 2006. "Cracks in the System: Twenty Years of the Unjust Federal Crack Cocaine Law." New York: American Civil Liberties

Union. Retrieved April 3, 2016. www.aclu.org/sites/default/files/field_document/cracksinsystem_20061025.pdf.

63  ACLU, "Hearing on Reports," 6.

64  Vagins and McCurdy, "Cracks in the System."

65  Clear, *Imprisoning Communities*, 8.

66  Travis, "Invisible Punishment," 22.

67  Ibid.

68  Dolovich, "Creating the Permanent Prisoner."

69  Ibid.

70  Davis, Angela. 1998. "Prosecution and Race: The Power and Privilege of Discretion." *Fordham Law Review* 67. Retrieved April 1, 2016. ir.lawnet.fordham.edu/flr/vol67/iss1/.

71  Travis, Jeremy, Bruce Western, and Steve Redburn. 2014. *The Growth of Incarceration in the United States: Exploring Causes and Consequences*. Washington, DC: National Academies Press. 98.

72  United States Department of Justice Civil Rights Division, *Invesigation of the Ferguson Police Department*.

73  Ibid.

74  Lawyers' Committee for Civil Rights of the San Francisco Bay Area. "Not Just a Ferguson Problem: How Traffic Courts Drive Inequality in California." Retrieved May 7, 2016. www.lccr.com/wp-content/uploads/Not-Just-a-Ferguson-Problem-How-Traffic-Courts-Drive-Inequality-in-California-4.20.15.pdf.

75  Clear, *Imprisoning Communities*, 54.

76  Pinto, Nick. 2015. "The Bail Trap." *New York Times*, August 13. Retrieved April 1, 2016. www.nytimes.com/2015/08/16/magazine/the-bail-trap.html?_r=0.

77  Rabuy, Bernadette and Daniel Kopf. 2015. "Prisons of Poverty: Uncovering the Pre-Incarceration Incomes of the Imprisoned." *Prison Policy Initiative*. Retrieved May 7, 2016. www.prisonpolicy.org/reports/income.html.

78  Clear, *Imprisoning Communities*, 4.

79  Ibid., 9; Western, *Punishment and Inequality*.

80  Petersilia, Joan. 2003. *When Prisoners Come Home: Parole and Prisoner Reentry*. New York: Oxford University Press; Festen, Marcia and Sunny Fischer. 2002. *Navigating Reentry: The Experiences and Perceptions of Ex-Offenders Seeking Employment*. Chicago, IL: Chicago Urban League; Nelson, Marta, Perry Deess, and Charlotte Allen. 1999. "The First Month Out: Post-Incarceration Experiences in New York City." New York: Vera Institute of Justice. vera.org/publications/the-first-month-out-post-incarceration-experiences-in-new-york-city.

81  Travis et al., *The Growth of Incarceration in the United States*.

82  Western, *Punishment and Inequality*, 112.

83  Saltzburg, Stephen. 2011. "Written Testimony of Stephen Saltzburg." *EEOC to Examine Arrest and Conviction Records as a Hiring Barrier*. Retrieved May 6, 2016. www.eeoc.gov/eeoc/meetings/7-26-11/saltzburg.cfm; see also Stiglitz, Joseph. 2016. *Rewriting the Rules of the American Economy: An Agenda for Growth and Shared Prosperity*. New York: W. W. Norton.

84  Western, *Punishment and Inequality*, 112.

85  Ibid.

86  Wakefield, Sara and Christopher Wildeman. 2014. *Children of the Prison Boom: Mass Incarceration and the Future of American Inequality*. New York: Oxford University Press. 18.

87  Dolovich, "Creating the Permanent Prisoner," 105.

88  Ibid., 106.

89  Annie E. Casey Foundation. 2016. "A Shared Sentence: The Devastating Toll of Parental Incarceration on Kids, Families and Communities." Baltimore, MD: Annie E. Casey Foundation. Retrieved April 27, 2016. www.aecf.org/m/resourcedoc/aecf-asharedsentence-2016.pdf.

90  Wakefield and Wildeman, "Children of the Prison Boom."

91  Ibid, 18.

92  Pew Center on the States. 2010. "Collateral Costs: Incarceration's Effect on Economic Mobility." Washington, DC: Pew Charitable Trusts. Retrieved May 5, 2016. www.pewtrusts.org/~/media/legacy/uploadedfiles/pcs_assets/2010/collateralcosts1pdf.

93  deVuono-Powell, Saneta, Chris Schweidler, Alicia Walters, and Azadeh Zohrabi. 2015. "Who Pays? The True Cost of Incarceration on Families." Oakland, CA: Ella Baker Center, Forward Together, Research Action Design.

94  Ibid.

95  Ibid.

96  Annie E. Casey Foundation, "Shared Sentence."

97  Pew Charitable Trusts, "Collateral Costs."

98  Glaze, Lauren E. and Lauren M. Maruschak. 2008. *Parents in Prison and Their Minor Children*. (Bureau of Justice Statistics Special Report). Washington, DC: U.S. Department of Justice. Retrieved May 5, 2016. www.bjs.gov/content/pub/pdf/pptmc.pdf.

99  Smyth, Julie. 2012. "Dual Punishment: Incarcerated Mothers and Their Children." *Columbia Social Work Review* Volume III: 33–45. cswr.columbia.edu/article/dual-punishment-incarcerated-mothers-and-their-children/.

100  Shlafer, R. & Poehlmann, J. 2010. "Attachment and Caregiving Relationships in Families Affected by Parental Incarceration." *Attachment & Human Development* 12(4): 395–415; Pew Charitable Trusts, "Collateral Costs"; Kampfner, D. 1995. "Posttraumatic Stress Reactions in Children of Imprisoned Mothers." In K. Gabel and D. Johnston, Eds. *Smyth Columbia Social Work Review*, Volume III. New York: Lexington. 89–100; Wakefield and Wildeman, Children of the Prison Boom, 122.

101  Ibid., 108–111.

102  DeFina, Robert and Lance Hannon. 2009. "The Impact of Mass Incarceration on Poverty." *Crime and Delinquency*. Retrieved April 25, 2016. papers.ssrn.com/sol3/papers.cfm?abstract_id=1348049.

103  Annie E. Casey Foundation, "Shared Sentence."

104  Clear, *Imprisoning Communities*, 10.

105  DeFina and Hannon, "Impact of Mass Incarceration."

106  Annie E. Casey Foundation, "Shared Sentence."

107  Ibid.

108  Justice Policy Institute. 2012. "Rethinking the Blues: How We Police in the U.S. and at What Cost." Washington, DC: Justice Policy Institute. Retrieved May 5, 2016. www.justicepolicy.org/uploads/justicepolicy/documents/rethinkingtheblues_final.pdf.

## 8 THE RACIAL RULES OF HEALTH

1 Bruce G. Link and Jo C. Phelan argue that individual risk factors must be contextualized by examining *what* puts people at risk, and that social factors such as socioeconomic status and social support are likely "fundamental causes" of disease. Many of the rules we address in this book have become fundamental causes of negative health outcomes. They "embody access to important resources, affect multiple disease outcomes through multiple mechanisms, and consequently maintain an association with disease even when intervening mechanisms change." Link, Bruce G. and Jo C. Phelan. 1995. "Social Conditions as Fundamental Causes of Disease." *Journal of Health and Social Behavior* (Extra Issue): 80–94.

2 The World Health Organization's constitution states: "The right to the highest attainable standard of health" requires a set of social criteria that is conducive to the health of all people, including the availability of health services, safe working conditions, adequate housing, and nutritious foods. We support the notion that achieving the right to health is closely related to that of other human rights, including the right to food, housing, work, education, nondiscrimination, access to information, and participation.

3 Robert Wood Johnson Foundation. 2009. "Issue Brief 6: Education and Health." Retrieved April 13, 2016. www.commissiononhealth.org/PDF/c270deb3-ba42-4fbd-baeb-2cd65956f00e/Issue%20Brief%206%20Sept%2009%20-%20Education%20 and%20Health.pdf.

4 Families USA. 2014. "African American Health Disparities Compared to Non-Hispanic Whites." Retrieved April 30, 2016. familiesusa.org/sites/default/files/ product_documents/HSI-Health-disparities_african-americans-social-facebook_ 062414_final%255b1%255d.png.

5 Ibid.

6 Ibid.

7 Centers for Disease Control and Prevention (CDC). 2014. "Health Disparities in HIV/AIDS, Viral Hepatitis, STDs, and TB." Retrieved April 30, 2016. www.cdc .gov/nchhstp/healthdisparities/africanamericans.html; see also CDC. 2016. "HIV Among African Americans." Retrieved May 6, 2016. www.cdc.gov/hiv/group/ racialethnic/africanamericans/.

8 CDC, "Health Disparities."

9 According to the CDC, in 2010, blacks represented 69 percent of all reported cases of gonorrhea, with a rate of infection 18.7 times the rate among whites, and the rate of chlamydia among black women was more than seven times the rate among white women (1,536.5 and 205.1 per 100,000 women, respectively). The rate among black men was close to eleven times the rate among white men (761.8 and 69.9 cases per 100,000 men, respectively).

10 Beavis, Anna L., Patti E. Gravitt, and Anne F. Rositch. 2017. "Hysterectomy-Corrected Cervical Cancer Mortality Rates Reveal a Larger Racial Disparity in the United States." *Cancer* 123(6): 1044-1050.

11 CDC. 2015."Cervical Cancer Rates by Race and Ethnicity." Retrieved May 6, 2016. www.cdc.gov/cancer/cervical/statistics/race.htm; see also CDC. 2015."Breast Cancer Rates by Race and Ethnicity." Retrieved May 6, 2016. www.cdc.gov/cancer/breast/ statistics/race.htm; See also CDC. 2016. "Pregnancy Mortality Surveillance System."

Retrieved May 6, 2016. www.cdc.gov/reproductivehealth/maternalinfanthealth/pmss.html.

12 Center for Reproductive Rights. 2014. "Reproductive Injustice: Racial and Gender Discrimination in U.S. Healthcare." Retrieved February 16, 2016. www.reproductiverights.org/sites/crr.civicactions.net/files/documents/CERD_Shadow_US.pdf.

13 MacDorman, Marian F., Donna L. Hoyert, and T. J. Mathews. 2013. "Recent Declines in Infant Mortality in the United States, 2005–2011." Hyattsville, MD: Centers for Disease Control and Prevention. Retrieved April 1, 2016. www.cdc.gov/nchs/data/databriefs/db120.pdf.

14 Matthews, T. J., Marian F. MacDorman, and Marie E. Thoma. 2015. "Infant Mortality Statistics from the 2013 Period Linked Birth/Infant Death Data Set. Division of Vital Statistics." *National Vital Statistics Report* 64(9): 1–28. Retrieved May 6, 2016. www.cdc.gov/nchs/data/nvsr/nvsr64/nvsr64_09.pdf; see also CDC. 2016. "Sudden Unexpected Infant Death and Sudden Infant Death Syndrome." Retrieved April 1, 2016. www.cdc.gov/sids/data.htm; see also American Lung Association. 2012."Trends in Asthma Morbidity and Mortality." Retrieved April 1, 2016. www.lung.org/assets/documents/research/asthma-trend-report.pdf.

15 Harrison-Quintana, Jack, Chris Quach, and Jaime Grant. 2008. "Injustice at Every Turn: A Report of the National Transgender Discrimination Survey, a Look at Multiracial Respondents." *National LGBTQ Task Force*. Retrieved January 25, 2017. www.thetaskforce.org/static_html/downloads/reports/reports/ntds_multiracial_respondents.pdf.

16 Washington, Harriet. 2008. *Medical Apartheid: The Dark History of Medical Experimentation on Black Americans from Colonial Times to the Present.* New York: Anchor.

17 Ibid.

18 Ibid, Page 37.

19 Ibid, Page 42.

20 Ibid.

21 Ibid, Page 44.

22 Kluchin, Rebecca M. 2011. *Fit to be Tied: Sterilization and Reproductive Rights in America 1950–1980.* New Brunswick, NJ: Rutgers University Press.

23 Ibid.

24 Johnson, Corey G. 2013. "Female Inmates Sterilized in California Prisons Without Approval." Center for Investigative Reporting. Retrieved April 17, 2016. cironline.org/reports/female-inmates-sterilized-california-prisons-without-approval-4917.

25 North Carolina Office of Justice for Sterilization Victims. 2014. "N.C. Justice for Sterilization Victims Foundation." Retrieved April 17, 2016. www.sterilizationvictims.nc.gov/documents/JS-brochure.pdf?id=635965257712480616.

26 Smith, David Barton. 2005. "Racial and Ethnic Health Disparities and the Unfinished Civil Rights Agenda." *Health Affairs* 24(2): 317–324.

27 Ibid, Page 319.

28 Johnson, "Female Inmates Sterilized"; also see Hoffman, Beatrix. 2012. *Health Care for Some: Rights and Rationing in the United States Since 1930.* Chicago, IL: University Of Chicago Press.

29 Institute of Medicine. 2009. "Americas Uninsured Crisis: Consequences for Health and Health Care." Retrieved May 6, 2016. iom.nationalacademies.org/~/media/Files/

Report%20Files/2009/Americas-Uninsured-Crisis-Consequences-for-Health-and-Health-Care/Americas%20Uninsured%20Crisis%202009%20Report%20Brief.pdf.

30 Center on Budget and Policy Priorities and Georgetown Health Policy Institute: Center for Children and Families. 2012. "Expanding Coverage for Parents Helps Children: Children's Groups Have a Key Role in Urging States to Move Forward and Expand Medicaid." Retrieved May 6, 2016. www.cbpp.org//sites/default/files/atoms/files/expanding-coverage-for-parents-helps-children7-13.pdf.

31 Hayes, Susan, Pamela Riley, David C. Radley, and Douglas McCarthy. 2015. "Closing the Gap: Past Performance of Health Insurance in Reducing Racial and Ethnic Disparities in Access to Care Could Be an Indication of Future Results." Washington, DC: Commonweath Fund. Retrieved May 6, 2016. www.commonwealthfund.org/~/media/files/publications/issue-brief/2015/mar/1805_hayes_closing_the_gap_reducing_access_disparities_ib_v2.pdf; see also Institute of Medicine, "Americas Uninsured Crisis."

32 Duckett, Philethea and Samantha Artiga. 2013. "Health Coverage for the Black Population Today and Under the Affordable Care Act." Washington, DC: Kaiser Family Foundation. Retrieved April 1, 2016. kff.org/disparities-policy/fact-sheet/health-coverage-for-the-black-population-today-and-under-the-affordable-care-act/.

33 Hayes, Susan, Pamela Riley, David C. Radley, and Douglas McCarthy. 2015. "Closing the Gap: Past Performance of Health Insurance in Reducing Racial and Ethnic Disparities in Access to Care Could Be an Indication of Future Results." Washington, DC: Commonweath Fund. Retrieved May 6, 2016. www.commonwealthfund.org/~/media/files/publications/issue-brief/2015/mar/1805_hayes_closing_the_gap_reducing_access_disparities_ib_v2.pdf.

34 *Ibid.*

35 U.S. Department of Health and Human Services. 2015. "The Affordable Care Act is Working." Retrieved April 27, 2016 (www.hhs.gov/healthcare/facts-and-features/fact-sheets/aca-is-working/index.html); See also U.S. Department of Health and Human Services. 2015. "The ACA is Working for the African-American Community." Retrieved April 27, 2016 (www.hhs.gov/healthcare/facts-and-features/fact-sheets/aca-working-african-american-community/).

36 Ibid.

37 Obamacare Facts. "Federal Poverty Level Guidelines." Retrieved May 6, 2016. obamacarefacts.com/federal-poverty-level/.

38 Flynn, Andrea. 2015. "The Affordable Care Act on Trial." *The Next New Deal.* Retrieved April 27, 2016. rooseveltinstitute.org/affordable-care-act-trial/.

39 Ibid.

40 Garfield, Rachel and Anthony Damico. 2016. "The Coverage Gap: Uninsured Poor Adults in States that Do Not Expand Medicaid – an Update." Retrieved April 13, 2016. kff.org/health-reform/issue-brief/the-coverage-gap-uninsured-poor-adults-in-states-that-do-not-expand-medicaid-an-update/.

41 Artiga, Samantha, Anthony Damico, and Rachel Garfield. 2015. "The Impact of the Coverage Gap for Adults in States Not Expanding Medicaid by Race and Ethnicity." Washington, DC: Kaiser Family Foundation. Retrieved May 6, 2016. kff.org/disparities-policy/issue-brief/the-impact-of-the-coverage-gap-in-states-not-expanding-medicaid-by-race-and-ethnicity/; see also Wiltz, Teresa. 2015. "Many African-Americans Fall Into a Health 'Coverage Gap.'" Washington, DC: Pew Charitable

Trusts. Retrieved May 6, 2016. www.pewtrusts.org/en/research-and-analysis/blogs/stateline/2015/1/26/many-african-americans-fall-into-a-health--coverage-gap.

42 Kaiser Family Foundation. 2014. "Distribution of the Nonelderly with Medicaid by Race/Ethnicity." Retrieved May 6, 2016. kff.org/medicaid/state-indicator/distribution-by-raceethnicity-4/; see also Macartney, Suzanne, Alemayehu Bishaw, and Kayla Fonteno. 2013. "Poverty Rates for Selected Detailed Race and Hispanic Groups by State and Place: 2007–2011." Washington, DC: U.S. Census Bureau. Retrieved April 27, 2016. www.census.gov/prod/2013pubs/acsbr11-17.pdf.

43 Decker, Sandra. 2012. "In 2011 Nearly One-Third Of Physicians Said They Would Not Accept New Medicaid Patients, but Rising Fees May Help." *Health Affairs* 31(8): 1673–1679. Retrieved April 27, 2016. content.healthaffairs .org/content/31/8/1673.short; see also Center for Reproductive Rights. 2014. "Reproductive Injustice: Racial and Gender Discrimination in U.S. Healthcare." Retrieved May 6, 2016. www.reproductiverights.org/document/reproductive-injustice-racial-and-gender-discrimination-in-us-health-care.

44 Smedley, Brian D., Adrienne Y. Stith, and Alan R. Nelson. 2002. "Unequal Treatment: Confronting Racial and Ethnic Disparities in Health Care" (full printed version). Washington, DC: National Academies Press. Retrieved April 1, 2016. www .nationalacademies.org/hmd/Reports/2002/Unequal-Treatment-Confronting-Racial-and-Ethnic-Disparities-in-Health-Care.aspx#sthash.xxqb15hr.dpuf.

45 Center for Reproductive Rights. 2010. "Whose Choice? How the Hyde Amendment Harms Poor Women." Retrieved May 6, 2016. www.reproductiverights.org/sites/crr .civicactions.net/files/documents/Hyde_Report_FINAL_nospreads.pdf.

46 Park, Edwin. 2016. "Medicaid Block Grant Would Slash Federal Funding, Shift Costs to States, and Leave Millions More Uninsured." Washington, DC: Center on Budget and Policy Priorities. Retrieved January 25, 2017. www.cbpp.org/research/health/medicaid-block-grant-would-slash-federal-funding-shift-costs-to-states-and-leave.

47 Ibid.

48 Landsbaum, Claire. 2016. "Pregnancy-Related Deaths Doubled in Texas After Abortion Clinics Closed." *New York Magazine* (August 18). Retrieved January 25, 2017. nymag.com/thecut/2016/08/pregnancy-related-deaths-doubled-in-texas.html.

49 Williams, David R. and Chiquita Collins. 2001. "Racial Residential Segregation: A Fundamental Cause of Racial Disparities in Health." *Public Health Reports* 116(4): 404. Retrieved May 6, 2016. www.ncbi.nlm.nih.gov/pmc/articles/PMC1497358/.

50 Turner, Margery Austin and Karina Fortuny. 2009. "Residential Segregation and Low-Income Working Families." Urban Institute. Retrieved May 6, 2016. www .urban.org/sites/default/files/alfresco/publication-pdfs/411845-Residential-Segregation-and-Low-Income-Working-Families.PDF; see also Pais, J., Scott J. South, and Kyle Crowder. 2012. "Metropolitan Heterogeneity and Minority Neighborhood Attainment: Spatial Assimilation or Place Stratification?" *Social Problems* 59(2): 258. Retrieved May 6, 2016. www.ncbi.nlm.nih.gov/pmc/articles/PMC3359053/; see also Massey, Douglas A. and Nancy A. Denton. 1993. *American Apartheid: Segregation and the Making of the Underclass*. Cambridge, MA: Harvard University Press.

51 Joint Center for Political and Economic Studies Health Policy Institute. 2012. "Place Matters for Health in Cook County: Ensuring Opportunities for Good

Health for All, a Report on Health Inequities in Cook County, Illinois." Retrieved May 6, 2016. www.chicagobusiness.com/assets/downloads/JointCenterReport.pdf.

52 Kramer, Michael and Carol Hogue. 2009. "Is Segregation Bad for Your Health?" *Epidemiologic Reviews* 31(1): 178–194. Retrieved May 6, 2016. epirev.oxfordjournals.org/content/31/1/178.full.

53 Landrine, Hope and Irma Corral, I. 2009. "Separate and Unequal: Residential Segregation and Black Health Disparities." *Ethnicity & Disease* 19(2): 179–184. Retrieved May 6, 2016. www.ishib.org/journal/19-2/ethn-19-02-179.pdf.

54 Olden Kenneth and Sandra L. White. 2005. "Health-Related Disparities: Influence of Environmental Factors." *Medical Clinics of North America* 89(4): 721–738, cited in Landrine and Corral, "Separate and Unequal."

55 Landrine and Corral, "Separate and Unequal."

56 Ibid.

57 Robert Wood Johnson Foundation. 2014. "Education: It Matters More to Health than Ever Before." Retrieved April 1, 2016. www.rwjf.org/content/dam/farm/reports/issue_briefs/2014/rwjf409883.

58 Robert Wood Johnson Foundation. 2009. "Education Matters for Health." Retrieved April 13, 2016. www.commissiononhealth.org/PDF/c270deb3-ba42-4fbd-baeb-2cd65956f00e/Issue%20Brief%206%20Sept%2009%20-%20Education%20and%20Health.pdf.

59 Ibid.

60 Jackson, Fleda Mask. 2007. "Race, Stress, and Social Support: Addressing the Crisis in Black Infant Mortality." Joint Center for Political and Economic Studies. Accessed April 1, 2016. jointcenter.org/sites/default/files/RACE%20AND%20STRESS%20FINAL%20-%2017%20pages.pdf.

61 Smedley, Brian D., Adrienne Y. Stith, and Alan R. Nelson. 2002. "Unequal Treatment: Confronting Racial and Ethnic Disparities in Health Care" (full printed version). Washington, DC: National Academies Press. Retrieved April 1, 2016. www.nationalacademies.org/hmd/Reports/2002/Unequal-Treatment-Confronting-Racial-and-Ethnic-Disparities-in-Health-Care.aspx#sthash.xxqb15hr.dpuf.

62 Staats, Cheryl, Kelly Capatosto, Robin A. Wright, and Danya Contractor. 2015. "State of Science: Implicit Bias Review 2015." Retrieved April 1, 2016. kirwaninstitute.osu.edu/wp-content/uploads/2015/05/2015-kirwan-implicit-bias.pdf.

63 Ibid.

64 Ibid.

65 Center for Reproductive Rights. 2014. "Reproductive Injustice: Racial and Gender Discrimination in U.S. Healthcare." Retrieved April 1, 2016. www.reproductiverights.org/sites/crr.civicactions.net/files/documents/CERD_Shadow_US_6.30.14_Web.pdf.

66 HealthCare.Gov. N.d. "Transgender health care." Washington, DC: U.S. Centers for Medicare & Medicaid Services. healthcare.gov/transgender-health-care/; National Center for Transgender Equality. 2012. "National Transgender Discrimination Survey: A Look at Black Respondents." Washington, DC: NCTE. transequality.org/issues/resources/national-transgender-discrimination-survey-look-black-respondents.

67 Harvard University Center on Developing Child. N.d. "Key Concepts: Toxic Stress." Retrieved May 6, 2016. developingchild.harvard.edu/science/key-concepts/toxic-stress/.

68 Ibid.
69 Kemeny, Margaret. 2003. "The Psychobiology of Stress." *Current Directions in Psychological Science* 12(4): 124–129. Retrieved May 6, 2016. cdp.sagepub.com/content/12/4/124.short.
70 Nuru-Jeter, A., T. P. Dominguez, W. P. Hammond, Hammond Wizdom Powell, Leu Janxin, Marilyn Skaff, Susan Egerter, Camara P. Jones, and Paula Braveman. 2009. "It's the Skin You're In: African-American Women Talk About Their Experiences of Racism. An Exploratory Study to Develop Measures of Racism for Birth Outcome Studies." *Maternal and Child Health Journal* 13(1): 29–39. Retrieved on May 6, 2016. link.springer.com/article/10.1007/s10995-008-0357-x#/page-1; see also Geronimus, Arline T., Margaret T. Hicken, Jay A. Pearson, Sarah J. Seashols, Kelly Brown, and Tracey D. Cruz. 2010. "Do US Black Women Experience Stress-Related Accelerated Biological Aging? A Novel Theory and First Population-Based Test of Black–White Differences in Telomere Length." *Human Nature* 21(1): 19–38. Retrieved May 6, 2016. www.ncbi.nlm.nih.gov/pmc/articles/PMC2861506/.
71 Geronimus Arline T., Margaret T. Hicken, Dayne Keene, and John Bound. 2006. " 'Weathering' and Age Patterns of Allostatic Load Scores Among Blacks and Whites in the United States." *American Journal of Public Health.* 96(5): 826–833. Retrieved May 6, 2016. ajph.aphapublications.org/doi/abs/10.2105/AJPH.2004.060749.
72 Geronimus, Arline T., Margaret T. Hicken, Jay A. Pearson, Sarah J. Seashols, Kelly Brown, and Tracey D. Cruz. 2010. "Do US Black Women Experience Stress-Related Accelerated Biological Aging? A Novel Theory and First Population-Based Test of Black–White Differences in Telomere Length." *Human Nature* (Hawthorne, NY) 21(1): 19–38; see also Blount, Linda Goler. 2015. "Congratulations! Now Be Afraid." *Black Women's Health Imperative.* Retrieved May 1, 2016. www.bwhi.org/blog/2015/05/10/home/congratulations-now-be-afraid/.
73 Ibid.; Nuru-Jeter et al., "It's the Skin."
74 Jackson, Fleda Mask. 2001. "Examining the Burdens of Gendered Racism: Implications for Pregnancy Outcomes Among College-Educated African American Women." *Maternal and Child Health Journal* 5(2): 95-107.
75 Geronimus et al., " 'Weathering." Page 832.
76 Langley-Evans, Simon C. 2006. "Developmental Programming of Health and Disease." *Proceedings of the Nutrition Society* 65(1): 97–105. Retrieved April 2, 2016. www.ncbi.nlm.nih.gov/pmc/articles/PMC1885472/; Shonkoff, Jack P., Andrew S. Garner, Committee on Psychosocial Aspects of Child and Family Health, Committee on Early Childhood, Adoption, and Dependent Care, Section on Developmental and Behavior Pediatrics, Benjamin S. Siegel, Mary I. Dobbins, Marian F. Earls, Andrew S. Garner, Laura McGuinn, John Pascoe, and David L. Wood. 2012. "The Lifelong Effects of Early Childhood Adversity and Toxic Stress." *Pediatrics* 129(1): e232–e246. Retrieved May 1, 2016. pediatrics.aappublications.org/content/129/1/e232.
77 Eriksson Johan G. 2010. "Early Programming of Later Health and Disease: Factors Acting During Prenatal Life Might Have Lifelong Consequences." *Diabetes* 59(10): 2349–2350. Retrieved April 2, 2016. www.ncbi.nlm.nih.gov/pmc/articles/PMC3279565/.
78 Bowers, Mallory E. and Rachel Yehuda. 2016. "Intergenerational Transmission of Stress in Humans." *Neuropsychopharmacology* 41(1): 232–244.

79  Felitti, Vincent J., Robert Anda, Dale Nordenberg, David Williamson, Allison M. Spitz, Valerie Edwards, Mary P. Koss, and James S. Marks. 1998. "Relationship of Childhood Abuse and Household Dysfunction to Many of the Leading Causes of Death in Adults. The Adverse Childhood Experiences (ACE) Study." *American Journal of Preventive Medicine* 14(4): 245–258.

80  Birney, Ewan. 2015. "Study of Holocaust Survivors Finds Trauma Passed on Children's Genes." *The Guardian*. Retrieved May 6, 2016. www.theguardian.com/science/2015/aug/21/study-of-holocaust-survivors-finds-trauma-passed-on-to-childrens-genes.

81  Kluchin, Rebecca. 2011. *Fit to Be Tied: Sterilization and Reproductive Rights in America, 1950–1980*. Piscataway, NJ: Rutgers University Press.

82  Blount, Linda Goler. 2015. "Testimony of Linda Goler Blount, President and CEO, Black Women's Health Imperative." Reproductive Justice Initiative Hearing at the National Press Club.

83  Flynn, Andrea. 2013. "The Title X Factor: Why the Health of America's Women Depends on More Funding for Family Planning." *The Next New Deal*. Retrieved April 27, 2016. rooseveltinstitute.org/title-x-factor-why-health-americas-women-depends-more-funding-family-planning/.

84  Ibid.

85  Texas Policy Evaluation Project. 2015. "Abortion Wait Times in Texas: The Shrinking Capacity of Facilities and the Potential Impact of Closing Non-ASC Clinics." Retrieved May 1, 2016. sites.utexas.edu/txpep/files/2016/01/Abortion_Wait_Time_Brief.pdf.

86  Reproductive Health Technologies Project. 2015. "Two Sides of the Same Coin: Integrating Economic and Reproductive Justice." Retrieved on May 6, 2016. www.rhtp.org/abortion/documents/TwoSidesSameCoinReport.pdf.

87  Ross, Loretta. 2011. "Understanding Reproductive Justice." Retrieved May 3, 2016. www.trustblackwomen.org/our-work/what-is-reproductive-justice/9-what-is-reproductive-justice.

88  Ibid.

89  Gennuso, Keith P., Amanda Jovaag, Bridget B. Catlin, Matthew Rodock, and Hyojun Park. 2016. "Assessment of Factors Contributing to Health Outcomes in the Eight States of the Mississippi Delta Region." *Preventing Chronic Disease* 13: 150440.

90  Robert Wood Johnson Foundation. 2011. "Exploring the Social Determinants of Health." Retrieved April 12, 2016. www.rwjf.org/content/dam/farm/reports/issue_briefs/2011/rwjf70448.

91  Robert Wood Johnson Foundation. 2011. "Exploring the Social Determinants of Health." Retrieved April 12, 2016. www.rwjf.org/content/dam/farm/reports/issue_briefs/2011/rwjf70448.

92  Ibid.

93  Hajat, Anjum, Jay S. Kaufman, Kathryn M. Rose, Arjumand Siddiqi, and James C. Thomas. 2010. "Long-Term Effects of Wealth on Mortality and Self-Rated Health Status." *American Journal of Epidemiology* 173(2): 192–200.

94  Ibid.

95  Robert Wood Johnson Foundation. 2011. "Exploring the Social Determinants of Health." Retrieved April 12, 2016. www.rwjf.org/content/dam/farm/reports/issue_briefs/2011/rwjf70448.

96 Pickett, Kate and Richard Wilkinson. 2011. *The Spirit Level: Why Greater Equality Makes Societies Stronger*. New York: Bloomsbury Press.
97 Sanger-Katz, Margot. 2015. "Income Inequality: It's Also Bad for Your Health." *New York Times*. Retrieved May 6, 2016. www.nytimes.com/2015/03/31/upshot/income-inequality-its-also-bad-for-your-health.html?partner=rss&emc=rss&abt=0002&abg=1&_r=0.
98 Nuru-Jeter, Amani and Williams T, LaVeist. 2014. "Distinguishing the Race-Specific Effects of Income Inequality and Mortality in U.S. Metropolitan Areas." *International Journal of Health Services* 44(3): 435–456. Retrieved May 6, 2016. joh.sagepub.com/content/44/3/435.short.
99 Thorpe, Roland J., Patrick Richard, Janice V. Bowie, Thomas A. LaVeist, and Darrell J. Gaskin. 2013. "Economic Burden of Men's Health Disparities in the United States." *International Journal of Men's Health* 12(3): 195. Retrieved April 1, 2016. www.mensstudies.info/OJS/index.php/IJMH/article/view/655.
100 LaVeist, Thomas A., Darrell J. Gaskin, and Patrick Richard. 2009. "The Economic Burden of Health Inequalities in the United States." Washington, DC: Joint Center for Political and Economic Studies. Retrieved April 1, 2016. www.ndhealth.gov/heo/publications/The%20Economic%20Burden%20of%20Health%20Inequalities%20in%20the%20United%20States.pdf.
101 Peek, Monica. 2014. "Poverty's Association with Poor Health Outcomes and Health Disparities." *Health Affairs Blog*. Retrieved April 12, 2016. healthaffairs.org/blog/2014/10/30/povertys-association-with-poor-health-outcomes-and-health-disparities/.

## 9  THE RACIAL RULES OF DEMOCRATIC PARTICIPATION

1 Kusnet, David. 1992. *Speaking American: How the Democrats Can Win in the Nineties*. New York: Thunder's Mouth Press. See also Keyssar, Alexandra. 2000. *The Right To Vote*. Philadelphia: Basic Books.
2 Klinkner, Philip A. and Rogers M. Smith. 2002. *The Unsteady March*. Chicago, Il: University of Chicago Press; Waldman, Michael. 2016. *The Fight To Vote*. New York: Simon & Schuster.
3 Smith, Rogers M. 1997. *Civic Ideals: Conflicting Visions of Citizenship in US History*. Chelsea, MI: Book Crafters.
4 Woodward, C. Vann. 1955. *The Strange Career of Jim Crow* New York: Oxford University Press.
5 Foner, Eric. 1988. *Reconstruction: America's Unfinished Revolution*. New York: Harper & Row.
6 History, Art & Archives, U.S. House of Representatives. N.d. "Black Americans in Congress." Retrieved January 10, 2017. history.house.gov/Exhibitions-and-Publications/BAIC/Black-Americans-in-Congress/.
7 Kousser, J. Morgan. 1974. *The Shaping of Southern Politics*. New Haven, CT: Yale University Press.
8 Black Past: A Reference Guide to African American History. N.d. "Grandfather Clause, The (1898-1915)." www.blackpast.org/aah/grandfather-clause-1898–1915.
9 Shapiro, Andrew. 1993. "Challenging Criminal Disenfranchisement Under the Voting Rights Act: A New Strategy." *Yale Law Journal* 103(2): 537–566.

10  Naidu, Suresh. 2012. "Suffrage, Schooling, and Sorting in the Post-Bellum U.S. South." Cambridge, MA: National Bureau of Economic Research. Working Paper No. 18129. Retrieved May 7, 2016. www.nber.org./papers/w18129.

11  Carmines, Edward G. and James A. Stimson. 1989. *Issue Evolution: Race and the Transformation of American Politics*. Princeton, NJ: Princeton University Press; Edsall, Mary D. and Thomas Byrne Edsall. 1991. *Chain Reaction: The Impact of Race, Rights and Taxes on American Politics*. New York: W. W. Norton; Haney-Lopez, Ian. 2014. *Dog Whistle Politics*. New York: Oxford University Press.

12  Brown-Dean, Khalilah, Zoltan Hajnal, Christina Rivers, and Ismail White. 2015. "50 Years of the Voting Rights Act: The State of Race in Politics." Washington, DC: Joint Center for Political and Economic Studies. Retrieved May 8, 2016. jointcenter.org/sites/default/files/VRA%20report%2C%203.5.15%20%281130%20am%29%28updated%29.pdf.

13  Reed Jr, Adolph. 1999. *Stirrings in the Jug: Black Politics in the Post-Segregation Era*. Minneapolis: University of Minnesota Press; Thompson, J. Phillip. 2006. *Double Trouble: Black Mayors, Black Communities and the Call for Deep Democracy*. New York: Oxford University Press.

14  Knickrehm, Kay M. and Devin Bent. 1988. "Voting Rights, Voter Turnout, and Realignment: The Impact of the 1965 Voting Rights Act." *Journal of Black Studies* 18(3): 283–296. Retrieved January 11, 2017. www.jstor.org/stable/2784508?seq=3#page_scan_tab_contents.

15  Brennan Center for Justice. 2013. "The Voting Rights Act: Protecting Voters for Nearly Five Decades." New York: NYU School of Law. Retrieved January 11, 2017. www.brennancenter.org/analysis/voting-rights-act-protecting-voters-nearly-five-decades.

16  Pattillo-McCoy, Mary. 1999. *Black Picket Fences*. Chicago, IL: University of Chicago Press; Waldinger, Roger. *Still the Promised City?* Cambridge, MA: Harvard University Press.

17  Harris, Fredrick, Valeria Sinclair-Chapman, and Brian D. McKenzie. 2006. *Countervailing Forces in African–American Civic Activism, 1973–1994*. New York: Cambridge University Press.

18  Alexander, Michelle. 2010. *The New Jim Crow: Mass Incarceration in the Age of Colorblindness*. New York: New Press.

19  Uggen, Christopher, Sarah Shannon, and Jeff Manza. 2012. "State-Level Estimates of Felon Disenfranchisement in the United States, 2010." Washington, DC: Sentencing Project. Retrieved May 8, 2016. www.sentencingproject.org/doc/publications/fd_State_Level_Estimates_of_Felon_Disen_2010.pdf; Mauer, Marc and Christopher Uggan. 2013. "The Missing Black Voters," *Huffington Post*, July 28, 2013. Retrieved May 8, 2016. www.huffingtonpost.com/marc-mauer/the-missing-black-voters_b_3280102.html.

20  Uggen et al., "State-Level Estimates."

21  Uggen, Christopher and Jeff Manza 2002. "Democratic Contraction? Political Consequences of Felon Disenfranchisement in the United States." *American Sociological Review* 67 (6): 777–803.

22  Chung, Jean. 2016. "Felony Disenfranchisement: A Primer." Washington, DC: Sentencing Project. Retrieved January 11, 2017. www.sentencingproject.org/publications/felony-disenfranchisement-a-primer/.

23 Office of the Pardon Attorney. N.d. "Frequently Asked Questions Concerning Executive Clemency." U.S. Department of Justice. Retrieved January 11, 2017. www .justice.gov/pardon/frequently-asked-questions-concerning-executive-clemency.

24 Weaver, Vesla. 2014. "The Only Government I Know: How the Criminal Justice System Degrades Democratic Citizenship." *Boston Review*, June 10. Retrieved May 8, 2016. bostonreview.net/us/vesla-m-weaver-citizenship-custodial-state-incarceration.

25 Pinderhughes, Dianne. 1995. "Black Interest Groups and the 1982 Voting Rights Extension." In W. Parent and H Perry, Eds. *Blacks and the American Political System*. Gainesville: University Press of Florida.

26 Civil Rights Division. N.d. "About the National Voter Registration Act." Washington, DC: U.S. Department of Justice. Retrieved January 11, 2017. www.justice.gov/crt/ about-national-voter-registration-act.

27 Schwartz, John. 2013. "Between the Lines of the Voting Rights Act Opinion." *New York Times*, June 25. Retrieved January 11, 2017. www.nytimes.com/ interactive/2013/06/25/us/annotated-supreme-court-decision-on-voting-rights-act.html.

28 Brennan Center for Justice, "Voting Rights Act."

29 Childress, Sarah. 2013. "With Voting Rights Act Out, States Push Voter ID Laws." *PBS Frontline*, June 26. Retrieved January 11, 2017. www.pbs.org/wgbh/frontline/ article/with-voting-rights-act-out-states-push-voter-id-laws/.

30 Kaleem, Jaweed. 2016. "How Did the Weakened Voting Rights Act Affect Election Results?" *Los Angeles Times*, November 8. Retrieved January 11, 2017. www.latimes .com/nation/politics/trailguide/la-na-election-day-2016-how-did-the-weakened-voting-rights-act-1478670026-htmlstory.html.

31 Guinier, Lani. 1994. *Tyranny of the Majority: Fundamental Fairness in Representative Democracy*. New York: Free Press

32 Ibid.

33 Weisere, Wendy R. and Erik Opsal. 2014. "The State of Voting in 2014." Brennan Center for Justice, June 17. Retrieved May 7, 2016. www.brennancenter.org/ analysis/state-voting-2014.

34 Brennan Center for Justice. 2016. "Voting Restrictions in Place for the First Time in Presidential Election in 2016." Retrieved May 9, 2016. www.brennancenter.org/ sites/default/files/analysis/New_Restrictions_2016.pdf.

35 Brennan Center for Justice. 2016. "New Voting Restrictions in Place for 2016 Presidential Election." Retrieved March 1, 2017. www.brennancenter.org/ voting-restrictions-first-time-2016.

36 Hajnal, Zoltan, Nazita Lajevardi, and Lindsay Nielson. 2016. "Voter Identification Laws and the Suppression of Minority Votes." Retrieved January 5, 2017. pages.ucsd. edu/~zhajnal/page5/documents/VoterIDLawsSuppressionofMinorityVoters.pdf.

37 Minnite, Lorraine C. 2010. *The Myth of Voter Fraud*. Ithaca, NY: Cornell University Press; Levitt, Justin. 2012. "The New Wave of Election Regulation: Burden Without Benefit." *Issue Brief*, June 2012. Washington, DC: American Constitution Society for Law and Policy. acslaw.org/sites/default/files/Levitt_-_New_Wave_of_Election_ Regulation.pdf.

38 Strasser, Annie-Rose. 2012. "Pennsylvania Republican: Voter ID Laws Are 'Gonna Allow Governor Romney To Win." *Think Progress*, June 25. Retrieved January 13, 2017. thinkprogress.org/pennsylvania-republican-voter-id-laws-are-gonna-allow-governor-romney-to-win-52abae23b772#.k8q94s9og.

39  Famighetti, Christopher. 2016. "Long Voting Lines: Explained." New York: Brennan Center for Justice. Retrieved January 11, 2017. www.brennancenter.org/analysis/long-voting-lines-explained.

40  Hajnal, Zoltan L. 2009. "Who Loses in American Democracy: A Count of Votes Demonstrates the Limited Representation of African Americans." *American Political Science Review* 103(1): 37–57.

41  Wins, Michael and Manny Fernandez. 2016. "Stricter Rules for Voter IDs Reshape Races." *New York Times*, May 2. A1.

42  United States Government Accountability Office. 2014. "Issues Related to State Voter Identification Laws." Retrieved May 7, 2016. www.gao.gov/assets/670/665966.pdf.

43  Hobby, Bill, Mark P. Jones, Jim Granato, and Renée Cross. 2015. "The Texas Voter ID Law and the 2014 Election: A Study of Texas's 23rd Congressional District." Retrieved May 6, 2016. bakerinstitute.org/files/9541/.

44  Hajnal et al., "Voter Identification Laws."

45  Shapiro, Ian. 2003. *The State of Democratic Theory*. Princeton, NJ: Princeton University Press.

46  Ibid, Page 144-145.

47  Marshall, T. H. 1950. *Citizenship and Social Class*. Cambridge, MA: Cambridge University Press.

48  Cascio, Elizabeth and Ebonya Washington. 2012. "Valuing the Vote: The Redistribution of Voting Rights and State Funds Following the Voting Rights Act of 1965." Cambridge, MA: National Bureau of Economic Research. Working Paper No. 17776. www.nber.org/papers/w17776.

## 10  WHAT WILL IT TAKE TO REWRITE THE HIDDEN RULES OF RACE?

1  Johnson, Lyndon B. 1965. "To Fulfill These Rights." Commencement Address at Howard University. Retrieved April 1, 2016. www.lbjlib.utexas.edu/johnson/archives.hom/speeches.hom/650604.asp.

2  Ostry, Jonathan D., Andrew Berg, and Charalambos G. Tsangarides. 2014. "Redistribution, Inequality, and Growth." IMF Staff Discussion Note. February 2014. www.imf.org/external/pubs/ft/sdn/2014/sdn1402.pdf.

3  *Economic Report of the President, January, 1962*. Washington: Government Printing Office, 1962. Retrieved May 5, 2016. www.presidency.ucsb.edu/economic_reports/1962.pdf.

4  Benner, Chris and Manuel Pastor. 2015. "Brother, Can You Spare Some Time? Sustaining Prosperity and Social Inclusion in America's Metropolitan Regions." *Urban Studies* 52 (7, September 5): 1339–1356. Retrieved May 5, 2016. usj.sagepub.com/content/early/2014/09/03/0042098014549127.

5  powell, john a., Stephen Menendian & Jason Reece. 2009. "The Importance of Targeted Universalism." *Poverty & Race*. March/April 2009. Retrieved May 4, 2016. www.prrac.org/full_text.php?text_id=1223&item_id=11577&newsletter_id=104&header=Miscellaneous&kc=1.

6  Haney López, Ian. *Dog Whistle Politics*. 2014. New York: Oxford University Press

7  Tippett, Rebecca, and Avis Jones-DeWeever, Maya Rockeymoore, Darrick Hamilton, and William Darity, Jr. 2014. "Beyond Broke: Why Closing the Racial

Wealth Gap is a Priority for National Economic Security." Washington, DC: Center for Global Policy Solutions. Retrieved April 1, 2016. globalpolicysolutions.org/resources/beyond-broke-report/.

8  Coates, Ta-Nehisi. 2014. "The Case for Reparations." *Atlantic* (June). Retrieved April 1, 2016. www.theatlantic.com/magazine/archive/2014/06/the-case-for-reparations/361631/.

9  Commission to Study Reparation Proposals for African-Americans Act of 2015. HR 40, 114th Congress. 2015. Retrieved May 5, 2016. www.govtrack.us/congress/bills/114/hr40.

10  Voting Rights Advancement Act of 2015. HR 2867. 114th Congress. 2015. Retrieved May 5, 2016. www.congress.gov/bill/114th-congress/house-bill/2867.

11  The Leadership Conference on Civil and Human Rights. N.d. "VRA for Today: Restore the Voting Rights Act Now." Retrieved May 5, 2016. vrafortoday.org/current-legislation/.

12  No Money Bail Act of 2016. H.R. 4611. 114th Congress. 2016. Retrieved May 5, 2016. www.congress.gov/bill/114th-congress/house-bill/4611/text.

13  Black Youth Project 100. 2016. "BYP 100's Agenda to Build Black Futures." Retrieved May 5, 2016. agendatobuildblackfutures.org/our-agenda/.

14  Stiglitz, Joseph E. 2015. "*Rewriting the Rules of the American Economy: An Agenda for Growth and Shared Prosperity.*" New York: Roosevelt Institute. 80.

15  Black Youth Project 100, "Agenda to Build Black Futures."

16  Toobin, Jeffrey. 2015. "The Milwaukee Experiment." *New Yorker* (May 11). Retrieved April 29, 2016. www.newyorker.com/magazine/2015/05/11/the-milwaukee-experiment.

17  Stemen, Don. 2007. "Reconsidering Incarceration: New Directions for Reducing Crime." New York: Vera Institute of Justice. Retrieved April 29, 2016. vera.org/sites/default/files/resources/downloads/veraincarc_vFW2.pdf.

18  Warren, Dorian T., Chirag Mehta, and Steve Savner. 2016. "Unlocking Opportunities in the Poorest Communities: A Policy Brief." Washington, DC: Center for Community Change. Retrieved April 30, 2016. www.communitychange.org/wp-content/uploads/2016/02/Unlocking-Opportunities-policy-brief-2-2-16-1.pdf.

19  Silvers, Damon. "A Blueprint for 21st Century Infrastructure." Forthcoming. New York: Roosevelt Institute.

20  Randolph, A. Philip. 1966. "100 Billion Freedom Fund," *The Crisis* 73: 18–23.

21  john a. powell, Stephen Menendian, and Jason Reece. 2009. "The Importance of Targeted Universalism." *Poverty & Race* (March/April). Accessed April 27, 2016. www.prrac.org/full_text.php?text_id=1223&item_id=11577&newsletter_id=104&header=Miscellaneous&kc=1.

22  Jargowsky, Paul A. 2015. "The Architecture of Segregation: Civil Unrest, the Concentration of Poverty, and Public Policy." New York: Century Foundation. Accessed April 27, 2016. tcfdotorg.atavist.com/architecture-of-segregation.

23  Ibid.

24  Poo, Ai-Jen. 2016. *The Age of Dignity: Preparing for the Elder Boom in a Changing America.* New York: New Press.

25  Warren, Dorian T. 2015. "Putting Families First: Good Jobs for All." Washington, DC: Center for Community Change. Retrieved April 27, 2016. www.goodjobsforall.org/wp-content/uploads/2015/06/PFA-GJFA-Launch-Report.pdf.

26 Organization for Economic Co-operation and Development. 2014. "Trade Union Density." Retrieved April 29, 2016. stats.oecd.org/Index.aspx?DataSetCode=UN_DEN.

27 See Stiglitz's *Rewriting the Rules*, pages 76–78, for more thorough discussion, and Weil, Fissured Workplace.

28 Congress.gov. 2015. H.R. 2972 – Equal Access to Abortion Coverage in Health Insurance (EACH Woman) Act of 2015. Retrieved April 29, 2016. www.congress .gov/bill/114th-congress/house-bill/2972.

29 "Targeted Regulation of Abortion Providers (TRAP)." 2015. New York: Center for Reproductive Rights. Retrieved May 5, 2016. www.reproductiverights.org/project/ targeted-regulation-of-abortion-providers-trap.

30 We here draw on the extensive work of William Darity and Darrick Hamilton, whose scholarship has contributed to a broader understanding of the drivers of the wealth gap and the potential for child trust accounts to reduce a number of unequal black–white outcomes. Hamilton, Darrick, William Darity, Jr., Anne E. Price, Vishnu Sridharan, and Rebecca Tippett. 2015. "Umbrellas Don't Make it Rain." Oakland, CA: Insight Center for Community Economic Development. Retrieved April 29, 2016. www.insightcced.org/report-umbrellas-dont-make-it-rain/.

31 Boshara, Ray, William R. Emmons, and Bryan J. Noeth. 2015. "The Demographics of Wealth: How Age, Education and Race Separate Thrivers from Strugglers in Today's Economy." St. Louis, MO: St. Louis Federal Reserve. Retrieved May 5, 2016. www.stlouisfed.org/~/media/Files/PDFs/HFS/essays/HFS-Essay-1-2015-Race-Ethnicity-and-Wealth.pdf.

32 Hamilton, Darrick and William Darity, Jr. 2010. "Can 'Baby Bonds' Eliminate the Racial Wealth Gap in Putative Post-Racial America?" *Review of Black Political Economy* 37: 207–216. Retrieved May 5, 2016. www.whiteprivilegeconference.com/ pdf/WPC14_baby_bonds.pdf.

33 Sloan, Carrie. 2016. "How Wall Street Caused a Water Crisis in America's Cities." *The Nation* (March 11). Retrieved May 5, 2016. www.thenation.com/article/how-wall-street-caused-a-water-crisis-in-americas-cities/; Hill, Anita. 2011. *Reimagining Equality: Stories of Gender, Race and Finding Home*. Boston: Beacon Press; Stiglitz, *Rewriting the Rules*, 41–42; FedUp: The National Campaign for a Strong Economy. 2015. "Whose Recovery? A National Convening on Inequality, Race, and the Federal Reserve." Brooklyn, NY: Center for Popular Democracy. Retrieved May 5, 2016. populardemocracy.org/sites/default/files/whose%20recovery.pdf.

34 Federal Deposit Insurance Corporation. 2014. "2013 FDIC National Survey of Unbanked and Underbanked Households." Retrieved May 5, 2016. www.fdic.gov/ householdsurvey/2013execsumm.pdf.

35 Orfield, Gary, John Kucsera, and Genevieve Siegel-Hawley. 2012. "E Pluribus ... Separation Deepening Double Segregation for More Students." Los Angeles, CA: Civil Rights Project. Retrieved May 5, 2016 civilrightsproject.ucla.edu/ research/k-12-education/integration-and-diversity/mlk-national/e-pluribus ... separation-deepening-double-segregation-for-more-students.

36 Keleher, Terry. 2009. "Racial Equity Impact Assessment Toolkit." New York and Oakland, CA: Race Forward. Retrieved May 5, 2016. www.raceforward.org/ practice/tools/racial-equity-impact-assessment-toolkit.

37 Ibid.

## CONCLUSION

1 Lilla, Mark. 2016. "The End of Identity Liberalism," *New York Times*, November 18. Retrieved February 1, 2017. www.nytimes.com/2016/11/20/opinion/sunday/the-end-of-identity-liberalism.html?_r=0; Burnham, Linda. 2017. "Liberals, Don't Fall into the Right's 'Identity Politics' Trap." *The Guardian*, February 10. Retrieved March 1, 2017. www.theguardian.com/commentisfree/2017/feb/10/liberals-right-identity-politics-progressive.

2 Movement for Black Lives. 2016. "Platform." Retrieved March 1, 2017. policy.m4bl.org/platform/; Women's March on Washington. 2017. "Unity Principles." Retrieved March 1, 2017. www.womensmarch.com/principles/.

# Index

abortion, 134, 141, 142, 166, 211n86, 217n29
activism, 1, 15, 30, 83, 88, 117, 170
    Black Lives Matter, 1, 53, 57, 58
    Civil Rights Movement, 16, 24, 25, 26, 28,
        33, 84, 90, 109, 116, 131, 179n35
    Fight for 15, 1, 90
    Movement for Black Lives, 104, 108, 170,
        173, 185n3, 218n2
affirmative action, 8, 30, 32, 33, 46, 78, 83, 84,
    85, 92, 168, 192n27
Asian Americans, 12, 24, 37, 73, 94, 95, 144
assets, 2, 5, 8, 63, 64, 65, 67, 74, 75, 130,
    189n59, 200n5, 202n55, 204n92,
    206n14, 209n51, 215n42

bias, 4, 6, 8, 28, 30, 31, 39, 72, 73, 75, 78, 85,
    87, 104, 109, 120, 127, 128, 137, 138,
    165, 209n62
black elected officials, 20, 26, 33, 41, 84, 114,
    148, 151, 162
Black Lives Matter. *See* activism
*Brown v. Board of Education. See*
    Supreme Court

civil rights, 10, 18, 21, 26, 31, 33, 34, 70, 78, 83,
    85, 106, 115, 116, 131, 145, 148, 150
Civil Rights Act, 8, 20, 25, 36, 82, 83, 97, 131,
    151, 193n41
Civil Rights Movement. *See* activism
Civil War, 18, 19, 21, 81, 145, 178n21,
    187n30, 191n18
colorblind policy. *See* racial rules,
    race-neutral rules
criminal justice system, 3, 10, 13, 27, 41, 53,
    57, 58, 68, 92, 108, 109, 110, 111, 112,
    113, 114, 115, 116, 117, 118, 119, 120,
    121, 122, 125, 126, 134, 142, 149, 150,
    155, 156, 163, 171, 172, 173
crime rates, 70, 95, 110, 114, 116
death penalty, 42, 118
mass incarceration, 2, 10, 13, 65, 80, 86,
    106, 108, 109, 110, 111, 113, 116, 117,
    118, 120, 121, 122, 123, 124, 125, 126,
    149, 150, 157, 163, 200n18, 203n77,
    204n89, 214n24
police, 1, 13, 41, 56, 108, 109, 112, 116, 118,
    119, 125, 149, 150, 162, 163, 164, 170,
    172, 200n6
prison, 10, 33, 104, 108, 109, 110, 111, 112,
    113, 114, 115, 116, 117, 118, 119, 120,
    121, 122, 123, 124, 125, 126, 130, 149,
    150, 163, 164, 177n25, 180n59, 192n30,
    199n48, 200n10, 200n13, 200n3, 200n7,
    200n9, 201n26, 201n27, 201n29, 201n38,
    202n46, 202n49, 203n77, 204n100,
    204n90, 204n98, 206n24
sentencing, 8, 109, 112, 116, 117, 118, 119,
    121, 158, 163, 169, 202n49
War on Drugs, 111, 117, 119, 162, 163, 169

deindustrialization, 10, 26, 29, 30, 32, 33, 34,
    77, 83, 84, 87, 88, 89, 116, 148
Democratic Party, 22, 23, 69, 82, 147, 148, 171,
    187n31, 212n1
discrimination, 2, 4, 5, 8, 9, 11, 23, 25, 27, 28, 30,
    33, 42, 46, 47, 48, 49, 50, 58, 63, 70, 71,
    75, 78, 80, 82, 84, 85, 86, 89, 92, 102, 109,
    129, 131, 133, 134, 137, 138, 139, 142,
    150, 151, 157, 161, 162, 164, 168, 169,
    171, 172, 184, 203n2, 206n15, 208n13

economic inequality, 1, 6, 11, 12, 14, 17, 23, 26, 63, 77, 104, 138, 143, 155, 159, 171
economic mobility, 4, 16, 45, 47, 70, 84, 105, 122
education, 2, 4, 6, 13, 23, 27, 28, 29, 30, 31, 34, 38, 41, 44, 45, 55, 57, 58, 60, 63, 67, 68, 69, 70, 75, 77, 78, 79, 80, 82, 83, 86, 92, 93, 94, 95, 96, 97, 98, 99, 100, 101, 102, 104, 105, 106, 109, 119, 120, 122, 126, 127, 134, 135, 136, 138, 145, 147, 155, 156, 160, 163, 164, 166, 170, 172, 175n5, 191n12, 196n12, 196n18, 197n28, 199n47, 205n2, 217n35

financial crisis of 2008, 1, 8, 70, 72

gender, 2, 4, 6, 7, 10, 11, 13, 35, 39, 51, 57, 58, 59, 64, 78, 81, 82, 83, 84, 86, 87, 113, 128, 133, 139, 145, 155, 159, 162, 165, 171, 172, 173, 175n2, 175n5, 190n7, 190n9, 191n12, 193n43, 200n13, 208n43

health, 2, 8, 13, 14, 27, 28, 34, 41, 42, 43, 59, 70, 74, 77, 79, 81, 82, 88, 92, 93, 96, 98, 104, 106, 112, 113, 121, 122, 123, 126, 127, 128, 129, 131, 132, 134, 135, 136, 137, 138, 140, 141, 142, 143, 144, 155, 156, 160, 165, 166, 171, 173, 191n9, 205n1, 205n2, 207n32, 207n40, 208n41, 208n43, 208n46, 209n53, 209n66, 210n70, 210n76, 211n83, 212n101, 212n97
  insurance coverage, 85, 131, 132, 133, 134, 135, 138, 142, 173, 207n30, 207n32, 207n40, 207n41, 208n41, 208n42, 208n43, 208n46
  maternal and infant mortality, 124, 128, 141, 142, 143, 144
  reproductive rights, 112, 128, 130, 135, 138, 140, 141, 142, 166, 201n27, 208n43, 211n87
  toxic stress, 139, 142
hiring and promotion, 4, 6, 29, 30, 47, 48, 49, 50, 83, 84, 85, 86, 87n†, 123, 159, 165
Hispanic and Latino Americans, 12, 24, 30, 32, 45, 58, 60, 64, 66, 72, 73, 80, 90, 94, 95, 96, 100, 103n‡, 105, 106, 107, 110, 111, 119, 120, 124, 144, 153, 168, 205n4, 208n42
housing, 24, 25, 26, 27, 28, 57, 63, 65, 67, 68, 69, 70, 73, 74, 100, 101, 104, 109, 120, 121, 122, 125, 135, 144, 160, 168, 179n41, 187n32, 187n32, 187n33, 187n33, 188n40, 188n44, 205n2

homeownership, 2, 23, 27, 63, 64, 65, 66, 67, 69, 72, 73, 74
redlining, 8, 69, 70, 71, 72, 73, 101

immigration, 13, 24, 42, 44, 45, 46, 47, 57, 60, 61, 142, 170, 171, 173, 185n4
income, 2, 3, 5, 6, 10, 12, 13, 17, 23, 27, 28, 31, 34, 36, 43, 44, 45, 46, 51, 57, 59, 63, 64, 65, 67, 69, 71, 72, 73, 74, 75, 77, 78, 80, 81, 91, 96, 103, 105, 112, 115, 120, 121, 122, 123, 124, 127, 132, 133, 134, 135, 136, 138, 141, 142, 143, 154, 155, 157, 159, 160, 162, 164, 165, 166, 167, 170, 172, 190n5, 203n77, 212n97, 212n98
integration, 27, 93, 98, 99, 172, 196n12, 196n18, 197n28, 199n47, 217n35
interpersonal racism, 9, 128

Jim Crow laws, 3, 8, 10, 13, 16, 18, 22, 23, 24, 32, 49, 67, 68, 87, 93, 96, 108, 109, 115, 122, 129, 130, 131, 146, 148, 150, 156, 172, 196n14, 200n4, 212n4, 213n18

labor unions and law, 3, 6, 7, 8, 11, 16, 23, 30, 31, 34, 77, 81, 82, 83, 87, 88, 89, 92, 160, 165, 170, 194n52
LGBTQ rights, 24, 53, 56, 58, 111, 113, 114, 128, 129, 138, 142, 206n15, 209n66

mass incarceration. *See* criminal justice system
middle class, 3, 34, 36, 63, 69, 70, 80, 82, 83, 84, 85, 88, 89, 105, 148, 154, 159, 165
minimum wage, 2, 6, 79, 82, 89, 158, 172
Movement for Black Lives. *See* activism

NAACP, 24, 97, 102, 152, 198n39
Native Americans, 45, 95
neoliberalism, 4, 12, 16, 28, 29, 31, 33, 78, 83, 84, 85, 134, 159, 165, 173
New Deal, 3, 23, 31, 67, 68, 69, 70, 81, 82, 85, 89, 158, 178n28, 178n29, 187n31, 192n20, 192n21, 207n38, 211n83

police. *See* criminal justice system
political representation. *See* black elected officials
poverty, 10, 11, 27, 32, 65, 66, 70, 80, 85, 94, 95, 96, 97, 99, 100, 101, 102, 106, 107, 112, 121, 123, 125, 132, 133, 134, 135, 136, 139, 141, 143, 154, 164, 186n18, 186n19, 196n13, 207n37
prison. *See* criminal justice system

public goods, 29, 42, 43, 44, 84, 147, 157, 159, 164
public sector employment, 30, 82, 83, 84, 88, 91

racial rules, 3, 5, 7, 8, 10, 11, 12, 13, 16, 18, 19, 24, 33, 34, 63, 67, 69, 70, 75, 77, 78, 79, 81, 88, 92, 94, 108, 109, 111, 113, 117, 126, 127, 129, 131, 138, 142, 143, 145, 146, 147, 149, 152, 156, 157, 158, 159, 160, 169, 170, 171, 172, 173
  exclusionary rules, 8, 15, 22, 82, 96, 109, 146, 156
  inclusionary rules, 7, 8, 9, 12, 18, 19, 21, 24, 56, 71, 78, 84, 90, 92, 93, 115, 131, 132, 155, 156, 157, 159, 160
  non-rules, 8, 70, 72, 73, 75, 152
  race-neutral rules, 1, 2, 3, 23, 28, 31, 44, 73, 75, 78, 80, 82, 85, 101, 116, 120, 146, 147, 149, 156, 158, 159, 162, 169, 173
Reconstruction, 16, 18, 19, 20, 21, 22, 24, 32, 33, 41, 68, 114, 115, 145, 146, 147, 148, 149, 172, 173, 177n11, 177n13, 177n9, 178n16, 178n22, 191n16, 212n5
redlining. *See* housing
reparations, 15, 131, 160, 161, 177n3, 187n23, 216n8
Republican Party, 18, 19, 20, 33, 194n60, 214n38

segregation, 2, 4, 10, 13, 17, 22, 24, 25, 27, 29, 31, 32, 68, 70, 73, 79, 85, 86, 93, 96, 99, 100, 101, 102, 103n‡, 105, 106, 131, 135, 138, 164, 168, 169, 171, 190n6, 193n43, 193n44, 199n53, 209n53, 216n22, 217n35
skin tone, 15, 42, 46
slavery, 3, 8, 10, 12, 15, 17, 18, 19, 20, 21, 34, 45, 67, 68, 70, 81, 82, 87, 108, 109, 114, 115, 129, 130, 131, 140, 145, 147, 156, 161, 172, 187n29, 200n7
South, the, 18, 19, 20, 21, 22, 23, 26, 31, 34, 68, 69, 81, 82, 83, 97, 105, 106, 114, 115, 116, 134, 146, 147, 148, 152, 178n28, 185n5, 192n21, 198n46, 212n7
stratification economics, 10, 13, 35, 36, 37, 38, 39, 40, 42, 43, 44, 46, 50, 51

structural racism, 1, 5, 9
Supreme Court, 21, 28, 96, 97, 100, 130, 133, 146, 148, 149, 151, 168, 178n19
  *Brown v. Board of Education*, 8, 24, 93, 96, 131, 148, 169, 195n1

targeted universalism, 9, 13, 14, 52, 54, 55, 56, 59, 61, 159, 164, 176n20, 215n5, 216n21
transgender people. *See* LGBTQ rights
trickle-down economics, 1, 33, 85, 88, 90, 159, 164, 167

unemployment, 2, 27, 30, 36, 41, 67, 69, 77, 79, 80, 82, 85, 88, 91, 116, 126, 165, 190n3
unions. *See* labor unions and law

voting, 19, 22, 23, 25, 27, 33, 43, 60, 109, 114, 145, 146, 147, 148, 149, 150, 151, 152, 153, 161, 162, 170, 172, 173, 179n41, 213n15, 214n27, 214n29, 214n30, 214n33, 214n35, 215n39
Voting Rights Act, 8, 25, 26, 28, 145, 146, 148, 149, 150, 151, 152, 155, 161, 212n9, 213n12, 213n14, 213n15, 214n27, 214n29, 214n30, 215n48, 216n11

War on Drugs. *See* criminal justice system
wealth, 2, 3, 8, 10, 13, 18, 19, 25, 27, 29, 32, 34, 36, 43, 44, 45, 46, 51, 52, 59, 63, 64, 65, 66, 67, 68, 69, 70, 72, 73, 74, 75, 78, 80, 81, 82, 92, 96, 101, 104, 105, 117, 120, 121, 122, 124, 134, 135, 142, 145, 154, 155, 158, 161, 162, 164, 166, 167, 170, 171, 186n5, 199n49, 217n30
welfare, 28, 81, 112, 117, 120, 123
women, 1, 2, 3, 23, 24, 28, 29, 30, 41, 42, 53, 56, 64, 65, 66, 72, 73, 78, 79, 80, 82, 89, 90, 91, 108, 110, 111, 112, 113, 114, 121, 124, 128, 130, 133, 134, 135, 137, 138, 139, 140, 141, 142, 143, 144, 145, 146, 162, 166, 171, 172, 173, 179n43, 185n2, 186n10, 186n13, 186n15, 186n18, 186n18, 186n6, 186n8, 189n47, 189n48, 190n9, 193n43, 195n69, 200n15, 200n20, 201n26, 201n27, 205n9, 208n45, 210n70, 210n72, 210n74, 211n82, 211n83, 218n2